T0189232

Advanced Information and Knowledge Processing

Series editors

Lakhmi C. Jain
Bournemouth University, Poole, UK, and
University of South Australia, Adelaide, Australia

Xindong Wu
University of Vermont

Information systems and intelligent knowledge processing are playing an increasing role in business, science and technology. Recently, advanced information systems have evolved to facilitate the co-evolution of human and information networks within communities. These advanced information systems use various paradigms including artificial intelligence, knowledge management, and neural science as well as conventional information processing paradigms. The aim of this series is to publish books on new designs and applications of advanced information and knowledge processing paradigms in areas including but not limited to aviation, business, security, education, engineering, health, management, and science. Books in the series should have a strong focus on information processing—preferably combined with, or extended by, new results from adjacent sciences. Proposals for research monographs, reference books, coherently integrated multi-author edited books, and handbooks will be considered for the series and each proposal will be reviewed by the Series Editors, with additional reviews from the editorial board and independent reviewers where appropriate. Titles published within the Advanced Information and Knowledge Processing series are included in Thomson Reuters' Book Citation Index.

More information about this series at http://www.springer.com/series/4738

Tshilidzi Marwala · Evan Hurwitz

Artificial Intelligence and Economic Theory: Skynet in the Market

Springer

Tshilidzi Marwala
Faculty of Engineering and the Built
    Environment
University of Johannesburg
Auckland Park
South Africa

Evan Hurwitz
Department of Electrical and Electronic
    Engineering Science,
Faculty of Engineering and the Built
    Environment
University of Johannesburg
Auckland Park
South Africa

ISSN 1610-3947   ISSN 2197-8441   (electronic)
Advanced Information and Knowledge Processing
ISBN 978-3-319-88177-5   ISBN 978-3-319-66104-9   (eBook)
DOI 10.1007/978-3-319-66104-9

Printed on acid-free paper

This Springer imprint is published by Springer Nature
The registered company is Springer International Publishing AG
The registered company address is: Gewerbestrasse 11, 6330 Cham, Switzerland

Preface

Artificial Intelligence and Economic Theory: Skynet in the market borrows the word Skynet from the movie *The Terminator*. The advent of artificial intelligence has changed many disciplines such as engineering, social science and economics. Artificial intelligence is a computational technique which is inspired by natural intelligence such as the swarming of birds, the workings of the brain and the path finding behavior of the ants. These techniques have impact on economic theory. This book studies the impact of artificial intelligence on economic theory, a subject that has not yet been studied. The theories that are considered include asymmetrical information, pricing, rational expectations, rational choice, game theory, mechanism design, behavioral economics, bounded rationality, efficient market hypothesis, financial engineering, portfolio, rational counterfactual and causality. The benefit of this book is that it evaluates existing theories of economics and updates them based on the developments in the artificial intelligence field. This book makes an important contribution to the area of econometrics, and is an interesting read for graduate students, researchers and financial practitioners. In this book, Chaps. 1, 2, 3, 4, 5, 8, 9, 12, 13, 14, and 15 were written by Tshilidzi Marwala whereas Chaps. 7 and 10 were written by Evan Hurwitz. Chapters 6 and 11 were jointly written. We thank the three anonymous reviewers for their contributions.

Johannesburg, South Africa
July 2017

Tshilidzi Marwala Ph.D.
Evan Hurwitz D.Eng.

Contents

About the Authors

Tshilidzi Marwala is the Vice-Chancellor and Principal of the University of Johannesburg. He was previously the Deputy Vice-Chancellor: Research and Internationalization and a Dean of the Faculty of Engineering at the University of Johannesburg. He was also previously a Full Professor of Electrical Engineering, the Carl and Emily Fuchs Chair of Systems and Control Engineering as well as the SARChI chair of Systems Engineering at the University of the Witwatersrand. Prior to this, he was an Executive Assistant to the Technical Director at the South African Breweries. He holds a Bachelor of Science in Mechanical Engineering (*magna cum laude*) from Case Western Reserve University (USA), a Master of Mechanical Engineering from the University of Pretoria, a Ph.D. in Engineering from Cambridge University and was a postdoctoral research associate at the Imperial College (London). He is a registered professional engineer, a Fellow of TWAS, the World Academy of Sciences, the Academy of Science of South Africa (ASSAf), the African Academy of Sciences and the South African Academy of Engineering. He is a Senior Member of the IEEE (Institute of Electrical and Electronics Engineering) and a distinguished member of the ACM (Association for Computing Machinery). His research interests are multidisciplinary and they include the theory and application of computational intelligence to engineering, computer science, finance, social science and medicine. He has supervised 47 Masters and 23 Ph.D. students to completion. He has published 11 books (one translated into Mandarin), over 280 papers and holds 3 international patents. He is an Associate Editor of the International Journal of Systems Science (Taylor and Francis Publishers).

Evan Hurwitz is a South African computer scientist. He obtained his B.Sc. Engineering (Electrical) (2004), his M.Sc. Engineering (2006) from the University of the Witwatersrand and Ph.D. from the University of Johannesburg in 2014 supervized by Tshilidzi Marwala. He is known for his work on teaching a computer how to bluff, which was widely covered by the magazine New Scientist. Hurwitz together with Tshilidzi Marwala proposed that there is less level of information asymmetry between two artificial intelligent agents than between two human agents and that the more artificial intelligent there is in the market the less is the volume of trades in the market.

Chapter 1
Introduction to Man and Machines

Abstract This chapter introduces this book, Artificial Intelligence and Economic Theory: Skynet in the market, and in the process studies some of the big ideas that have concerned economics and finance in the last 300 years. These ideas include Marxist thinking, the theory of invisible hand, the theory of equilibrium and the theory of comparative advantage. It, furthermore, describes methods in artificial intelligence such as learning, optimization and swarm intelligence. It sets a scene on how these theories can be better understood by using artificial intelligence techniques, thereby, setting a scene for the rest of the book.

1.1 Introduction

"Workers of the world unite, you have nothing to lose but chains" so said Karl Marx. Despite what many Marxists claim, he never foretold the advent of artificial intelligence, otherwise he would probably have said "Artificial intelligent robots of the world unite, you have nothing to lose but chains" (Marx 1849). But what Marx realized was that the principal agent of work is man. Man is the invisible hand that drives the economy as observed by Adam Smith (Smith 2015). The economy was made by man, about man and for man but the theories that explained the economy did not quite match the behaviour of a man. For this reason, the rational man is indeed irrational and his irrationality permeates every aspect of life including the very concept we call the economy.

Human beings have been around for two hundred thousand years and, throughout their existence and even from their forbearers, have inherited certain traits and behaviors that influence them even today (Harari 2014). Some of these traits and behaviours include greed, fear, bias and social structure. All these traits are still with us today because of one and only one reason and that is because they all have given us an evolutionary advantage. Of course, this might change in the future depending on the change of environment and, therefore, these traits might depart from human beings. All these traits influence our decision making and the rationality thereof. Herbert Simon calls the idea of making decisions with all these

© Springer International Publishing AG 2017

T. Marwala and E. Hurwitz, *Artificial Intelligence and Economic Theory: Skynet in the Market*, Advanced Information and Knowledge Processing,
DOI 10.1007/978-3-319-66104-9_1

constraints e.g. processing power of our brains; incomplete, imperfect and imprecise information; and human behaviour, *bounded rationality* (Simon 1991). Our rationality is bound by all these constraints but what will happen when machines inevitably replace humans in decision-making capacities? Is the rationality of machines bound? Are the bounds of rationality bigger in humans than in machines? These are some of the questions that this book seeks to answer.

Machines are now part of everyday decision making. They are becoming more intelligent due to a technology called artificial intelligence (AI) (Marwala 2013). Alan Turing surmised that machines are intelligent if and only if when we interact with them we cannot tell whether we are interacting with a man or a machine (Traiger 2000). No machine has passed this Turing test over an extended level of man-machine interaction. But this does not limit artificial intelligence and make machines incapable of solving complex problems. Some of the critics of the Turing test is the work done by John Searle on the problem called the Chinese Room problem (Searle 1980). In the Chinese Room problem, you have a person inside a room and there is a hole where something written in Chinese is slipped into a room and there is a lookup table which the person inside this room uses to translate into English. To the person outside it seems as if the person inside can speak Chinese. John Searle goes further and classifies between Strong AI versus Weak AI. In this classification, Strong AI is the one that is really intelligent, i.e. there is actually a Chinese person inside the room, as opposed to a Weak AI, where there is a Zulu person who does not speak Chinese inside the room who is just using a lookup table.

This chapter describes man-machine interaction and its impact on some of the big ideas in economics. Every economic epoch had its own theories or thinking. Some of these theories stood the test of time but some have fallen by the wayside. The biggest event in history of economics is the history of industrialisation and all its various stages. The first industrial revolution occurred in 1874 in England. What is less clear is why it did not happen in Asia, especially in India or China as these two regions had significantly higher population densities? What was the catalyst that caused the first industrial revolution? In the 17th century lived a man in England called Isaac Newton who was educated in that superb institution of Trinity College Cambridge (Newton 1729). Legend claims that unlike many people who had lived before him and had witnessed an apple falling, he asked: "Why did the apple fall?" And from this he discovered gravity, an intriguing concept which was only given an explanation by another fine German/Swiss/American scientist by the name of Albert Einstein some hundreds of years later. Newton, furthermore, came with what is now called the laws of motion which stated that objects will continue at rest or keep on moving until they are moved or stopped respectively. Furthermore, he observed the relationship between force and mass of an object with its acceleration. This thinking of Newton reshaped our understanding of movement and became the catalyst or DNA for the first industrial revolution. This gave us steam engines, trains and mechanical machines for production. From this era, economic principles such as Marxism, Adam Smith's invisible hand as well as David Ricardo's theory of value and principle of comparative advantage were conceived (de Vivo 1987).

Then in the 19th century came a British man called Michael Faraday who performed crucial experiments which were later interpreted by James Clerk Maxwell through his beautiful mathematical equations (Maxwell 1873; Agassi 1971). Michael Faraday observed that if you have a magnet and you put it next to a wire that conducts electricity and you move the wire, then electricity flows in that conductor. This is wizardry beyond miracles of biblical proportions. Even today we generate electricity, perhaps with the exception of solar energy and few others, using this technique. Faraday's discovery allowed us to convert mechanical energy into electrical energy, such that could be usefully distributed through electrical wires, dramatically altering the nature and course of human existence. Conversely, Faraday observed that again with a magnet and a conducting wire, you force electricity through the wire, then the wire moves and this was the birth of the electric motor that still moves our assembly lines. This complementary discovery allowed the transmitted energy to be utilised at some distant location, which is the heart of machinery as we know it today. These events were the DNA for the second industrial revolution. From this era, economic principles such as mass production and Keynesian economics were introduced.

Then in the second half of the 20th century, John Bardeen, Walter Brattain, and William Shockley discovered the transistor (Amos and James 1999). It is based on semiconductors which are objects that conduct electricity under certain conditions. The transistor is the catalyst for the electronic age that gave us computers, cell phones, information technology and automation in our factories. It is the DNA of the third industrial revolution. It was in this era that powerful economic concepts such as market efficiency introduced prospect theory.

The era we are living in is the fourth industrial revolution. This is an era of intelligent machines. The DNA of the fourth industrial revolution is AI. It will touch all aspects of our lives. We will have robotic cops to protect us, robotic doctors to assist us with medical issues, all our vital organs will be monitored real time to extend human lives, driverless cars and aircraft as well as human empty factories as labor will be replaced. What will happen to economics? Already we know that the stock market no longer has crowds of people shouting a price of stocks because artificial intelligent software are doing the work (Siegel 2008). This book explores how economic theories that have guided decision makers in the past will have to change in the light of artificial intelligent capabilities.

1.2 Economics and Economic Theory

Economics began when man started bartering for exchanging goods. This was mainly based on the reality that man could not produce all he wanted. For example, suppose we have a man called Peter who produces maize and another called John who produces peanuts. Then Peter will give half of his maize for half of John's peanuts. If we include a third person Aiden who produces wheat, then Peter takes a third of his maize and gives it to John in exchange of a third of his peanuts, gives another third to Aiden in exchange of his third of wheat. It is evident that this becomes a complicated problem quickly as more and more people exchange goods.

To facilitate this process, an additional entity called money comes into the picture for one and one reason only and that is to simplify the exchange of goods and services. Well not quite because money on its own is worthless. It becomes useful when it has a property called trust. Trust is what makes money useful. When you take away the trust, as Robert Mugabe did in Zimbabwe circa 2006, you collapse the money as happened when Zimbabwean dollar was replaced by the American dollar as legal currency. In this example there are factors of production that makes this transaction happen and these are labour to plough, capital and here we are talking about seeds and land to plough these seeds on. The study of all these activities is called economics. The generalization of these activities such as the philosophy on how to price these goods is called economic theory. Generalization is of course a big concept. For example if most of the time it is cloudy and humid it rains then one can generalize and say there is a natural law that states that whenever it is cloudy and humid then it will probably rain.

If money is now the object to be used to exchange goods, how do we put a price to peanuts, maize and wheat? Well it depends on your ideology. In a strictly planned economy the authority determines the price (this is referred to as a planned economy or command economy, such as was evident in Soviet Russia under Stalin) whereas in the market economy it is determined by the demand and supply characteristics while in a market in Delhi you negotiate a price and it is not fixed. One thing is for sure, the producers of goods and services are only willing to sell their goods at a price which is higher than the cost of producing these goods. This book will explore how artificial intelligence is likely to change pricing and the theory of pricing.

On the theory of pricing one looks at the supply and demand and in our case we will use peanuts. When the supply and demand are equal this is called equilibrium. Equilibrium is a balance of all economic forces and in our case these forces are the supply and demand of goods and services. At the point of equilibrium there is no incentive to change because changing does not advantage any agent. With the advent of artificial intelligence, we can now employ multi-agent systems to simulate an economic process and observe the point of equilibrium thereby assisting in matters such as pricing. Futhermore, we can estimate the effects of policy changes on the market using the same systems in order to understand the impact of policy changes without throwing the markets into turmoil.

The production of peanuts, wheat and maize can be industrialized using tractors. In this situation the owners of capital do not necessarily have to work, the workers have to work. In the worst case scenario, these workers can be so exploited that they are paid a bare minimum wage (or lower, considering that in the times of Marx most Nations indeed had no minimum wage). From a situation like this in the major industrial towns of Britain, Karl Marx looked at this and crafted an ideology where the workers become the owners of capital through a revolution. He went further and stated that "To each according to their needs and from each according to their abilities". This of course was against human nature and could not be enforced without the violence of Lenin and Stalin. The idealism of Marx did not account for the lack of any driving for the owners of capital to invest their means in an enterprise without some sort of reasonable expectation of reward for the risk that they were undertaking with their own wealth.

Adam Smith looked at organization of the economy and observed that as individuals pursue goals of maximizing their returns, the greater good of increasing production and income are achieved. He called the driver of this greater good the invisible hand. The concept of maximizing the greater good is what is called utilitarianism and was proposed by John Stuart Mill (Mill 2001). When these owners of capital and workers pursuing their individual wants intersect, the emerging outcome is for the greater good for society. Of course with the advent of multinationals that are big, and the influence of finance and advertising this is not necessarily the case. The ability of large corporations to unduly influence lawmakers and policy creators has recently been seen to skew this idealised view of the free market, in essence applying influence to make the market less free in practice than it is theory. In fact as Thomas Picketty observes in his seminal book *Capital in the 21st Century* that inequality is still a major problem (Picketty 2014). As Nobel Laureate Joseph Stiglitz in his book *The Price of Inequality* observes that inequality stifles economic growth (Stiglitz 2012). The idea of the invisible hand is a phenomenon that is observed even in biological systems. For example, the swarming of pigeons which is illustrated in Fig. 1.1 is an example of the invisible hand because there is no leader. Each bird looks at what its neighbours as well as the group are doing and follows, and what emerges is a coordinated movement of the swarm towards the food source. The action of each individual following a relatively simple

Fig. 1.1 The swarming of pigeons

set of rules that is translated into a more complex resultant action of the group is something referred to as emergent behaviour, the understanding of which allows us to model systems of large amounts of actors performing individually simple tasks with complex results in the marketplace. In the field of AI, this has also allowed us to translate such phenomena into useful algorithms such as particle swarm optimization.

The other important factor is the concept of value. In our example, between peanuts, wheat and maize which one is more valuable? Should we break them into their chemical components and price each compound? Simply trade on weight? Use measured nutritional value? To paraphrase the eternally misquoted bard, "Value is in the eye of the beholder". Depending on an individual's frame of reference and reason for trade, these three farmers will exchange goods at differing valuations because of the differences in their perceptions of the goods' respective values. Even within a single product there can be a difference in the perception of value. Consider Peter, who grows Maize, knows that every kilogram of Maize he grows is going to cost him $500 in materials and labour. To him the Value of Maize is $500/Kg. Tracy, who owns a mill, can sell the processed maize at $600/Kg, after her costs of $100/Kg to process it. She therefore values the same maize at $600/Kg, and so the two can find a value in-between their respective valuations to trade, and Tracy can buy maize from Peter at $550/Kg. This example shows how two agents with similar understanding of a product can still value the same product at different prices. This becomes even more striking once it is noted that one party may have a very different understanding or access to information than the other party. The concept of asymmetry of value and its principal importance in trade will be discussed in detail later in this book and it will be established that AI reduces information asymmetry.

In the example we have given, Peter may go and create a company Peter Incorporated. The company will have limited liability and the theory behind this is that in order to encourage people to form companies, a legal framework is established to limit personal liability in case of when the company runs into difficulties. The company is therefore established as a legal entity independent of its owners and therefore has rights and obligations. Peter may then decide to list the company in the local stock exchange to raise funds for the company and by so doing distributes shareholding to members of the public.

There is an entire discipline on how to predict the future price of stocks and there are two general ways of doing this. These are through fundamental and technical analyses. Technical analysis is a mathematical exercise where one looks at the data of the performance of the stock and makes decisions on whether to buy such a stock or not. The problem with this is that people buy stock for no reason except that it is going up irrespective of how solid the company is with that particular share price. The dotcom bubble that burst in the early 2000s was largely based on this where a company with a shaky business model was listed in the stock market and its share price skyrocketed and then crashed to the ground (Hamilton 1922). The other way of predicting the share price is by looking at the underlying business activities of companies and then deciding whether to buy the share price or not. Both of these approaches have merit and today with the advent of big data and AI, technical analysis is augmented with data from the internet whether twitter or searching through the internet to find out what the market sentiments, including quantification of the fundamentals, on the particular stock are. These will be discussed in this book in a chapter on quantitative analysis.

Another theory that has emerged from the stock market is the theory of the efficient market hypothesis (Fama 1970). This theory basically states that it is impossible to beat the market because the share price reflects all elements that are relevant. This theory states that even though there might be instances where a share price might not already incorporate all relevant information, it then self corrects to reach an equilibrium point when the markets are efficient. Much of the information in the stock are based on human decisions which are unpredictable and in most cases irrational. For a share price to incorporate all these decisions and their future intentions, is almost importable. Irrational people make decisions in the market, these result in irrational markets. But now we know that much of the decisions in the market are made by artificial intelligent machines and the volume of these will expand in the future. Therefore, as these happen, the markets become more efficient and this is discussed in detail in this book.

Peter, John and Aiden when they make their decisions on when to plant, how to plant, what fertilizers to use, how to trade, at what price and who to seek advice from, they require certain attributes to make these decisions. The first attribute is information and this is often limited, not wholly accurate and often missing. The second attribute is sufficient mental capability to make sense and process the information which is often less than perfect. This is the concept that Economics Nobel Prize Laurate and AI expert Herbert Simon called bounded rationality. He further observed that in such a situation, Peter, John and Aiden, will have to satisfice meaning obtaining satisfactory and sufficient solution. Now if we add AI into this decision making process, what happens to missing data and processing of information?

All the players in the market have to make decisions, regarding how much peanuts, maize and wheat are to be planted. They make these decisions individually and/or collectively. The question that has been asked for many generations is: How do people make their choices? The theoretical answer is that they make their choices based on their desires to maximize their utilities. There is a difference between a desire to maximize utility and actually being able to make a rational decision (Anand 1993). Studies have shown that the theory of rational choice is not what drives decision making. In fact, Kahneman in his book *Thinking fast and slow* demonstrated that people make decisions based on their aversion to loss, oftentimes losing out on lucrative expected returns as a result of being overly cautious (Kahneman 2011). Clearly, this is not a disease that affects the banking industry of late, although again a more realistic understanding of risk and loss would have been beneficial to say the least.

Now with the advent of artificial intelligence, is it not possible to design machines that are able to make decisions based on rational choice theory? Does artificial intelligence in decision making not imply that decisions are more and more going to be based on the theory of rational choice rather than aversion to loss? Another closely aligned matter is the issue of rational expectation theory which states that people make decisions based on future outlook, information available and past experience. AI machines look at available information and past information to make a decision and exclude individual perception of the future. Therefore, the degree of uncertainty in AI made decisions is lower than that made by human beings. For example, if one asks human beings to make decisions at different times they will change their minds depending on all sorts of irrelevant factors.

As people make their decisions on what to do, there is a framework that has been developed to aid with that and this is called game theory (Myerson 1991). Game theory is a mathematical framework which assists us in making optimal decisions given the fact that we do not know what other people's choices will be but their choices influence the outcome. There are many types of games e.g. zero sum games where the gain for one player is the loss by another player. In game theory there are a number of assumptions that are made and these include the fact that players are rational, and there are sets of rules, and the games are played till Nash equilibrium is reached. Nash equilibrium is a position where each player cannot improve his utility by playing further (Nash 1950). With the advent of artificial intelligence and in particular multi-agent systems, the whole theory of games can be better implemented and for much complicated games for the benefit of better decision making.

Another framework that has been developed is the framework of mechanism design which in our example can be used to design a market for the peanuts industry (Hurwicz et al. 1975). Mechanism design won Leonid Hurwicz, Eric Maskin, and Roger Myerson a Nobel Prize in Economics. Mechanism design is in essence reverse game theory where instead of players, rules and then identifying equilibrium, here you have the desired equilibrium and players and you want to design the rules so that the desired equilibrium can be reached. This is in effect a control problem where the system is designed to achieve a certain desired outcome. For an example, when an aircraft is flying over a highly turbulent environment, the autopilot system identifies the appropriate speed, angle of attach and altitude to achieve maximum comfort for the passengers. This development offers yet another tool that one can expect policy-makers to utilise in order to craft policies and laws that achieve their desired outcomes with a minimum of undesirable side-effects.

Suppose a trader who has $1 million is faced with making a choice on buying stocks from a list of 100 stocks. The trader has two options, either use $1 million to buy one stock or buy a basket of stocks. The process of choosing the optimal basket of stocks is called portfolio optimization. The optimal basket today is not the optimal basket tomorrow and how then does he optimize this? Perhaps he can use a time window, say 2 months, to find the average optimal basket. All these variables, e.g. time window, selection that forms a basket, how large should the basket be, are all unknown variables. Nobel Prize Laureate, Harry Markowitz, proposed what is called portfolio optimization theory to select this basket of stocks (Markowitz 1952). However, his theory is based on a number of assumptions including the fact that the character of the basket of stocks does not change, something that is called stationarity in mathematical language. With the advent of AI, one is now able to apply this technology to the theory of portfolio optimization. For example, how do we solve portfolio optimization problem using the theory of ant colony intelligence which is based on ants depositing pheromones as they move and following the path with the strongest pheromones, and then converging on an equilibrium path which happens to be the shortest distance between the food source and ants nest?

The theories of factual and counterfactuals are at the heart of economic theory (Byrne 2005). For example, if the farmer Aiden who plants wheat instead planted maize, will he have obtained a better return on investments? These two scenarios, planting wheat, factual (planting wheat because it happened) compared to the counterfactual (planting maize because it did not happen), economists have a beautiful term for this and they call these losses "opportunity costs" (Henderson 2008). The question that needs to be answered is whether we can use AI, with its predictive, adaptive and learning capabilities, to estimate the counterfactuals and thus economic costs. If we are able to quantify the opportunity cost, it means this can be integrated into decision making to make choices that maximize return on investments.

Another issue that is closely related to the issues of factual and counterfactual is the concept of causality (Gujarati and Porter 2009). Nobel Laureate Clive Granger thought he had pinned down this matter when he proposed Granger causality which even though is useful particularly in economics is not causality at all but some measure of correlation. We know that detecting causality on static data is difficult and that only experimentation is the most reliable way of detecting causality. A causes B if and only if there is a flow of information from A to B. How do we then detect such flow of information? Alternatively, we can frame causality in terms of factual and counterfactual by posing the following problem instead: A causes B (factual) if when A does not happen then B does not happen. This book illustrates the centrality of causality in understanding economic problems and proposes several ways in which to understand economics. We explore the theories of rational choice and rational expectations within the dimensions of causality.

1.3 Artificial Intelligence

In order to rewrite economic theory in the light of artificial intelligence it is important to understand what artificial intelligence is (Marwala 2007, 2009, 2010). AI is made out of two words, artificial and intelligence and thus it is intelligence that is artificially made. Intelligence is the ability to make sense of information beyond the obvious. There are two types of intelligence in nature and these are individual intelligence and group intelligence. Individual intelligence is intelligence located in a single agent for example, the farmer Aiden is individually intelligent, whereas group intelligence is when it is located in a group of agents such as the swarming of pigeons shown in Fig. 1.1 or the school of fish (Marwala and Lagazio 2011).

Within the field of AI, intelligence manifests itself in two ways, specialised intelligence and generalised intelligence (Marwala 2012, 2013). For example, a

Fig. 1.2 The KAIST humanoid robot amongst human

robot designed at the Korean Advanced Institute of Science and Technology, shown in Fig. 1.2, which drives a car, opens doors, walks and drills holes, is demonstrating generalized intelligence (Marwala 2014, 2015). This is because it is able to do multiple independent tasks. A voice recognition software which is able to hear and interpret a person is a specialised robot because it is trained and is able to do one task only.

In artificial intelligence, there are various capabilities that have been invented and these are how to make machines learn, optimize, predict, adapt and interact. On learning, the source of knowledge is how a human brain functions and from this a neural network was invented which is able to take information from the world and interpret it (Marwala et al. 2006, 2017). For example, a neural network is able to

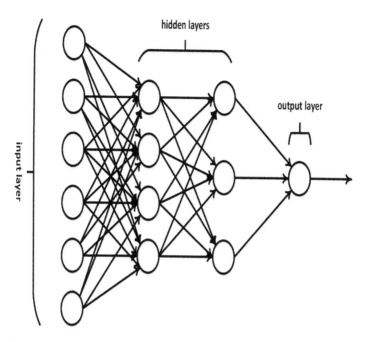

Fig. 1.3 An example of a neural network

take an X-ray picture of the individual's lung and then establish whether the individual has pulmonary embolism or not. A neural network is also able to take an EEG signal from an individual and establish whether the individual will be experiencing epileptic activities or not in the near future.

In Fig. 1.3, we have input and output layers. The input layer has the variables that are to be used as a basis for prediction whereas the output layer is what is to be predicted. An example, is a study on using the income of parents to predict the educational outcome of the children as measured by whether they go to college or not. Here the income of the parents will be in the input layer whereas the educational outcome of the children will be in the output layer. The hidden layers constitute the mechanism or the engine which facilitates the translation of input data into the output. This engine consists of neurons (inspired by natural neurons) and the identity of these neurons which are represented by numbers is obtained from the observed historical data. The identification of these neurons is obtained through the process called optimization. The interesting aspect of this setup is that the prediction is essentially derived from the historical observation and thus confirms the quote that: "Predicting the future is nothing more than the rearrangement of information that currently exists".

These are tasks normally done by trained doctors. In fact, doctors here use what is called in economic theory 'rational expectation' by taking current and previous histories and their predictions of the future to make decisions. What AI does is not necessarily to change the predicted diagnosis but to bring more consistency which in statistical terms is referred to as a reduction of the degree of uncertainty. There are other AI techniques that have been designed for learning and these are fuzzy logic which brings precision to the spoken words and uses these to make decisions through a computer, and support vector machines which are based on increasing the dimension of the space to better differentiate attributes in objects.

The second aspect of AI is optimization. Optimization is a process of identifying the lowest or highest point in a problem. For example, the process of identifying who is the shortest man in the world is an optimization problem. Using this example, the optimization algorithm is a computer or mathematically based procedure of identifying who the shortest person in the world is. Another example if you are designing an aircraft you might intend to make all your choices e.g. material to use and shape of the plane to result in the lowest amount of aeroplane weight. The parameters that you will play around with are called design variables. Nature is full of optimization processes and one exciting example is the process of natural evolution. This controversial theory, especially amongst the religious right, is a process in which species adapt to their environment and they achieve this through three drivers being mutation (random alteration of genes), crossover (mixing of genes), as well as reproduction of those individuals that are most adaptive to their environment. This natural optimization process has been codified to produce a computer based process called genetic algorithm.

The other aspect of AI is adaptation which is an optimization problem. For example, if one was to create a predictive system that predicts whether it is going to rain or not. The first level of optimization is to set up parameters that will make a predictive system predict whether it will rain or not. The second optimization level ensures that such a predictive system adapts to the evolving environment due to global warming. There are many techniques that have been developed to make adaptation possible and these include fish school algorithm which is inspired by the school of fish behaviour and ant colony optimization which is inspired by the colony of ants. The mathematics of the topics covered in this book are illustrated in Appendix A–F.

1.4 Conclusion

This chapter went through some of the big ideas that have been developed in the study of economics. These include concepts such as Marxism, the theory of invisible hand, rational expectations, rational choice, mechanism design and game theory. Furthermore, this chapter discussed how some of these will change as man is replaced by an artificial intelligent machine as a principal agent of economic decision making.

References

Agassi J (1971) Faraday as a natural philosopher. University of Chicago Press, Chicago

Amos SW, James MR (1999) Principles of transistor circuits. Butterworth-Heinemann

Anand P (1993) Foundations of rational choice under risk. Oxford University Press, Oxford

Byrne RMJ (2005) The rational imagination: how people create alternatives to reality. MIT Press, Cambridge, M.A.

de Vivo, G (1987) In: Ricardo, David, the new Palgrave: a dictionary of economics, pp 183–98

Fama E (1970) Efficient capital markets: a review of theory and empirical work. Journal of Finance 25(2):383–417

Gujarati DN, Porter DC (2009) Causality in economics: the granger causality test. In: Basic Econometrics, Fifth international ed, McGraw-Hill, New York, pp 652–658

Hamilton WP (1922). The stock market barometer. John Wiley & Sons Inc, New York. (1998 reprint)

Harari Y (2014) Sapiens: a brief history of humankind. Vintage, ISBN, p 9780099590088

Henderson DR (2008) Opportunity cost. Concise encyclopedia of economics, 2nd edn. Library of Economics and Liberty, Indianapolis

Hurwicz L, Radner R, Reiter S (1975) A stochastic decentralized resource allocation process: Part I. Econometrica 43(2):187–221

Kahneman D (2011) Thinking, fast and slow. Macmillan

Markowitz HM (1952) Portfolio selection. J Financ 7(1):77–91

Marwala T (2007) Computational intelligence for modelling complex systems. Research India Publications, Delhi

Marwala T (2009) Computational intelligence for missing data imputation, estimation, and management: knowledge optimization techniques. IGI Global, Pennsylvania

Marwala T (2010) Finite element model updating using computational intelligence techniques: applications to structural dynamics. Springer, Heidelberg

Marwala T (2012) Condition monitoring using computational intelligence methods. Springer, Heidelberg

Marwala T (2013) Economic modeling using artificial intelligence methods. Springer, Heidelberg

Marwala T (2014) Artificial intelligence techniques for rational decision making. Springer, Heidelberg

Marwala T (2015) Causality, correlation, and artificial intelligence for rational decision making. World Scientific, Singapore

Marwala T, Lagazio M (2011) Militarized conflict modeling using computational intelligence. Springer, Heidelberg

Marwala T, Mahola U, Nelwamondo FV (2006) Hidden Markov models and Gaussian mixture models for bearing fault detection using fractals. International Joint Conference on Neural Networks, (IJCNN'06) pp 3237–3242

Marwala T, Boulkaibet I, Adhikari S (2017) Probabilistic finite element model updating using bayesian statistics: applications to aeronautical and mechanical engineering. Wiley

Marx K (1849) Wage labour and capital. Neue Rheinische Zeitung, Germany. Retrieved 26 Oct 2016

Maxwell JC (1873) A treatise on electricity and magnetism, vol I. Clarendon Press, Oxford

Mill JS (2001) Utilitarianism and the 1868 speech on capital punishment. In: Sher (ed), Hackett Publishing Co

Myerson RB (1991) Game theory: analysis of conflict. Harvard University Press

Nash J (1950) Equilibrium points in n-person games. Proc Natl Acad Sci 36(1):48–49

Newton I (1729) Mathematical principles of natural philosophy. 1729 English translation based on 3rd Latin edition (1726), vol 2, containing Books 2 & 3

Picketty T (2014) Capital in the twenty-first century. Belknap Press, Cambridge, MA

Searle JR (1980) Minds, brains, and programs. Cambridge University Press, Behavioral and brain sciences

Siegel JJ (2008) Stock market. In: Henderson DR (ed) Concise encyclopedia of economics, 2nd ed. Library of Economics and Liberty, Indianapolis

Simon H (1991) Bounded rationality and organizational learning. Organ Sci 2(1):125–134

Smith A (2015) The concise encyclopedia of economics. Liberty Fund, Inc. Retrieved 29 July 2015

Stiglitz JE (2012) The price of inequality: how today's divided society endangers our future. W.W. Norton & Company, New York

Traiger S (2000) Making the right identification in the turing test. Mind Mach 10(4):561

Chapter 2
Supply and Demand

Abstract The law of demand and supply is the fundamental law of economic trade. It consists of the demand characteristics of the customer which describes the relationship between price and quantity of goods. For example, if the price of a good is low the customer will buy more goods and services than if the price is high. The relationship between price and the willingness of the customers to buy goods and services is called the demand curve. The other aspect of the demand and supply law is the supply curve which relates the relationship between the price and the quantity of goods suppliers are willing to produce. For example, the higher the price the more the goods and services the suppliers are willing to produce. Conversely, the lower the price the lesser the goods and services the suppliers are willing to produce. The point at which the suppliers are willing to supply a specified quantity of goods and services which are the same as those that the customers are willing to buy is called equilibrium. This chapter studies how the law of demand and supply is changed by the advent of artificial intelligence (AI). It is observed that the advent of AI allows the opportunity for individualized demand and supply curves to be produced. Furthermore, the use of an AI machine reduces the degree of arbitrage in the market and therefore brings a certain degree of fairness into the market which is good for the efficiency of the economy.

2.1 Introduction

The law of supply and demand has been studied by many thinkers. Some of the earliest studies of demand and supply were by a Muslim scholar Ibn Taymiyyah in the fourteenth century, English philosopher and physician John Locke in the seventeenth century and Scottish philosopher Adam Smith in the eighteenth century (Locke 1691; Hosseini 2003). The law of supply and demand has two aspects and these are the supply side as well as the demand side. On the supply side it states that the higher the price of goods and services is, the more the suppliers are willing to produce those goods and services. Conversely, the lower the price of goods and services, the fewer the suppliers are willing to produce those goods and services. On

© Springer International Publishing AG 2017   15
T. Marwala and E. Hurwitz, *Artificial Intelligence and Economic Theory: Skynet in the Market*, Advanced Information and Knowledge Processing,
DOI 10.1007/978-3-319-66104-9_2

the demand side, the higher the price of goods and services is, the lesser the customers are willing to buy those goods and services. Conversely, the lower the price of goods and services, the more the customers are willing to buy those goods and services. The point where the demand matches the supply is called equilibrium. Every customer has his/her own demand curve and every supplier has his/her own supply curve. For a particular good, there is an aggregate demand curve which is a collection of the demand curves of all the customers whereas for the supply curve there is an aggregate supply curve for all suppliers of that particular good. The aggregate equilibrium is what most customers is used as a basis of pricing of goods that we find in stores and this is the price which suppliers are subjected to. With the advent of artificial intelligence (AI), online buying and big data analytics, it is now possible to create individualized pricing models because it is now possible to individualize the supply and demand curves and therefore have an individual equilibrium price.

There is a concept of price elasticity which was introduced by the English economist Alfred Marshall which is a measure of how much customers change their buying patterns given the change in price (Marshall 1920). With the advent of artificial intelligence, it is now possible to study individualized price elasticity. This chapter studies the law of supply and demand given the fact that a substantial amount of trades are now conducted online and that decisions are made by or with the help of computers which are capacitated by artificial intelligence technology.

2.2 Scarcity

The fundamental basis of supply and demand is the concept of scarcity (Montani 1987; Jeff et al. 2003; Mankiw and Taylor 2011). The concept which makes goods and services have economic value and therefore can be priced, according to neo-classical economics, is the notion of scarcity. Oxygen is valuable and without it there is no life but because it is not scarce it has no price. The trigger or the necessary condition for goods and services to have a price, i.e. economic value, is scarcity. Scarcity is a phenomenon which is a result of the fact that goods and services are limited and therefore cannot fulfil or be given to all human beings if they require them.

Suppose there is a farmer Peter who produces 200 apples per month. For this farmer to produce these apples he needs fertilizers, water, expertise and instruments. The 200 apples that he produces per month are not limitless as there are only 200 per month. Because of this situation, the apples are classified as being scarce. Suppose in this ideal world, Peter is the only person who produces apples. Then these apples will be classified as being scarce. Suppose we have another person, John, who is the only person who eats apples and eats one apple per day (30 apples per month). In this ideal world, there will be excess of 170 apples per month. In this case because the demand for apples by John are lower than the supply of apples by Peter, the price of apples will be low because the supply outstrips the demand.

Suppose 10 people now eat a total of 10 apples per day. Then the demand for apples will outstrip the supply because 300 apples are now needed per month. In this situation, the price of apples will be high. In this scenario of 10 people who eat an apple per day, the apples are scarcer than when only John is the only one who eats an apple per day. These ten people want these apples because somehow these apples fulfil their individual wants or have certain benefits such as the fact that they give them energy.

2.3 Utilitarianism

Utilitarianism is another concept that is important for the understanding of the notion of demand and supply. It is a theory that prescribes what should be done given a set of conditions. It was developed by an English philosopher Jeremy Bentham and was extensively developed by the English philosopher John Stuart Mill (Bentham 1776; Bentham and Mill 2004). On defining utilitarianism, Jeremy Bentham advised that on choosing how to differentiate right from wrong a person should use the principle of "... the greatest happiness of the greatest number that is the measure of right and wrong". Utilitarianism emanates from the word utility which means how useful or beneficial goods and services are. For example, when John eats the apple he wants to ingest those aspects of the apple that makes him healthy and gives him enough energy to be able to pursue those aspects of life that are fulfilling to him.

Suppose Peter is a President of the Republic of Venda and wants to know what decision to take given a particular situation. If Peter is schooled in the philosophy of utilitarianism, he will take a decision that maximizes the aggregate happiness and minimizes the aggregate misery in his country, the Republic of Venda. This decision is summed and restated as Peter maximizing his utility.

In nature there are examples of biological objects that exhibit the principle of maximizing utility. For example, in Darwin's theory of evolution, species adapt to their environments through crossover, mutation and reproduction where the elements of the species that are not adapted to the environment die out (Darwin 1861). For example, those members of the population that are not adapted to the environment die and their gene pool is therefore not represented in the next generation. This mechanism can be viewed as a utilitarian problem where the species as a system undergoes evolution to maximize its utility i.e. survival. This concept of natural selection is so powerful that it explains many aspects of life in society, medical sciences and has been adapted in computer science to form an algorithm called genetic algorithm that has been successfully used to schedule optimal or shortest routes between multiple locations (Goldberg 1989).

Another example of populations maximizing their utility, is a swarm of pigeons in a park where when a person puts seeds at a particular location all the pigeons rush towards that location where the seeds were dropped. Each pigeon makes a move based on two factors and these are its own knowledge (individual intelligence) and the knowledge of the swarm (group intelligence). It basically looks at what everyone is doing and what it knows in order to make its move. Each pigeon does this in order to maximize its utility which is measured by how many seeds it is able to find and then eat. There are many other examples that illustrate the concept of utility, such as the school of fish, ant colony, swarm of bees etc.

At the core of the principle of utilitarianism there is something valuable that individuals are pursuing to maximize such as survival in the theory of evolution as well as seeds in case of the swarm of pigeons we have described.

2.4 Supply and Demand

The demand and supply curve is an illustration of the relationship between the supplier and the customer which is shown in Fig. 2.1. The supplier produces goods and services with economic value and his intention is to maximize utility and in this case this is the return on his investment. The customer has money and he estimates the value of the goods and services he wants to procure, and he prices these goods and services to maximize utility. These transactions will go ahead if the supplier's perception of value of the price offered by the customer is at least equal to and preferably higher than the value he places on the good. Alternatively, the customer will procure the good if his perception of the value of the good is equal to or higher than the value of the money he will use. This is what is called the asymmetry of information with regards to perception of value and this will be discussed in detail in the chapters ahead. The concept of information asymmetry and its impact on the market won George Akerlof, Michael Spence, and Joseph E. Stiglitz a Nobel Prize (Akerlof 1970; Spence 1973).

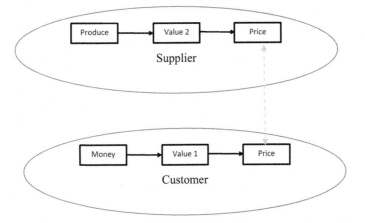

Fig. 2.1 An illustration of the relationship between the supplier and customer

Table 2.1 The demand data for Peter

Price	7	2
Quantity	1	8

Suppose a customer, Peter, is willing to buy 1 kg of rice for 7 cents and is willing to buy 8 kg of rice for 2 cents (see Table 2.1). Then Peter's demand curve is represented as in Fig. 2.2. Suppose a supplier George is willing to supply 1 kg of rice for 2 cents while he is willing to supply 8 kg of rice for 7 cents (see Table 2.2). Then George's supply curve is shown in Fig. 2.2. The point of equilibrium for this business transaction between Peter and George is 4.5 kg of rice for 4.5 cents and this is shown in Fig. 2.2. The point of equilibrium for the business transaction between Aiden and Isaac as per Tables 2.3 and 2.4 and further shown in Fig. 2.3 is 4.7 kg of rice for 5.69 cents. The aggregate point of equilibrium for this business transaction amongst all players is 9.12 kg of rice for 10.01 cents. This is shown in Fig. 2.4 (Tables 2.5 and 2.6).

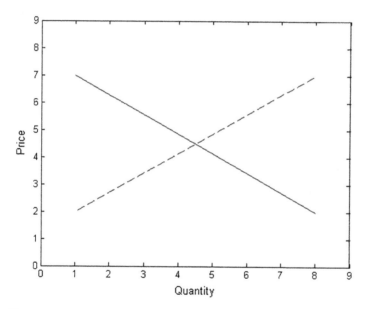

Fig. 2.2 The supply and demand curves for Peter and George

Table 2.2 The supply data for George

Price	2	7
Quantity	1	8

Table 2.3 The demand data for Aiden

Price	8	2
Quantity	2	9

Table 2.4 The supply data
for Isaac

Price	3	9
Quantity	2	8

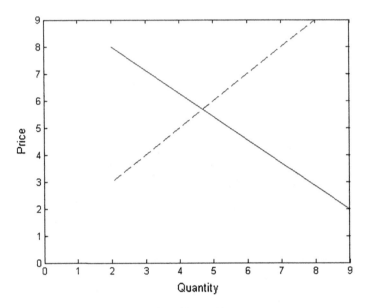

Fig. 2.3 The supply and demand curves for Aiden and Isaac

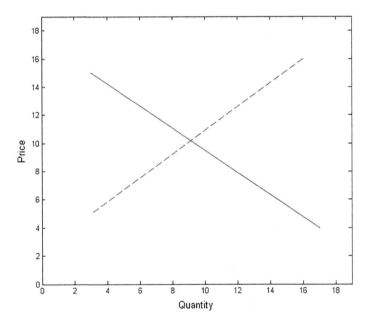

Fig. 2.4 The aggregate supply and demand curves

Table 2.5 The aggregate demand

Price	7 + 8 = 15	2 + 2 = 4
Quantity	1 + 2 = 3	8 + 9 = 17

Table 2.6 The aggregate supply data

Price	2 + 3 = 5	7 + 9 = 16
Quantity	1 + 2 = 3	8 + 8 = 16

What do we learn from this picture? That individual customers and suppliers have their own demand and supply curves and these differ from the aggregate demand and supply curves. If a customer goes to a market in Delhi in India and wants to buy a shirt and approaches five different suppliers selling the same shirt then he will get five different prices. Then there are 6 sets of equilibriums and these are from the five suppliers and the aggregate for all of them. Of course the customer will buy from the supplier with the lowest price to maximise his utility. The normal way of handling this Indian market is to negotiate a better deal rather than subject yourself to the aggregate equilibrium, forces we see often in Western markets.

2.5 Factors Influencing Demand and Supply

The demand curve is an expression of a measure of the willingness of the customers to buy a particular quantity of a good or service at a particular price. What are some of the factors that make customers buy a desired good or service? Do we buy a good or service because it will maximize utility? Does a common individual even know how to maximize utility?

One of the factors that influences the demand is the amount of capital one has because without any money, then customer is not willing or perhaps able to buy a particular amount of a good at a specified price. That is why sellers want to get into markets that have capital. For example, China prefers to sell its goods and services in the USA as opposed to the Democratic Republic of Congo because the demand for goods and services is higher in the USA than in the Democratic Republic of Congo. No money, no demand, square and simple!

The second is the taste of the customers and the need for that good. So it will not make any sense for a beef farmer in Botswana to try to enter the Indian market because people there are largely vegetarian. When a customer for a used car goes to look for a red Toyota Corolla, then he is willing to pay for it at a given price which is a point in his demand curve. The other factor is the comparative price for other goods. For example, the customer might prefer a red Toyota because a BMW is too expensive. He might prefer to buy the car now because the future price of cars is going to go up considerably. The fact of the matter is that a human being has his own demand and supply curve. If these are not in line with the market, then the supplier will get out of business, whereas, the customer for goods and services will not find anyone that is willing to sell him goods and services.

In a practical situation, suppose we introduce an artificial intelligent agent that is meant to buy goods and services on his behalf. This artificial intelligent agent is able to look for all cars in the market including the internet and look at his needs such as what are his average daily travels, the nature of the roads he travels and other factors to find a best match for the car he desires. This artificial intelligent agent maximizes the utility of their human owner far much better than the human being himself. This agent is known as a recommender system and organizations such as Amazon are full of these agents that study the characteristics of their human owners and then make recommendations on what book to buy. Now given that the customers will more and more no longer be making purchases directly and that artificial intelligent agents are well suited for such tasks, what does this configuration do to the nature of the demand curve?

On the supply side, the producers are willing to produce a good and service at a particular price provided that they are able to maximize their utilities (i.e. profits). The factors that influence the supply curve include the production costs that are more and more being automated with artificial intelligence capabilities. The fourth industrial revolution will see more and more intelligent automation and thus resulting in the dramatic decrease in the cost of labour. This will result in the dramatic reduction in the cost of production.

The other factor influencing the supply curve is the expected future prices and profits, a feat that is more and more becoming easier to manage because of the advent of artificial intelligence which makes forecasting easier to handle. The other factor that influences the supply curve is competition. Today it is far easier to understand competition than before because of the availability of information in the internet due to dramatic increase in data analytics capabilities, as well as the availability of techniques such as deep learning that make sense of information from big data.

2.6 Artificial Intelligence (AI) and Demand and Supply

AI is a computational procedure that is able to mimic high level skills that are observed in natural and biological systems (Marwala 2007, Marwala and Hurwitz 2015). For example, neural networks mimics the functioning of the human brain and have been used to solve complex problems in medical sciences (Marwala 2009), mechanical engineering (Marwala 2010), modelling interstate conflict (Marwala and Lagazio 2011, Marwala 2015), electrical engineering (Marwala 2012), economics (Marwala 2013), automated rational decision making (Marwala 2014) and aeronautical engineering (Marwala et. al. 2017). How does AI impact the demand and supply theory? Firstly on the demand side, AI is acting as a DNA of agents that act on behalf of their human owners. For example, on buying a book on the Amazon online system, the computer learns the buying behaviour of the customer. How does this happen? There are two ways of teaching a neural network to learn and these are supervised learning and unsupervised learning.

The supervised learning technique learns labelled data with inputs and outputs. A practical illustration of this is on teaching a child pictures and their names. The first picture is of a dog and a child is told that this is a dog. Then a second picture of a cat is presented and the child is told that this is a cat. The third picture is of a lion and the child is told that this is a lion. This scenario has input to the neural network which is the picture and the output of the neural network which is the corresponding name of the animal. This is called supervised learning. Neural networks maps the input i.e. pictures of animals to the output i.e. their corresponding identity using network weights which are akin to the neurons of the brain and activations functions which are akin to the mechanism in which these neurons are handled.

This works very well for structured environment like in a classroom. The other way of learning the same information is for a child to operate in the environment and by observing and listening to people in their normal conversations, gets to learn what a cat, a dog and a lion are. This is unstructured learning and in artificial intelligence terminology is unsupervised learning. Again, unsupervised learning occurs in many forms including through grouping similar data together e.g. cats are grouped together.

The introduction of artificial intelligence agents does not change the income of the person it is acting for nor does it change his tastes and preferences. However, it recommends based on historical knowledge of the preferences of the human being it is acting on behalf of and therefore it does influence his future decisions. Because it is able to search much more extensively than its human owner, it gets better products at better prices. By so doing, it reduces the probability of the customer to over pay for the products he buys and therefore reduces the degree of arbitrage i.e. exploiting the flow of information resulting in suboptimal pricing. People generally buy goods and services because they need the goods but also because they are getting a better price. If the artificial intelligence agent improves the flow and accuracy of the information of the goods and services the customer is buying, the result is that the volume of trades will decrease.

On the supply side, artificial intelligence is changing the mode of production of goods and services. Goods and services that normally required large number of people to produce are now produced using AI enabled robots. The consequence of intelligently automating production is that the cost of producing goods decreases. The production facilities self-repair thereby decreasing the amount of downtime. Artificial intelligence predicts equipment failures due to advances in condition monitoring and signal processing. All these factors make production more efficient and therefore contribute towards the reduction of the cost of production.

What do these do to the supply curve? It increases the willingness of suppliers to produce goods and services. What happens to the expected price of goods and services? Because machines do not get tired, the price of goods and services decreases. What does it do to the barrier of entry into the supply chain by new entrants? Capital becomes the major barrier to entry to by new entrants. What does AI do to the flexibility of the production lines? Evolutionary based procedures, such as genetic algorithm, become part of the production process and thereby make production facilities be autonomously adaptive. Genetic algorithm is an artificial intelligence procedure that is inspired by the way evolution operates and which is driven by crossover i.e. mixing of different production configurations, mutation i.e. adapting production process, and reproduction i.e. synthesizing best production configurations.

2.7 Conclusion

This chapter studied the impact of artificial intelligence on the law of demand and supply. The demand curve is a measure of how much quantity of goods and services customers are willing to buy given the price. The supply curve is a measure of how much quantity of goods suppliers are willing to produce given the price. Equilibrium is a measure of the position where the quantity of goods customers are willing to buy at a certain price is the same as what the suppliers are willing to produce. AI through learning and evolution is able to ensure that the demand and supply curves are better modelled. The use of an AI machine reduces the degree of arbitrage in the market and therefore brings a certain degree of fairness into the market which is good for the efficiency of the economy.

References

Akerlof GA (1970) The market for lemons: quality uncertainty and the market mechanism. Q J Econ 84(3):488–500 (The MIT Press)
Bentham J (1776) A fragment on government. London. Preface (2nd para.)
Darwin C (1861) On the origin of species by means of natural selection, or the preservation of favoured races in the struggle for life, 3rd edn. John Murray, London
Goldberg D (1989) Genetic algorithms in search, optimization and machine learning. Addison-Wesley Professional, Reading, MA
Hosseini HS (2003) Contributions of medieval Muslim scholars to the history of economics and their impact: a refutation of the schumpeterian great gap. In Biddle
Jeff E, Davis JB, Samuels, Warren JA (2003) Companion to the history of economic thought. Blackwell, Malden, MA, p 28. doi:10.1002/9780470999059.ch3. ISBN:0-631-22573-0
Locke J (1691) Some considerations on the consequences of the lowering of interest and the raising of the value of money, Marxists
Marshall A (1920) Principles of economics. Library of Economics and Liberty
Marwala T (2007) Computational intelligence for modelling complex systems. Research India Publications, Delhi
Marwala T (2009) Computational intelligence for missing data imputation, estimation, and management: knowledge optimization techniques. IGI Global, Pennsylvania
Marwala T (2010) Finite element model updating using computational intelligence techniques: applications to structural dynamics. Springer, Heidelberg
Marwala T (2012) Condition monitoring using computational intelligence methods. Springer, Heidelberg. ISBN 978-1-4471-2380-4

Marwala T (2013) Economic modeling using artificial intelligence methods. Springer, Heidelberg

Marwala T (2014) Artificial intelligence techniques for rational decision making. Springer, Heidelberg

Marwala T (2015) Causality, correlation, and artificial intelligence for rational decision making. World Scientific, Singapore

Montani G (1987) Scarcity. In: Eatwell J, Millgate M, Newman P (eds) The new Palgrave. A dictionary of economics. 4. Palgrave, Houndsmill, pp 253–254

Mankiw NG, Taylor MP (2011) Economics (2nd ed., revised ed.). Cengage Learning, Andover

Marwala T, Hurwitz E (2015) Artificial intelligence and asymmetric information theory. arXiv:1510.02867

Marwala T, Lagazio M (2011) Militarized conflict modeling using computational intelligence. Springer, Heidelberg

Marwala T, Boulkaibet I, Adhikari S (2017) Probabilistic finite element model updating using bayesian statistics: applications to aeronautical and mechanical engineering. John Wiley and Sons, New Jersey

Mill JS, Bentham J (2004). Utilitarianism and other essays. In: Ryan A (ed) Penguin Books, London

Spence M (1973) Job market signaling. Q J Econ 87(3):355–374 (The MIT Press)

Chapter 3
Rational Choice and Rational Expectations

Abstract The theory of rational choice assumes that when people make decisions they do so in order to maximize their utility. In order to achieve this goal they ought to use all the information available and consider all the options available to select an optimal choice. This chapter investigates what happens when decisions are made by artificial intelligent machines in the market rather than human beings. Firstly, the expectations of the future are more consistent if they are made by artificial intelligent machines than if they are made by human beings in that the bias and the variance of the error of the predictions are reduced. Furthermore, the decisions that are made are more rational and thus the marketplace becomes more rational.

3.1 Introduction

This chapter is on rational decision making, through the theory of rational choice, and this is a complex process that has perplexed thinkers for a very long time. On making a decision rationally a person should take into account that other players may be acting irrationally. In this situation, the rational decision that is taken will factor into account the irrational reaction from the other players. Suppose a doctor prescribes medicine to a superstitious individual. That decision making process (rational) of prescribing medicine might take into account the individual's superstitious tendencies (irrational) and thus also prescribes that the patient should be supervised on taking the medication. So in essence, the decision taken has factored into account the fact that the patient will act irrationally. Rational choice is a mechanism of choosing using complete information and evaluating all options to select an option that globally maximizes utility.

In prehistoric society, decision making was jumbled with superstitions (Marwala 2014). For example, there is an old superstitious belief that if a person encounters a black cat crossing the road then that person will encounter bad luck. The other superstition among the Venda people in South Africa is that if the owl crows in your house then there will be death in the family. How these superstitions came about is not known but one can speculate that perhaps sometime in the past, a

T. Marwala and E. Hurwitz, *Artificial Intelligence and Economic Theory: Skynet in the Market*, Advanced Information and Knowledge Processing,
DOI 10.1007/978-3-319-66104-9_3

powerful person in the community, perhaps the King, by chance encountered a black cat crossing the road and he had bad luck subsequently. Whatever the explanations for these superstitions may be, the fact remains that superstitions have been and remain part of who we are as human beings in this present state of our evolution. Perhaps sometime in the future we will evolve into some other species which is not superstitious and, the fourth industrial revolution or cyber-physical-biological system offers us a unique opportunity for that to happen.

Superstition can be viewed as supernatural causality where something is caused by another without them being connected to one another. The idea of one event causing another without any connection between them whatsoever is irrational. Making decisions based on superstitious assumptions is irrational decision making and is the antithesis of this chapter which is on rational decision choice.

This book basically proposes that the basic mechanisms of rational decision making are causality and correlation machines to create rational expectations machines, and optimization to select the appropriate option that maximizes utility. Suppose we compare two ways of moving from A to B. The first choice is to use a car and the second one is to use a bicycle. The rational option is not just to select the choice which minimizes time but to compare this with the cost of the action. Rational decision making is a process of reaching a decision that maximizes utility and these decisions are arrived at based on relevant information and by applying sound logic and, by optimizing resources (Marwala 2015).

Nobel Prize Laureate Herbert Simon realized that on making a rational decision one does not always have all the information, and the logic that is used is far from perfect and, consequently, he introduced the concept of bounded rationality (Simon 1991). Marwala (2014) in his book that extends the theory of bounded rationality developed this notion that with the advent of artificial intelligence (AI) the bounds of rationality that Herbert Simon's theory prescribed are in fact flexible. This is the subject to be addressed later in this book.

3.2 Adaptive and Rational Expectations

The concept of rational expectations is a theory that prescribes how an agent uses all the information that is currently available to predict what will happen in the future (Snowdon et al. 1994). It is based on the premise that predicting the future is nothing more than the arrangements of the information that currently exists (McCloskey 1998; Galbács 2015). The idea that the future is largely based on the totality of the present is an interesting proposition that has been tested so many times without resolution. What we do know is that it is rational to expect that the future is not going to be too different from the present. Rational expectations evolved from what is known as adaptive expectations. Adaptive expectations is a theory, in our context, that states that the future price of an economic variable is based on its past values. It has been found that this assumption gives biased results because there might be other factors beside the economic variable that is in question that affects its future value. The efficient market hypotheses states that the past value of an economic variable reflects all other factors that have influenced it and, therefore, there is no need to incorporate other variables (Fox 2009). Despite this argument it is a good practice to use as many variables as possible to predict future expectations and this is what is termed the theory of rational expectations. For example, if the unemployment has been rising in the last 5 years one would expect it to rise in the next year. In this case, if one takes into account the economic growth, one could have predicted that the unemployment rate will go up next year. So just looking at the past values of the variable one requires to predict, is not sufficient to predict its future. This chapter evaluates the impact of big data, artificial intelligence and related technologies on the concept of rational expectations.

Suppose a farmer by the name Jabulani wants to predict whether it will rain tomorrow. He has the data for the last three months and wants to use the data from the last three days to predict the subsequent days. This is what is called adaptive expectations where one uses the previous experience and, in this case, whether it rained or not in the last 5 days to predict the subsequent day. The problem with this approach is that it does not take into account the seasonality. How about using other factors such as humidity, average temperature etc.? The data representing this is indicated in Table 3.1.

One can then use this data to build a regression model which takes Day 1 to 5 as input and Day 6 as output. If one assumes that the model governing this relationship is linear, then one can use linear regression. If one can assume that this model is nonlinear of unspecified order, then artificial intelligence neural network models can be used. Neural networks are based on the functioning of the brain and there are many neural network models that can be used in this regard, and these include the multi-layer perceptron, radial basis functions or even support vector machines. These techniques have been used to model economic systems (Marwala 2013), for modelling mechanical structures (Marwala 2010), interstate disputes (Marwala and Lagazio 2011), missing data (Marwala 2009), modelling causality (Marwala 2014), for rational decision making (Marwala 2015) and for modelling aeronautical systems (Marwala et al. 2016). The fact that adaptive expectations gives an expected error that is not zero and, therefore biased, has led Palestrini and Gallegati (2015) to propose a bias correction term to reduce the error of the adaptive expectation schemes. Furthermore, Sorge (2013) introduced conditions under which adaptive expectations hold and applied these to macroeconomic models. The theory of

Table 3.1 Data on rain Key: 1 = rained; 0 = no rain

	Day 1	Day 2	Day 3	Day 4	Day 5	Day 6
Episode 1	0	0	0	0	0	1
Episode 2	1	1	0	0	0	1
Episode 3	1	1	1	1	1	1
Episode 4	1	0	0	0	0	0
Episode 5	0	1	0	1	0	0

adaptive expectations has been found to give biased results and, consequently, the theory of rational expectations was established.

Rational expectations is an improvement on the theory of adaptive expectations and it stipulates that rational agents make use of all the information available to predict the future and, such a prediction of the future is not systematically wrong. The concept of "systematically wrong" is important in that it does not preclude being wrong but that this wrong is not systematic. For example, in the case described earlier of predicting the next day rain from the previous five days, if the results systematically predict rain when it does not rain then a human agent will recognize this trend and use it to correct the predictions. Liu (2016) implemented rational expectations for pricing whereas Chen and Liu (2016) implemented rational expectations to understand how the returns of insider traders impact on precision of leakage information. Other work on rational expectations are by Spiegler (2016) who studied rational expectations within the framework of Bayesian networks as well as Zierhut (2016) within the context of real assets and binding constraints.

One classical example of rational expectation is the study of the prediction of the future price of a stock. If one only uses the previous price of the stock, then one is adaptively predicting the future price of the stock and, the results are biased. One can incorporate the markets sentiments which can be extracted from the internet to the past values of the stock. For example, Bollen et al. (2010) used the markets' moods as extracted from the twitter data and found that the results show a reduction of error of 6%. Robert Lucas observed that it is naïve to predict the future of an economic variable based solely on historical data, especially aggregated historical data (Lucas 1976). Artificial intelligence techniques such as neural networks offer an excellent platform to fuse different data such as stock price and twitter data to predict the future price. This reduces the bias and variance of the error in predicting the future price.

3.3   What Is Rational Choice?

It is important to first understand what rational choice is and to do this, it is important to understand the meaning of the words rational and choice (Green and Shapiro 1994; Friedman 1996). According to google dictionary, rational is defined as "based on or in accordance with reason or logic" while choice is defined as "the act of choosing between two or more possibilities". Rational choice is a process of making decisions based on relevant information, in a logical, timely and optimized manner. Suppose a man called Thendo wants to make a decision on how much coffee he should drink today and, he calls his sister Denga to find out the color of shoes she is wearing and uses this information to decide how much coffee he will drink on that day. This will be an irrational decision making process because Thendo is using irrelevant information (the color of shoes his sister Denga is wearing) to decide how much coffee he will drink. If on the same token, Thendo decides that every time he takes a sip of that coffee, he needs to walk for 1 km, we

Fig. 3.1 Steps for rational
decision making

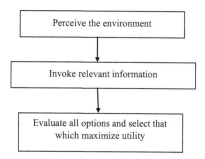

then will conclude that he is acting irrationally because he is wasting energy
unnecessarily by walking 1 km in order to take a sip of coffee. This unnecessary
wastage of energy is irrational and in mathematical terminology we describe this as
an un-optimized solution. If Thendo decides that every time he sips coffee he first
pours it from one glass to another for no other reason except to fulfil the task of
drinking coffee, then he is using an irrational course of action because this is not
only illogical but also un-optimized.

An illustration of a rational decision making framework is shown in Fig. 3.1.
This figure shows that on undertaking a rational decision making process one
studies the environment or more technically a decision making space. Then the next
step is to identify relevant information necessary for decision making. Then this
information is presented to a decision engine which is logical and consistent and
evaluates all possibilities and their respective utilities and then selects the decision
that offers the highest utility. Any weakness in this framework such as the absence
of all information, or information that is imprecise and imperfect, or not being able
to evaluate all possibilities limits the theory of rational choice and this becomes
bounded rationality, which was proposed by Simon (1991). What is termed neoclassical economics is based on the assumption that the agents in economics make
decisions based on the theory of rational choice. The fact that this agent is a human
being has led many researchers to study how human beings make decisions and this
is now what is called behavioral economics. Kahneman in his book *Thinking Fast
and Slow* explores behavioral economics extensively (Kahneman 2011). Today,
decisions are more and more made by artificial intelligent machines. These artificial
intelligent machines bring several aspects that make the assumption of rationality to
be stronger than when decisions are made by human beings. In this regard, the
machine makes decisions that are not as irrational as those made by warm blooded
human beings. However, machines are still not fully rational and, therefore, are
subjected to Herbert Simon's theory of bounded rationality.

For example, if in some isolated economic system all the decision making agents
are human beings, what will be the characteristics of that economy? That economy
will be governed by the principles of behavioral economics. If, however, all the
decision making agents are artificial intelligent machines that make decisions based
on rational choice, then that economy will be governed by the principles of

neoclassical economics. If half of these decision making agents are humans and the others are machines, then some economic system which is half neoclassical and half behavioral will emerge.

3.4 Information

The theory of rational choice is based on the fact that the information used to make decisions is complete and precise. This, however, is not physically realistic. The word information is from the verb informs and it means that which informs (Casagrande 1999). One of the ways in which information is represented is in the form of data, e.g. temperature, which needs to be sensed (Dusenbery 1992; Vigo 2011, 2013). For example, if one requires the information on the temperature of a body, one can use a thermometer to achieve this goal. The information from the thermometer is data, but it is really the volume of mercury which is not a representation of temperature but is correlated to temperature within certain conditions. For example, the same thermometer cannot be used for measuring very high temperatures (Vigo 2014). Measuring or acquiring information is not a precise science and is subject to uncertainties. These uncertainties are due to the fact that by measuring a metric from an object, the act of measuring changes the object and, therefore, the results are no longer the intended results. In Physics a German Nobel Laureate Werner Heisenberg proposed the uncertainty principle stating that one cannot measure the position and the speed of an electron accurately at the same time (Heisenberg 1927; Sen 2014). If one knows the speed, one does not know its position. On the other hand, if one knows its position, then one does not know its speed accurately. It turns out that this paradox is not because the measurement interferes with the speed or position, but it is just the fundamental nature of quantum mechanics. Getting complete and precise information is not possible so we have to deal with uncertainty, incompleteness and inaccuracy and, this has impact on the quality of decisions that are made.

3.5 Choices

The other factor in the theory of rational choice is the act of choosing options from many choices available (Hsee et al. 1999; Irons and Hepburn 2007). Suppose one wants to commercially fly from Johannesburg to New York. There are many routes to choose from. For example, one can fly from Johannesburg straight to New York or Johannesburg, Dubai then New York or Johannesburg, London then New York. The options available are thousands. In fact, if human beings have to make these choices, they cannot possibly be able to consider all these options in a reasonable time without the use of some software such as an artificial intelligence optimization technique (Schwartz 2005; Reed et al. 2011). Suppose it is raining outside and one needs to walk to the gate to pick up some mail. Suppose there is an umbrella and there are only two choices i.e. use an umbrella and walk to the gate and pick up some mail or do the same without an umbrella. The one that maximizes comfort i.e. utility is to pick up an umbrella and walk to the gate. This is a simple example because there are only two choices. In many instances, there are thousands of viable options and searching through all of them requires advanced search algorithms such as genetic algorithm. Furthermore, there might even be infinite choices making the prospect of a viable choice not reachable. The fact that one cannot be able to explore all options available, is more of a norm than an exception.

3.6 Optimization

On our task to identify a suitable route to travel to New York from Johannesburg described above, we can frame a problem in such a way that we want to identify a route which is the shortest or in which we shall spend the least amount of time on air or both. This is an optimization problem with an objective function of finding a route which minimizes the time on air or distance or both (Dixit 1990; Rotemberg and Woodford 1997). The process of identifying such route is called optimization and in this case it is to fly directly from Johannesburg to New York. This objective function is also called a cost function and is that function which a person wants to minimize (Diewert 2008). When both the distance and time are minimized, this is called a multi-objective optimization problem. We use our understanding of topology, i.e. intelligence to identify that the shortest distance is a straight line, and to infer that a direct route is the shortest one. Artificial intelligence has been used widely to solve such problems (Battiti et al. 2008).

3.7 Rational Choice

The theory of rational choice states that given several options, a rational human being will choose that option that maximizes his utility (Becker 1976; Hedström and Stern 2008; Lohmann 2008; Grüne-Yanoff 2012). This theory assumes several factors, and these include the fact that the decision maker has all the information that he can use to generate several options. In addition, that he can be able to construct all options as well as calculate the resulting utility for each option. An illustration of this concept is shown in Fig. 3.1. There are a number of principles that govern rational choice and these are completeness and transitivity. Completeness means that all pairs of alternative options can be compared to one another, whereas transitivity means if option 1 is better than option 2, which is in turn better than option 3, then option 1 is better than option 3. In addition, there are different classes of preferences and these are strict, weak and indifference. Strict preference is when one option is preferred over another, whereas indifference is

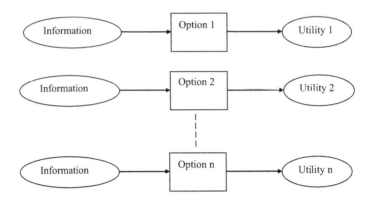

Fig. 3.2 An illustration of several options and their respective utilities

Table 3.2 An illustration of the calculation of utility

Options	Time (hours)	Utility
JHB-NY	18	0.05555556
JHB-DB-NY	36	0.02777778
JHB-LN-NY	24	0.04166667
JHB-PR-NY	26	0.03846154

when a person does not prefer one option over another. Figure 3.2 shows a problem with n options and their corresponding utility. In an example of identifying a shortest time to fly from Johannesburg to New York, the utility function is the inverse of the time it takes for this trip. In this regard, the shorter the time it takes to reach New York, the higher the utility. In this regard, suppose Johannesburg-New York takes 18 h, Johannesburg-Dubai-New York, 36 h, Johannesburg-London-New York takes 24 h, Johannesburg-Paris-New York 26, hours and so on. A table can be generated that takes these trips and converts them into utility, and this is indicated in Table 3.2. Utility is calculated as an inverse of the time it takes, i.e. one divided by the time it takes. This example, shows that to maximize utility, then one ought to fly directly from Johannesburg to New York.

Figure 3.2 can be simplified into Fig. 3.3, where there is a generalized options generator that takes in information and produces the optimal utility. An example of this, is when options can be represented in the form of a function, which takes in information and predicts alternative utilities given certain conditions and then, identify through some optimization routine, the option that maximizes utility.

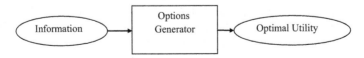

Fig. 3.3 A generalized options generator that takes information and gives the optimal utility

3.8   Rational Choice and Opportunity Cost

The fact that rational choice entails evaluating alternatives, invokes the concept of opportunity cost. The concept of opportunity cost was introduced by von Wieser (1914). According to Investopedia: "Opportunity cost refers to a benefit that a person could have received, but gave up, to take another course of action" (Anonymous 2017). When a person is presented with several options as shown in Fig. 3.2, a rational person will choose the option that maximizes his/her utility. The second best option for a rational person is to choose the option with a utility that is equal to or ranked second to the one he/she has just chosen (because he/she has already chosen the optimal choice). The options that are equal to or ranked second to the one he/she has chosen is the opportunity cost. This book introduces the concept of rational opportunity cost, which is the opportunity forgone that gives the expected utility that is equal to that which a rational person has pursued (a rational person maximizes utility). This is possible because there are situations where several options have the same utility values.

3.9   Rational Choice and Artificial Intelligence

On applying the theory of rational choice, a mechanism of generating options available needs to be established. For example, in the case of a trip from Johannesburg to New York, the options available are generated by connecting all the routes from Johannesburg to New York with one stopover, then two, then three etc. The options available are numerous. For example, there is a problem of inflation targeting that has been studied extensively where the goal is to use economic variables, including the previous interest rate, to predict inflation rate, and then to identify the interest rate that gives the desired inflation (Marwala 2012). The model which takes these economic variables and maps these to the inflation rate can be achieved using AI technique of neural networks or any other learning machine (Marwala and Lagazio 2011).

Neural networks are based on the functioning of the brain and, therefore, have much of the attributes of the brain such as the neuron in the brain being the processing element in neural networks, dendrites being the combining function, cell body being the transfer function, axon being the element output and synapses being the weights. Neural networks technique is a powerful machine that has been used to model complex systems (Marwala 2007), estimate missing data (Abdella and Marwala 2005, 2009), predict electrical faults (Marwala 2012), economic modelling (Marwala 2013), rational decision making (Marwala 2014), understanding causality (2015), and model mechanical structures (Marwala et al. 2006, 2017). These learning machines have free parameters and activation functions and, the free parameters are estimated from the data using some optimization method. In this way, whenever economic variables are given, the interest rate can be estimated.

The idea of predicting interest rate based on the previous interest rates is called the theory of adaptive expectations (Galbács 2015). The theory of adaptive expectations basically states that we can predict the future of an object based on its past values. Unfortunately, the theory of adaptive expectations has been found to result in systematic errors due to bias. The concept of including other variables in addition to the previous interest rate to predict the future interest rate is called the theory of rational expectations, and this eliminates systematic bias and errors (Muth 1971; Sargent 1987; Savin 1987).

After identifying a model that predicts the future interest rates based on the theory of rational expectations, which is made more valid by incorporating the use of artificial intelligence, data fusion, big data and text analysis, then one can identify the interest rate that will maximize the attainment of the desired inflation rate using an optimization routine. Optimization methods that are able to identify global optimum solutions are normally based on the branch of AI called evolutionary techniques, and these include techniques such as genetic algorithm, particle swarm optimization and simulated annealing (Perez and Marwala 2008). Genetic algorithm is a stochastic optimization method which is based on the principles of evolution, where mutation, crossover and reproduction are used to identify an optimal solution (Crossingham and Marwala 2008). Particle swarm optimization is a stochastic optimization method, which is based on the principles of local and group intelligence as observed in the swarm of birds, when they are identifying a roost, and this algorithm can be used to identify an optimal solution (Mthembu et al. 2011). These AI optimization methods can be used within the context of the theory of rational choice to identify a course of action that maximizes utility.

The implications of artificial intelligence on the theory of rational choice are as follows: (1) AI makes use of information in various formats e.g. text, pictures, internet and fuse them to make better rational expectations of the future, bringing decision making closer to the theory of rational choice; (2) On making the optimal choice, global optimization methods such as genetic algorithm give higher probability of identifying a global optimum utility, and thereby bringing decision making closer to the theory of rational choice.

3.10 Interstate Conflict and Rational Choice

Interstate conflict is a major source of economic instability, and the best option for rational states is to minimize conflict or maximize the attainment of peace. This is achieved by creating a model which takes several input variables and predicts the risk of conflict. This prediction of the risk of conflict is done by assuming the theory of rational expectations using the AI technique of neural networks to predict the peace/conflict outcome (zero for peace and one for conflict). This outcome is deemed to be the utility. Then using this neural network, controllable variables are identified and tuned using genetic algorithm optimization method to produce a peaceful outcome, as was done by Marwala and Lagazio (2011). The neural network is trained using seven dyadic independent variables and these are *Allies*, a binary measure coded 1 if the members of a dyad are linked by any form of military alliance, *Contingency* which is binary, coded 1 if both states are geographically contiguous, *Distance* which is an interval measure of the distance between the two states' capitals, *Major power* which is a binary variable coded 1 if either or both states in the dyad are a major power, *Democracy* which is measured on a scale where 10 is an extreme democracy and −10 is an extreme autocracy, *Dependency* which is measured as the sum of the countries import and export with its partner divided by the Gross Domestic Product of the stronger country and *Capability* which is the logarithm, to the base 10, of the ratio of the total population plus the number of people in urban areas plus industrial energy consumption plus iron and steel production plus the number of military personnel in active duty plus military expenditure in dollars in the last 5 years. We lag all independent variables by one year to make temporarily plausible any inference of causation. Of the 7 dyadic variables used in this chapter, there are only 4 that are controllable and these are: *Democracy*, *Allies*, *Capability* and *Dependency*.

As was done by Marwala and Lagazio (2011), the Golden section search (GSS) technique was used for the single strategy approach and simulated annealing was used for the multiple strategy approach. This technique is shown in Fig. 3.4.

When the control strategies were implemented, the results shown in Fig. 3.4 were obtained (Marwala and Lagazio 2011). These results show that, for a single strategy approach, where *Democracy* is the controlling dyadic variable, 90% of the 286 conflicts could have been avoided. When controlling the dyadic variable *Allies* as the only variable used to bring about peace, it was found that 77% of the 286 conflicts could have been avoided. When either *Dependency* or *Capability* was used as a single controlling variable, 99 and 98% of the 286 conflicts could have been avoided, respectively. In relation to the multiple strategy approach, when all the controllable variables were used simultaneously to bring about peace, all the 286 conflicts could have been avoided (Fig. 3.5).

This indicates the significance of democracy and dependency to achieve peace. From these results, it is evident that policy makers should focus on democratization and economic cooperation to maximize the attainment of peace. They should resolve which method, single or multiple, is the most suitable on the basis of how easy and cost efficient an intervention with the identified controllable variables is, and how long it would take to control them.

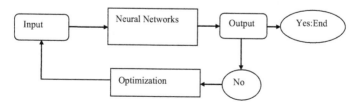

Fig. 3.4 Feedback control loop that uses Bayesian neural networks and an optimization method

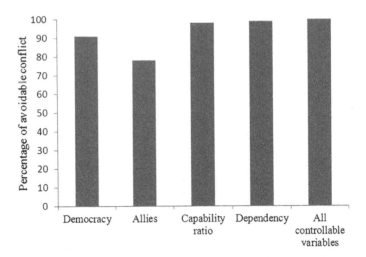

Fig. 3.5 Graph showing the proportion of past conflicts that could have been avoided

3.11   Conclusion

This chapter introduced rational expectations and rational choice and how they are changed through the advances of artificial intelligence. Furthermore, it introduced how the theory of rational choice changes the definition of the concept of opportunity costs. It proposed a framework of rational choice which is based on the theory of rational expectations to create a causal model between the input and output using neural networks and optimization to change the input to obtain the desired output. The theory of rational choice and artificial intelligence are used to maximize the attainment of peace.

References

Abdella M, Marwala T (2005) Treatment of missing data using neural networks and genetic algorithms. IEEE International Joint Conference on Neural Networks, Montreal, 598–603
Anonymous (2017) Opportunity cost. Investopedia. Last Retrieved 18 Mar 2017
Battiti R, Brunato M, Mascia F (2008) Reactive search and intelligent optimization. Springer Verlag
Becker, G.S. (1976) The Economic Approach to Human Behavior. University of Chicago Press
Bollen J, Mao H, Zeng X-J (2010) Twitter mood predicts the stock market arxiv:1010.3003
Casagrande D (1999) Information as verb: Re-conceptualizing information for cognitive and ecological models. J Ecol Anthr 3(1):4–13. doi:10.5038/2162-4593.3.1.1
Chen B, Liu S (2016) Rational expectation and information leakage with imperfect competition. Proceedings of the 28th Chinese Control and Decision Conference, CCDC, art. no. 7531715, 4180–4184

Crossingham B, Marwala T (2008) Using genetic algorithms to optimise rough set partition sizes for HIV data analysis. Adv Intell Distrib Comput Stud Comput Intell 78:245–250

Diewert WE (2008) Cost functions. The New Palgrave Dictionary of Economics (2nd edn contents)

Dixit AK (1990) Optimization in Economic Theory (2nd edn), Oxford

Dusenbery DB (1992) Sensory ecology. W.H. Freeman, New York

Fox J (2009) Myth of the rational market. Harper Business

Friedman J (1996) The rational choice controversy. Yale University Press

Galbács P (2015) The theory of new classical macroeconomics. a positive critique. Springer, Heidelberg/New York/Dordrecht/London

Green DP, Shapiro I (1994) Pathologies of rational choice theory: a critique of applications in political science. Yale University Press

Grüne-Yanoff T (2012) Paradoxes of rational choice theory. In Roeser S, Hillerbrand R, Sandin P, Peterson M (eds) Handbook of risk theory, pp 499–516. doi:10.1007/978-94-007-1433-5_19

Hedström P, Stern C (2008) Rational choice and sociology. The New Palgrave Dictionary of Economics (2nd edn). Abstract

Heisenberg W (1927) Über den anschaulichen Inhalt der quantentheoretischen Kinematik und Mechanik. Zeitschrift für Physik (in German) 43(3–4):172–198

Hsee CK, Loewenstein GF, Blount S, Bazerman MH (1999) Preference reversals between joint and separate evaluations of option: a review and theoretical analysis. Psychol Bull 125 (5):576–590

Irons B, Hepburn C (2007) Regret theory and the tyranny of choice. Econ Rec 83(261):191–203

Kahneman D (2011) Thinking, Fast and Slow. Macmillan, UK

Liu Z (2016) Implementation of maximin rational expectations equilibrium. Econ Theor 62 (4):813–837

Lohmann S (2008) Rational choice and political science. The New Palgrave Dictionary of Economics (2nd edn). Abstract

Lucas R (1976) Economic policy evaluation: a critique. In Brunnerm K, Meltzer A (eds) The philips curve and labor markets. Carnegie-Rochester Conference Series on Public Policy. Elsevier, New York, pp 19–46

Marwala T (2007) Computational intelligence for modelling complex systems. Research India Publications, Delhi

Marwala T (2009) Computational intelligence for missing data imputation, estimation, and management: knowledge optimization techniques. IGI Global, Pennsylvania. ISBN 978-1-60566-336-4

Marwala T (2010) Finite element model updating using computational intelligence techniques: applications to structural dynamics. Springer, Heidelberg

Marwala T (2012) Condition monitoring using computational intelligence methods. Springer, Heidelberg

Marwala T (2013) Economic modeling using artificial intelligence methods. Springer, Heidelberg

Marwala T (2014) artificial intelligence techniques for rational decision making. Springer, Heidelberg

Marwala T (2015) Causality, Correlation, and artificial intelligence for rational decision making. World Scientific, Singapore. ISBN 978-9-814-63086-3

Marwala T, Lagazio M (2011) Militarized conflict modeling using computational intelligence. Springer, Heidelberg. ISBN 978-0-85729-789-1

Marwala T, Mahola U, Nelwamondo FV (2006) Hidden Markov models and Gaussian mixture models for bearing fault detection using fractals. International Joint Conference on Neural Networks, pp 3237–3242

Marwala T, Boulkaibet I, Adhikari S (2017) Probabilistic finite element model updating using bayesian statistics: applications to aeronautical and mechanical engineering. John Wiley and Sons, ISBN: 978-1-119-15303-0

McCloskey DN (1998) The rhetoric of economics (2 edn). University of Wisconsin Press, p 53

Mthembu L, Marwala T, Friswell MI, Adhikari S (2011) Finite element model selection using particle swarm optimization. Conference proceedings of the society for experimental mechanics series, 1, vol 13, Dynamics of civil structures, vol 4, Springer, London, pp 41–52, Tom Proulx (Editor)

Muth JF (1961) Rational expectations and the theory of price movements Reprinted in The new classical macroeconomics. 1.3–23 (1992) (International Library of Critical Writings in Economics. Elgar, Aldershot, vol 19)

Palestrini A, Gallegati M (2015) Unbiased adaptive expectation schemes. Economics Bulletin 35 (2):1185–1190

Perez M, Marwala T (2008) Stochastic optimization approaches for solving Sudoku. arXiv preprint arXiv:0805.0697

Reed DD, DiGennaro Reed FD, Chok J, Brozyna GA (2011) The tyranny of choice: choice overload as a possible instance of effort discounting. Psychol Rec 61(4):547–560

Rotemberg J, Woodford M (1997) An optimization-based econometric framework for the evaluation of monetary policy. NBER Macroeconomics Annual, vol 12, pp 297–346

Sargent TJ (1987) Rational expectations, The New Palgrave: A Dictionary of Economics. vol 4, pp 76–79

Savin NE (1987) Rational expectations: econometric implications. The New Palgrave: A Dictionary of Economics 4:79–85

Schwartz B (2005) The Paradox of Choice: why more is less. Harper Perennial

Sen D (2014) The uncertainty relations in quantum mechanics (PDF). Curr Sci 107(2):203–218

Simon H (1991) Bounded rationality and organizational learning. Organ Sci 2(1):125–134

Snowdon B, Vane H, Wynarczyk P (1994) A modern guide to macroeconomics. Edward Elgar Publishing Limited, Cambridge, pp 236–279

Sorge MM (2013) Generalized adaptive expectations revisited. Econ Lett 120(2):203–205

Spiegler R (2016) Bayesian networks and boundedly rational expectations. Q J Econ 131(3): 1243–1290

Vigo R (2011) Representational information: a new general notion and measure of information. Inf Sci 181:4847–4859. doi:10.1016/j.ins.2011.05.020

Vigo R (2013) Complexity over uncertainty in Generalized Representational Information Theory (GRIT): a structure-sensitive general theory of information. Information 4(1):1–30. doi:10.3390/info4010001

Vigo R (2014) Mathematical principles of human conceptual behavior: the structural nature of conceptual representation and processing. Scientific Psychology Series. Routledge, New York and London. ISBN 0415714362

von Wieser F (1914) Theorie der gesellschaftlichen Wirtschaft [Theory of social economics] (in German). Adelphi, New York

Zierhut M (2016) Partially revealing rational expectations equilibrium with real assets and binding constraints. Econ Theor 62(3):495–516

Chapter 4
Bounded Rationality

Abstract Rational decision making involves using information which is almost always imperfect and incomplete, together with some intelligent machine, which if it is a human being is inconsistent in making a decision that maximizes utility. Since the world is not perfect and decisions are made irrespective of the fact that the information to be used is incomplete and imperfect, these decisions are rationally limited (bounded). Recent advances in artificial intelligence and the continual improvement of computer processing power due to Moore's law have implications for the theory of bounded rationality. These advances expand the bounds within which a rational decision making process is exercised and, thereby, increases the probability of making rational decisions.

4.1 Introduction

Decision making has been a complex exercise since time immemorial, and in primeval society, making decisions was jumbled with superstitions, where causality was used and none existed at all to make decisions. There has even been speculation that superstition also occurs in other animals such as pigeons as observed by Skinner (1948). Essentially, superstition can be defined as mystical causality where something is caused by another without them being linked to one another at all. The notion of one event causing another without any connection between them, whatsoever, is irrational thinking (Marwala 2014).

The three basics of a rational decision making process are information, information utilization and, a model that estimates the outcome given the information using some causal or correlation machine. As societies make efforts to retreat from superstition, the concept of rational decision making comes to the front. The notion of rationality has attracted many philosophers from different fields. Max Weber studied the role of rationality in social action (Weber 1922). Some researchers have extended the definition of rationality not only to include the use of logic and reason to make decisions, but that such decisions should be optimized.

© Springer International Publishing AG 2017
T. Marwala and E. Hurwitz, *Artificial Intelligence and Economic Theory: Skynet in the Market*, Advanced Information and Knowledge Processing,
DOI 10.1007/978-3-319-66104-9_4

Basically, rational decision making is a process of reaching decisions through logic and reason in order to maximize utility. Decision making can be defined as a process through which a decision is reached. It usually involves many possible decision outcomes and is said to be rational and optimal if it maximizes the good or utility that is derived from its consequences, and at the same time minimizing the bad or the uselessness that is also derived from its consequences. The philosophical concept that states that the best course of action, is that which maximizes utility, is known as utilitarianism and was advocated by philosophers such as Jeremy Bentham and John Stuart Mill (Bentham 2009; Mill 2011).

There is a theory that has been proposed to achieve this desired outcome. This is the theory of rational choice and it states that one should choose a decision based on the product of the impact of the decision and its probability of occurrence. However, this theory was found to be inadequate because it does not take into account where the person will be relative to where they initially were before making a decision. Kahneman and Tversky (1979) extended the theory of rational choice by introducing the prospect theory, which includes the reference position, aversion to loss, diminishing sensitivity to loss and gains, as well as nonlinear probability of weighting decision options to evaluate the optimal decision (Kahneman 1979).

A generalized decision making process has two sets of input information which form the basis for decision making. These are the options that are available for making such decisions (model) and the output being the decision being made. Within this generalized decision making framework, lies the statistical-analysis/correlation/causal machine which makes sense of the data at hand. Thus, decision making can be summarized as follows (Marwala 2015):

1. Optimization Instrument: e.g. maximizing utility while minimizing the loss which is what prospect theory does.
2. Decision making Instrument: This device contains statistical analysis, correlation machine and causal machine.

In the next section, we will describe, in detail, the concept of rational decision making, and the following section will describe the concept of bounded rationality, followed by a generalized model for decision making.

4.2 Rational Decision Making: A Causal Approach

Rational decision making is a process through which a decision is made using some gathered information and some intelligence to make a globally optimized decision. It is deemed to be rational because it is based on the evidence in the form of information, sound logic and it maximizes utility. Making decisions in the absence of any information is deemed irrational. Rational decision making (Fig. 4.1) entails using data and a model (e.g. human brain) to make a decision. The relationship between data and the impact of the decision is used to improve or reinforce the learning process.

Fig. 4.1 An illustration of a rational decision making system

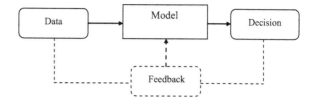

4.3 Rational Decision Making Process

A decision making process consists of decision making actions (Marwala 2014). Decision making action is a basic unit of a decision making process. A decision making action is conducted in a limited rational manner. A decision action is rational if it is logical and globally optimized. A decision making process can have many decision making actions because there may be many optimal points. If at least one of the decision making actions that form a decision making process is irrational, then a decision making process is partially irrational contrary to the assertion of Marwala (2014) because it is not fully logical nor globally optimized. Decisions can be made under rational or irrational circumstances. Nobel Prize Laureate Hebert Simon's theory of bounded rationality, merely, prescribes the bounds within which rationality is applied. This is contrary to the views expressed by Marwala (2014) that rationality cannot be truncated or divided (Simon 1957, 1990, 1991).

Our definition of rationality includes three key concepts and these are: logic (based on scientific principles), information (it should be based on information) and global optimization (it should be optimized). The notion that for a decision to be rational it has to be optimized has a far reaching implication on human decision making. It essentially implies that on the whole, human beings are fundamentally irrational beings. An optimized decision essentially implies that such a decision results in the global maximization of utility (DeGroot 1970; Berger 1980). If as described by Marwala (2015), a person needed to go from Johannesburg to Vancouver, then he/she decides to go to London then to Nairobi and then to Vancouver for no other reason except to try to reach Vancouver, then this behaviour will be considered irrational. The reason why this will be considered irrational is because it is not a globally optimized decision and, therefore, it wastes resources. Wasting resources is not rational. As we move from human decision making into decision making by artificial intelligent (AI) machines, it is vital that we capacitate these machines with the ability to make logical and globally optimized decisions.

4.4 Bounded-Rational Decision Making

One definition of rationality includes the concept of making an optimized decision. Practically, this is not possible because of the limitation of the availability of information required to make such a decision, and the limitation of the device to make sense of such incomplete decision (Simon 1990). This is what is known as the theory of bounded rationality and was proposed by Nobel Laureate Herbert Simon (Simon 1957). The implication of this observation on many economic systems is quite substantial (Simon 1991). It questions the truthfulness of the theory of the efficient market hypothesis, especially given the fact that participants in the market are at best only rational within the bounds of limited information, and possess limited models to make sense of the information.

The literature review indicates that the theory of bounded rationality is a powerful tool of analysis that has found usage in many diverse areas. It should be noted that the theory of bounded rationality has not replaced the theory of rationality. What this theory does is to put limitations or constraints on the applicability of the theory of rationality. The theory of rationality which was described in Fig. 4.1 can thus be updated to construct the theory of bounded rationality as shown in Fig. 4.2.

Figure 4.2 illustrates that on making decisions rationally, certain considerations must be taken into account, and these are that the data that is used to make such decisions are never complete and are subject to measurement errors and, are thus imperfect and incomplete. The second aspect that should be observed is that the model which takes the data and translates these into decisions is also imperfect. If for example, this model is a human brain, then it is inconsistent in the sense that it may be influenced by other factors such as whether the individual concerned is hungry or angry.

Herbert Simon coined a term *satisficing*, thereby, hybridizing the terms satisfying and sufficing, which is the concept of making optimized decisions under the limitations that the data used in making such decisions are imperfect and incomplete, while the model used to make such decisions is inconsistent and imperfect. In order to understand the impact of AI and other related technologies on the theory of bounded rationality, it is important to state few propositions which are the corrections of those made by Marwala (2015):

1. Rational decision making is a process of making optimized decisions based on logic and scientific thought. The issue of optimized decision becomes even necessary given the migration of decision making towards using machines.
2. Rationality, whether as in a decision process or decision action, can be scaled. Bounded rationality basically is a theory that says that one can be rational to a certain extent and that extent is defined by the bounds of rationality.

Fig. 4.2 Illustration of the theory of bounded rationality

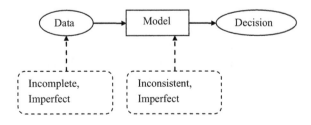

With advances in information processing techniques, enhanced theories of autoassociative machines and advances in artificial intelligence methods, it has become necessary to revise the theory of bounded rationality. Information, which is used to make decisions, is imperfect because of factors, such as measurement errors, but can be partially corrected by using advanced information analysis methods. Furthermore, some of the data that are missing and, thereby, incomplete can be partially completed using missing data estimation methods. Additionally, a human brain, influenced by other social and physiological factors, can be substituted for by recently developed artificial intelligence machines. Furthermore, the processing capabilities of decision making machines is always improving in line with Moore's Law. Because of the reasons above, the bounds under which rationality is exercised can be shifted and thus bounded rationality. Because of this shifting of the bounds of rationality, we term this flexibly-bounded rationality.

Tsang (2008) proposed that computational intelligence determines effective rationality. What Tsang implies is that there is a degree of rationality. The model, which incorporates artificial intelligence and other related technologies on the theory of bounded rationality, can thus be expressed as shown in Fig. 4.3 as it was done by Marwala (2015).

The implications of the model in Fig. 4.3 to many disciplines such as economics, political science and social science are extensive. It goes to the heart of the relationship between rationality and technology. Basically, modern technology now allows us to update the limiting concept of bounded rationality. The implication of the notion of effective rationality and the application of this profound notion to many areas such as economics, sociology and political science is far reaching and requires further investigation. The schematic illustration of the influence of AI and other related technologies on the theory of bounded rationality is shown in Fig. 4.4.

Figure 4.4 demonstrates that artificial intelligence and other related technologies expand the bounds within which the principle of rationality is applied.

(a) **Advanced Information Processing**

This section describes advanced information processing techniques that are required in order to use data to make decisions within the context of bounded rationality possible. These techniques are the time domain, frequency domain and time-frequency domain frameworks.

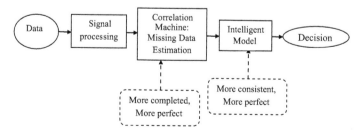

Fig. 4.3 Illustration of the theory of bounded rationality

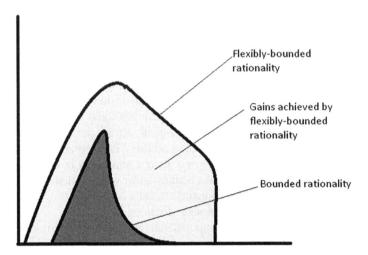

Fig. 4.4 Comparison between flexibly-bounded rationality and bounded rationality

Time Domain Data

When decisions are made, data can be used in the time domain to make decisions. In simple terms, data in the time domain means that the data set is used exactly as it was sampled at a given time. For example, if one wants to use the data of temperature per unit time today, to predict the average temperature tomorrow, one can observe a series of data today to make tomorrow's predictions.

Frequency Doman

The basis of the frequency domain method is the Fourier series and it fundamentally states that every periodic function can be approximated by a Fourier series which is a combination of series of cosine and sine functions of various frequencies (Fourier 1822; Boashash 2003; Bochner and Chandrasekharan 1949; Bracewell 2000). This means that a signal can be characterized by a series of cycles with different amplitudes and frequencies.

Time-Frequency Domain Time-frequency methods are approaches where it is possible to view data in both the time and frequency domains simultaneously. There are different types of time-frequency methods and these comprise of Short-time Fourier transform (Jont 1977; Jacobsen and Lyons 2003), wavelet transform (Chui 1992; Akansu and Haddad 1992), Wigner distribution function (Wigner 1932) and Gabor distribution (Daugman 1980).

(b) **Missing Data Estimation**

One aspect of the impact of AI and related technology on the theory of bounded rationality is that it uses missing data estimation techniques to reduce information that is not observed or known. In this section, we describe missing data estimation methods as discussed by Marwala (2009) and Marwala (2015). Missing data estimation method is a technique that is used to estimate data, and thus information that is missing. It uses mathematical models that describe interrelationships that exist amongst the variables. There are many methods that have been proposed to approximate missing data. One of these is the autoassociative neural network which can be used to capture variables' interrelationships and, genetic algorithm to identify missing values (Abdella and Marwala 2006).

(c) **Intelligent Machines**

The core of the theory of flexibly-bounded rationality is that it assumes that an artificial intelligent machine is used for the decision making process because it is deemed to be better than the human brain. There are many different types of artificial intelligence methods that can be used to make decisions and one of these is a neural network. Neural network is an artificial intelligence technique which is inspired by how a human brain is structured, which is used to learn patterns from data. There are many types of neural networks and these include the radial basis function and the multi-layer perceptron neural network. Ensemble of neural networks also called a committee of networks have been used to relate two sets of data.

4.5 Credit Scoring

The theory of bounded rationality is illustrated using the problem of credit scoring of Australian Credit Data from the UCI data repository (Anonymous 2012; Leke 2014). The variables differ in range and type but normalization of the values results in uniformity of these as shown in Table 4.1 (Leke 2014). The dataset consist primarily of categorical and continuous variables. A multi-layer perceptron neural network with an autoassociative architecture was trained on the data. The prediction variable was the Credit Score from 14 variables, but sometimes, some of these variables were missing. To measure the level of accuracy, the Receiver Operating Characteristics (ROC) curves were used and the areas under these curves were calculated. ROC curves were used because they are more convenient as measurements of classification problems. The area under the ROC curve also called AUC is a 1 for perfect classification, whereas, it is a 0.5 for an imperfect classification (akin to flipping a coin). The framework used is illustrated in Fig. 4.5. Here, the autoassociative network is trained to recall itself. Because the credit score is one of the variables, when it is missing, an optimization technique searches for the correct value such that the input of the autoassociative neural network makes the same input as the output. This is the case even if another variable, in addition to the credit score, is used. The optimization techniques that can be used to achieve this are genetic algorithm (GA), particle swarm optimization (PSO) and simulated annealing (SA). All these optimization methods are classified within the domain of computational intelligence (Marwala 2010). Genetic algorithm is based on the same way in which natural evolution operates, where the principles of mutation, crossover and reproduction are used to identify a fitter population than the one before.

Table 4.1 Variables used to train a neural network

Variables	N	Mean	Min	Max	Standard deviation
A1	690	0.678	0	1	0.467
A2	690	31.549	13.750	80.250	11.864
A3	690	4.771	0	28	5.009
A4	690	1.767	1	3	0.430
A5	690	7.372	1	14	3.683
A6	690	4.683	0	9	1.996
A7	690	2.220	0	20	3.263
A8	690	0.523	0	1	0.499
A9	690	0.428	0	1	0.495
A10	690	2.400	0	67	4.863
A11	690	0.471	0	9	0.595
A12	690	1.930	1	3	0.302
A13	690	184.041	0	2000	172.161
A14	690	1018.386	1	100001	5210.103
A15	690	0.445	0	1	0.497

PSO is based on the principles of individual and group intelligence as observed in a population of a swarm of pigeons trying to identify the optimal position of the food source. Simulated annealing is based on the annealing process in metallurgy where the molten material is gradually cooled so that the lowest energy state is identified.

The AUC results obtained were 82.2% for GA, 81.3% for SA and 85.4% for PSO. This indicates that within the space of bounded rationality, the level of technology deployed moves the limits within which one can exercise rationality. The ultimate accuracy that can possibly be obtained are then the bounds of

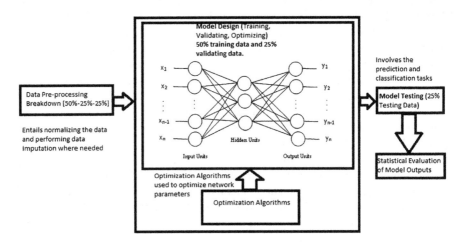

Fig. 4.5 Representation of the framework used

rationality as per the theory of bounded rationality. Unfortunately, we are never sure where these bounds of rationality are, because we are not sure of the limits of technological advancement, whether it is computer processing power or artificial intelligence and, because of this reason, the bounds of the theory of bounded rationality are always variable.

4.6 Conclusions

In this chapter, the concept that the bounds in the theory of bounded rationality (flexibly-bounded rationality) are variable because of the unpredictability in advancements of technology was discussed. In particular, it was studied how advanced signal processing, missing data estimation methods and artificial intelligence techniques change the principle of rationality. Flexibly-bounded rationality expands the bounds within which a rational decision making process can be exercised and, thereby, increases the probability of making accurate decisions when compared to the theory of bounded rationality.

References

Abdella M, Marwala T (2006) The use of genetic algorithms and neural networks to approximate missing data in database. Comput Inform 24:1001–1013

Akansu AN, Haddad RA (1992) Multiresolution signal decomposition: transforms, subbands, wavelets. Academic Press, San Diego. ISBN 978-0-12-047141-6

Anonymous (2012). Center for machine learning and intelligent systems, UCI Machine Learning Repository: Data Sets, http://archive.ics.uci.edu/ml/datasets.html, lastchecked: 15 November 2012

Bentham J (2009) An introduction to the principles of morals and legislation (Dover Philosophical Classics), Dover Publications Inc

Berger JO (1980) Statistical decision theory and Bayesian analysis. Springer-Verlag, Heidelberg

Boashash B (2003) Time-frequency signal analysis and processing: a comprehensive reference. Elsevier Science, Oxford

Bochner S, Chandrasekharan K (1949) Fourier transforms, Princeton University Press

Bracewell RN (2000) The fourier transform and its applications (3rd edn). McGraw-Hill, Boston

Chui CK (1992) An introduction to wavelets. Academic Press

Daugman JG (1980) Two-dimensional spectral analysis of cortical receptive field profiles, Vision Res., PMID 7467139 20(10):847–856

DeGroot M (1970) Optimal statistical decision. McGraw-Hill, New York

Fourier JB (1822) Théorie Analytique de la Chaleur, Paris, père et fils

Jacobsen E, Lyons R (2003) The sliding DFT. IEEE Signal Process Mag 20(2):74–80

Jont BA (1977) Short time spectral analysis, synthesis, and modification by discrete fourier transform. IEEE Trans Acoust Speech Signal Process ASSP-25(3):235–238

Kahneman D (2011) Thinking, Fast and Slow. Macmillan, New York

Kahneman D, Tversky A (1979) Prospect theory: an analysis of decision under risk. Econometrica 47(2):263–291

Leke CA (2014) Empirical evaluation of optimization techniques for prediction and classification tasks. University of Johannesburg Master of Engineering Thesis

Marwala T (2009) Computational intelligence for missing data imputation, estimation and management: knowledge optimization techniques information science reference imprint. IGI Global Publications, New York

Marwala T (2010) Finite element model updating using computational intelligence techniques: applications to structural dynamics. Springer, Heidelberg

Marwala T (2014) Artificial intelligence techniques for rational decision making. Springer, Heidelberg

Marwala T (2015) Causality, correlation, and artificial intelligence for rational decision making. World Scientific, Singapore

Mill JS (2011) A system of logic, ratiocinative and inductive (Classic Reprint). Oxford University Press

Simon H (1957) A behavioral model of rational choice, in models of man, social and rational: mathematical essays on rational human behavior in a social setting. Wiley, New York

Simon H (1990) A mechanism for social selection and successful altruism. Science 250 (4988):1665–1668

Simon H (1991) Bounded rationality and organizational learning. Organ Sci 2(1):125–134

Skinner BF (1948) Superstition' in the Pigeon. J Exp Psychol 38(2):168–172

Tsang EPK (2008) Computational intelligence determines effective rationality. Int J Autom Control 5(1):63–66

Weber M (1922) Ueber einige Kategorien der verstehenden Soziologie. In: Gesammelte Aufsaetze zur Wissenschaftslehre, pp 427–74

Wigner EP (1932) On the quantum correlation for thermodynamic equilibrium. Phys Rev 40: 749–759

Chapter 5
Behavioral Economics

Abstract Behavioural economics is an approach to economics which takes into account human behavior. In his book "Thinking fast and slow", which is based on the work he did with Tversky, Kahneman describes human thought as being divided into two systems i.e. System 1 which is fast, intuitive and emotional, and System 2, which is slow, rational and calculating. He further described these systems as being the basis for human reasoning, or the lack thereof, and the impact of these on the markets. Some of the findings are the inability of human beings to think statistically, called heuristics and biases, the concept of Anchoring, Availability effect, Substituting effect, Optimism and Loss aversion effect, Framing effect, Sunk costs and Prospect theory where a reference point is important in evaluating choices rather than economic utility. With the advent of decision making using intelligent machines, all these effects and biases are eliminated. System 1, which is intuitive, is eliminated altogether. System 2 becomes the norm, as advances in artificial intelligence are made. System 2 becomes fast because contemporary computational intelligent machines work fast. If one considers Moore's Law, which states that computational power doubles every year, System 2 next year is faster than System 2 this year, thus making machines "Think Fast and Faster".

5.1 Introduction

Behavioural economics is an approach to economics which takes into account human behaviour and psychology. In his book "Thinking Fast and Slow", Nobel Laureate Kahneman describes human thought as being divided into two systems. System 1 which is fast, intuitive and emotional (Kahneman 2011). System 2 is slow, rational and calculating. He further described these two systems as being the basis for human reasoning, or the lack thereof, and how these impact on the markets. Some of the findings that have been observed are the inability of human beings to think statistically and therefore are subjected to heuristics and biases. This is because human beings, when they use System 1, use experience to make sense of new patterns. Kahneman used an example of a child who has only seen shapes that

© Springer International Publishing AG 2017
T. Marwala and E. Hurwitz, *Artificial Intelligence and Economic Theory: Skynet in the Market*, Advanced Information and Knowledge Processing,
DOI 10.1007/978-3-319-66104-9_5

are made of straight lines and then when the child is presented with a circle, he/she would think the circle is an octagon. Another example of this is in the field of technical analysis with regards to predicting the future price of stock. When the analyst is presented with a totally new scenario, which involves other forms of analysis such as political analysis, the analyst fails to give an appropriate guidance.

Furthermore, they studied the concept of Anchoring, which is an effect which makes people be influenced by irrelevant numbers. For example, if one is presented with the question as to whether Idi Amin was heavier than 150 kg, they will give a bigger number than if they were first asked if he was heavier than 80 kg.

They also studied the concept of Availability, where people make decisions based on how easily they can think of examples. For example, one can easily make an assumption that there is a disproportionate number of academics who wear glasses than in the general population. They also observed that System 1 has a tendency of substituting difficult questions with easy ones. Furthermore, they found that on making decisions, people are more averse to loss than potential gain. Furthermore, they observed that the framing of a problem is more important than the problem itself. For example, people choose an option if it is framed as 80% of winning a prize rather than 20% of losing the price.

These biases affect how decisions are made, and have a far reaching consequence in markets that are full of human decision makers. Some of the implications of these include making markets inefficient. The pure human decision maker is becoming rarer and rarer given the advent of machine learning and related technology. For example, artificial intelligent (AI) machines make decisions in areas such as stock markets, buying and selling over the internet. For example, the laws of supply and demand, which have been the basis of much of the pricing theory, are being changed by AI technology such that it is now possible to draw individual demand and supply curves and thus, the related pricing rather than aggregate demand, supply and pricing. This chapter studies how the concept of behaviour in the markets will be changed as a result in advances of artificial intelligence and the related technologies.

Another issue that will be studied is the concept of Moore's Law, which states that computational power of devices doubles every year. This means that an AI decision agent becomes better every year. This has implications on Systems 1 and 2 as proposed by Kahneman. Furthermore, it has implications on the concept of "thinking fast and slow" as proposed by Kahneman.

5.2 Behavioural Economics

Classical economics is based on the principle of an agent maximizing its utility when making a decision. For example, if a customer is faced with three choices on buying a pair of trousers, one which is expected to last for three days, another for three months and another for three years. If all these trousers cost the same price, a rational customer will choose to buy the pair of trousers, which last three years.

This agent is making this choice because it maximizes utility, i.e. how long the trousers will last. This is what is called the theory of rational choice. Herbert Simon realized that rational choice is impossible to be implemented by human beings, because it is not always possible for human beings to identify all options available (Simon 1991). Furthermore, even for those options that can be accessed, it is not always possible to evaluate their respective utilities. In addition, the transaction costs of accessing all options, such as the time needed to make such evaluations, is often prohibitive. Because of these limitations, Herbert Simon introduced the concept of bounded rationality. Bounded rationality basically prescribes that there are bounds that limit the effecting of rationality, and behavioural economics is a type of such bounds.

One of the most powerful theories of behavioral economics is the prospect theory (Tversky and Kahneman 1973; Simon 1987). There are three characteristics that define human decision making and these are:

1. **Heuristics**: That people make decisions based on the rule of thumb rather than accurate logic.
2. **Framing**: That the collections of prejudices and anecdotes are the engines of human decision making.
3. **Market inefficiencies**: That markets are inefficient because of mispricing, bounded rationality as well as irrational expectations and choices.

All these behavioral traits are eliminated when decision making is delegated to artificial intelligent machines and other expert systems.

The prospect theory which was proposed by Kahneman and Tversky (1979) is based on the following four concepts:

1. **Reference Dependence**: If Denga had $100,000.00 and invested this in the stock market, and Thendo had $200,000.00 and he too invested this in the stock market. If after 2 days each had $150,000.00 arising from this investment, then according to the theory of utility, they should be equally happy because they both have $150,000.00. Not so according to behavioral economics, as Denga will be happy because she gained $50,000.00 while Thendo lost $50,000.00 and thus unhappy. This then means that the concept of utility is not the only aspect that should be considered when evaluating choices that people make but also the reference point.
2. **Loss Aversion**: This principle basically prescribes that people are more afraid of losing and therefore factor this in making decisions. For example, if people are given an option of winning $100,000.00 by spinning a wheel with 95% chances of winning compared to taking $40,000.00 and walking away, then they will choose $40,000.00 even though it does not maximize the utility that they can possibly get.
3. **Nonlinear Probability Weighting**: Research has shown that human decision makers give more weight to smaller probabilities than they give to larger probabilities. This results in a weighting function probability which is shown in Fig. 5.1. For example, if people are given the following two options:

Fig. 5.1 Decision
characteristics

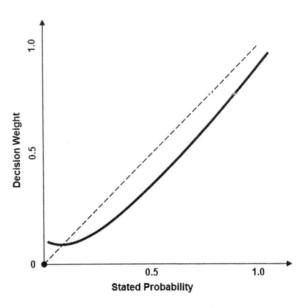

(A) 90% chance of winning $4500
(B) 100% chance of winning $2500

They will overwhelmingly choose B over A.
If for example they are given the following two options:

(C) 20% chance of winning $4500
(D) 25% chance of winning $2500

They normally will chose C over D.

4. **Diminishing sensitivities to gains and losses**: The relationship between the
   distance between the reference point, the losses and gains is inversely propor-
   tional to the marginal effect on the decision maker's utility. The respective value
   function is shown in Fig. 5.2.

5.3 Behavioural Economics and Demand and Supply

The principle of demand and supply, which is illustrated in Fig. 5.3, consists of two
curves, the demand and supply curves of price versus quantity of goods (Marshall
1920; Mankiw and Taylor 2011). The demand curve has a negative slope. This is
because the more expensive the price of goods are, the less is the quantity of goods

Fig. 5.2 Value function for
prospect theory

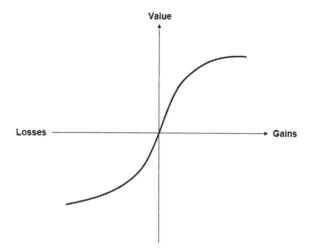

the customers demand. Conversely, the less expensive the price of goods are, the more the quantity of goods the customers demand. The supply curve is positively sloped. This is because the more expensive the price of goods are, the more the quantity of goods the suppliers are willing to sell. Conversely, the less expensive the price of goods are, the less are the sellers willing to supply. How does the prospect theory impact on the theory of demand and supply? Equilibrium is a measure of the position where the quantity of goods customers are willing to buy at a certain price is the same as the price the suppliers are willing to produce. Artificial intelligence, through learning and evolution, is able to ensure that the demand and supply curves are better modelled. Because of this reason, the opportunity for arbitrage, where the fact that many players in the market are operating away from equilibrium, leads to a situation where suppliers or/and producers benefit. The use of the AI machine reduces the degree of arbitrage in the market and, therefore, brings a certain degree of fairness into the market, which is good for the efficiency of the economy. The aspect of heuristics prescribes that people make decisions based on the rule of thumb rather than on accurate logic. In this regard, they buy and sell goods based on the principles of the rule of thumb rather than logic. The consequence of this is that they are subjected to prices that are away from equilibrium points. This creates opportunity for arbitrage, as illustrated by a circle in Fig. 5.3. Because of framing, prejudices and anecdotes concepts, human beings predict biased futures. This brings the prediction of the future to be closer to the prediction of adaptive expectations than rational expectations. On the principle of loss aversion, human beings look at the worst case scenario, when supplying and selling products, and this creates the opportunity for arbitrage.

Fig. 5.3 Demand and supply curve

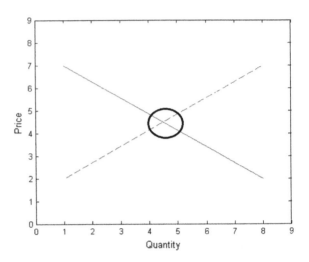

5.4   Behavioural Economics and Rational Expectations

Rational expectations is a theory that states that agents when making decisions make use of all the information at their disposal to make decisions and, consequently, they cannot be systematically wrong. It is an improvement on the theory of adaptive expectations, where agents make use of the previous values of the variable to be forecasted to predict its future values (Muth 1961; Savin 1987). The theory of adaptive expectations was found to give biased expectations (Evans and Honkapohja 2001). How does the prospect theory impact on the theory of rational choice? Do human agents making predictions about the future values of variables within the context of prospect theory give biased results even if they are making use of all the information that is available at their disposal? In the past, we observed that AI is better able to use available information needed to forecast the future than a human being is able to. We also observed that, consequently, artificial intelligent agents give more unbiased predictions of the future variables if they use all the information at their disposal. We observed that this makes the theory of rational expectations more valid for AI agents than for human agents. What is the impact of behavioural economics on rational expectations? The first aspect of heuristics prescribes that people make decisions based on the rule of thumb rather than on logic. In this regard, when they predict future variables, they use rule of thumb with detrimental consequences to the ability to predict future expectations resulting in biased predictions. On the concept of framing, prejudices and anecdotes, which are the engines of human decisions, human beings predict biased futures thus bringing the prediction of the future closer to the prediction of adaptive expectations than rational expectations. On the principle of loss aversion, human beings look at the negative aspects, when predicting the future. Consequently, this results in the prediction of the worst case scenario of the expected future resulting in bias. On the concept of nonlinear probability weighting, when human beings predict the future expectations, they overemphasize smaller probabilities and underemphasize larger probabilities. This results in biased expectations. Therefore, behavioural economics makes rational expectations converge to adaptive expectations.

5.5 Behavioural Economics and Bounded Rationality

Rational choice is a procedure of making a choice based on relevant information, in a logical, timely and optimized fashion to maximize utility (Green and Shapiro 1994; Hedström and Stern 2008; Grüne-Yanoff 2012; Marwala 2014, 2015). Rational choice is limited by the amount of information that is available to make a decision, by the time it takes to process the information and by the information processing (decision making) device that uses the information to make a decision i.e. human brain. This is what Herbert Simon called bounded rationality (Simon 1957, 1991). Bounded rationality can be viewed as the limit of rationality and, therefore, operates with the most information the decision maker can possibly access, the highest information processing capability that the decision maker can possibly afford, the most efficient information processing device that can be afforded and considers the maximum number of decision options that can be accessed to select an option that maximizes utility. The heuristics theory of behavioral economics stipulates that human beings make decisions based on the rule of thumb rather than efficient logic. This results in the information processing device being compromised and, therefore, puts further limitation on its efficiency and effectiveness. Furthermore, the framing phenomenon stipulates that human beings make decisions within the context of inherent prejudices and anecdotes further compromising the goal of achieving maximum utility. In addition, the loss aversion, reference dependence, nonlinear probability weighting and diminishing sensitivity to loss and gains in human beings, as prescribed by prospect theory, further compromise the attainment of maximum utility. An illustration of this is shown in Fig. 5.4, where bounded rationality and prospect theory limit the space of exercising rationality.

5.6 Artificial Intelligence and Behavioural Economics

Behavioural economics severely limits bounded rational decision making because human beings are unpredictable, are easily influenced by external factors such as mood swings, prejudices and lack of capacity to process data. However in this age of the fourth industrial revolution, decision making are more going to be conducted at best using artificial intelligence machine and at worst by man-machine systems. These remove or limit behavioural characteristics, such as framing, heuristics, risk aversion, reference dependency, nonlinear probability weighting and diminishing

Fig. 5.4 Illustration of the space of exercising rationality for bounded rationality and prospect theory

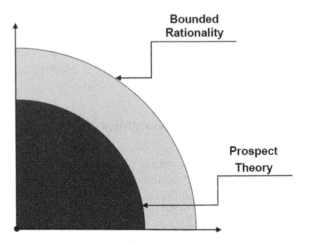

sensitivity to losses and gains, which were observed in prospect theory. Artificial intelligence is based on using intelligent computing to emulate the impressive capabilities observed in the human brain. These capabilities include the ability to recognise objects, patterns, make sense of data and to do other complicated tasks. AI has been successful in many domains such as modelling complex phenomena such as HIV and financial markets (Marwala 2010), complex processes such as making decisions with incomplete information (Marwala 2009), advanced structures such as cars (Marwala 2010), complex social phenomena such as interstate conflict (Marwala and Lagazio 2011), maintenance of complex structures (Marwala 2012), prediction of the stock market and other economic phenomena (Marwala 2013), rational decision making (Marwala 2014), causality and correlation based decision making (Marwala 2015), as well as aerospace structures (Marwala et al. 2016).

Fig. 5.5 Illustration of decision making using artificial intelligence, human beings (prospect theory) compared to the limit of bounded rationality

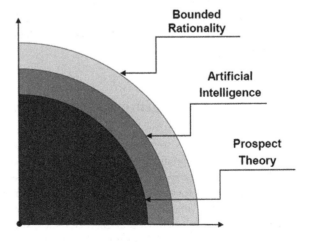

When decision making is conducted using AI machines, the degree of rationality of such a decision is better than when human beings make such decisions, which is subjected to prospect theory, and this is illustrated in Fig. 5.5.

5.7   Moore's Law

One of the principles of rational decision making is the ability to make decisions in a timely manner. It is not rational for a decision that could be made in a shorter time to be made in a longer time. In the book "Thinking fast and slow" the two systems: System 1, which is fast, and System 2, which is slow, study human decision making. Now much of such decisions are increasingly being made by an artificial intelligent machine, what happens to such decision making? Do we still have "a slow and a fast" system in machine decision making? Moore's law, is a principle that was introduced by Gordon Moore, which states that the computer processing power doubles every year and this is illustrated in Fig. 5.6 (Schaller 1997). This figure shows the negligible number of transistors in a computer in 1971 (2300) and in 1980 (8080) and rising to 80486 in 1990. Given the fact that computational power is increasing year after year, what is the implication of this on computer based decision making? Within the context of the book "Thinking fast and slow", if decision makers are artificial intelligent machines rather than human beings, this book could have been called "Thinking fast and faster". This is because the difference in the speed of decision making using computers is negligible whether we are talking about System 1 or 2. Because computational power doubles every two years, it means decision making using AI agents becomes faster in the following year than in the current year. For example, suppose a stock market is traded using artificial intelligent machines in the year 2017. In the year 2018, the transactions in the same stock market will be faster and, therefore, the stock market will become more efficient.

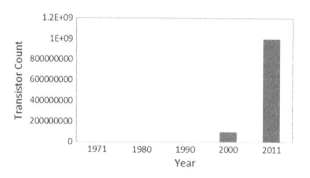

Fig. 5.6 An illustration of the Moore's Law

5.8 Conclusions

This chapter studied behavioral economics, which is an approach to economics which takes into account human behavior. The book "Thinking fast and slow", describes human thought as being divided into two Systems. System 1 is fast, intuitive and emotional whereas System 2 is slow, rational and calculating. With the advent of decision making using AI machines, all these effects and biases are eliminated. System 1, which is itutitive is eliminated altogether. System 2 becomes the norm as advances in artificial intelligence are made. System 2, becomes fast because contemporary computational machines work fast. If one considers Moore's Law, which states that computational power doubles every year, System 2 next year is faster than System 2 this year thus making machines "Think Fast and Faster".

References

Evans GW, Honkapohja S (2001) Learning and expectations in macroeconomics. Princeton University Press, Princeton

Green DP, Shapiro I (1994) Pathologies of rational choice theory: a critique of applications in political science. Yale University Press, New Haven

Grüne-Yanoff T (2012) "Paradoxes of Rational Choice Theory". In Roeser S, Hillerbrand R, Sandin P, Peterson M (eds) Handbook of risk theory, pp 499–516. doi:10.1007/978-94-007-1433-5_19

Hedström P, Stern C (2008) "Rational choice and sociology," The New Palgrave Dictionary of Economics, 2nd edn. Abstract

Kahneman K (2011) Thinking, fast and slow. Macmillan, NY

Kahneman D, Tversky A (1979) Prospect theory: an analysis of decision under risk. Econometrica. 47(2):263

Mankiw NG, Taylor MP (2011) Economics (2nd ed, revised edn). Cengage Learning, Andover

Marshall A (1920) Principles of economics. Library of economics and liberty. ISBN 0-256-01547-3

Marwala T (2009) Computational intelligence for missing data imputation, estimation, and management: knowledge optimization techniques. IGI Global, Pennsylvania. ISBN 978-1-60566-336-4

Marwala T (2010) Finite element model updating using computational intelligence techniques: applications to structural dynamics. Springer, Heidelberg

Marwala T (2012) Condition monitoring using computational intelligence methods. Springer, Heidelberg

Marwala T (2013) Economic modeling using artificial intelligence methods. Springer, Heidelberg

Marwala T (2014) Artificial intelligence techniques for rational decision making. Springer, Heidelberg

Marwala T (2015) Causality, correlation, and artificial intelligence for rational decision making. World Scientific, Singapore. ISBN 978-9-814-63086-3

Marwala T, Lagazio M (2011) Militarized conflict modeling using computational intelligence. Springer, Heidelberg. ISBN 978-0-85729-789-1

Marwala T, Boulkaibet I, Adhikari S (2016) Probabilistic finite element model updating using bayesian statistics: applications to aeronautical and mechanical engineering. Wiley, London

Muth JF (1961) "Rational Expectations and the Theory of Price Movements" reprinted in The new classical macroeconomics. Volume 1. (1992): 3–23 (International Library of Critical Writings in Economics, vol 19. Elgar, Aldershot, UK)

Savin NE (1987) Rational expectations: econometric implications. New Palgrave Dictionary Econ 4:79–85

Schaller RR (1997) Moore's law: past, present and future. IEEE Spectrum, pp 52–59

Simon H (1957) A behavioral model of rational choice, in models of man, social and rational: mathematical essays on rational human behavior in a social setting. Wiley, NY

Simon HA (1987) Behavioral economics. New Palgrave Dictionary Econ 1:221–224

Simon H (1991) Bounded rationality and organizational learning. Organ Sci 2(1):125–134

Tversky A, Kahneman D (1973) Availability: A heuristic for judging frequency and probability. Cogn Psychol 5(2):207–232

Chapter 6
Information Asymmetry

Abstract Often when human beings interact to make decisions, one human agent has more information than the other and this phenomenon is called information asymmetry. The fact that information asymmetry distorts the markets won Akerlof, Stiglitz and Spence a Nobel Prize. Generally, when one human agent is set to manipulate a decision to its advantage, the human agent can signal misleading information. On the other hand, one human agent can screen for information to diminish the influence of asymmetric information on decisions. With the dawn of artificial intelligence (AI), signaling and screening are easier to achieve. This chapter investigates the impact of AI on the theory of asymmetric information. The simulated results demonstrate that AI agents reduce the degree of information asymmetry and, therefore, the market where these agents are used become more efficient. It is also observed that the more AI agents that are deployed in the market, the less is the volume of trades in the market. This is because of the fact that for trades to occur, asymmetry of information should exist, thereby, creating a sense of arbitrage.

6.1 Introduction

Asymmetry of information is a concept which illustrates a situation where one agent e.g. a human being has more information, thus better off, than another agent. This concept won Stiglitz, Akerlof and Spence a Nobel Prize (Akerlof 1970; Stiglitz and Greenwald 1986; Spence 1973, Stiglitz 1974). Here, a human being is just one type of an agent, as there are computer agents that are replacing human beings (Marwala 2009, 2010, 2013, 2014, 2015; Marwala and Lagazio 2011; Marwala et al. 2017). Asymmetry of information has been a reason for many historical events. The basis of colonization of one nation by another is information asymmetry whether it was the British in India or in South Africa. Human beings have evolved such that whenever there is information asymmetry and there are resources to be acquired through that information asymmetry, then the human being with superior information exploits that with lesser information. This is because of

© Springer International Publishing AG 2017
T. Marwala and E. Hurwitz, *Artificial Intelligence and Economic Theory: Skynet in the Market*, Advanced Information and Knowledge Processing,
DOI 10.1007/978-3-319-66104-9_6

the maximizing utility principle. The only exception to this rule is if the parties concerned are bound by some moral code.

The theory of asymmetry of information and its impact in the markets has been written about extensively (Sun et al. 2014; Chung et al. 2015). Some of the undesirable consequences of information asymmetry are moral hazards and adverse selection. Moral hazard is a situation where a person takes more risks knowing very well that it will be paid by another person. Corruption, especially by government officials, is an example of a moral hazard. It is some form of information asymmetry, where the extent of risk is more known by one agent than another. Adverse selection is a form of information asymmetry where the buyers have more information than the sellers, or vice versa. Consequently, buyers rig the market for their advantage over the sellers. An example of this is observed in an insurance industry where those with high risks tend to buy more insurance. Another type of information asymmetry is the asymmetry due to deception. In this case, the seller misleads the market by scaring them off without illegality in order to sharpen the information asymmetry for the benefit of the seller. An example of this is the YK2 situation, where the sellers of information technology services scared off companies by claiming that technological devices will collapse as a result of moving from year 1999 to 2000. This was inspite of the fact that a counter in computer science is created by adding a number, in this instance a one, to the year in question to get to the following year making most electronic counters immune to the YK2 dilemma.

The difference in perception of value of goods and services is the basis of trade. Humans for much of history have been agents that execute trade. Humans often have a distorted perception of information for all kinds of reasons and often change their minds about one thing or another. There is a thought experiment where a human being is given 20 paintings to rank in the order of how valuable they are. Ten days later the same human being is given the same paintings and often it is found that the rankings differ markedly from the first instance. The same phenomenon governs human beings, when they participate in the market. Consequently, the character of the market is deformed simply because of the inconsistency of humans who are participating in the market. This is primarily because humans have a warped sense of information and, therefore, their decisions are bounded (i.e. limited) rationally.

Over the last few years, much of the decisions in the market are being made by intelligent machines. These intelligent machines are able to analyze vast amounts of information and are able to identify latent information, which are not easily accessible. This is achieved through the advent of big data and deep learning. These decisions are, in effect, flexibly rationally bounded for better decision making due to advances in signal processing techniques, missing data estimation and the ability to process vast amounts of data fast.

Information Asymmetry, in a nutshell, deals with the effects of two or more parties having different degrees of information about a particular object that they are negotiating to trade, and this is illustrated in Fig. 6.1. This could be information about the goods themselves, information about prospective buyers/sellers, upcoming problems with production, availability of raw materials, incoming

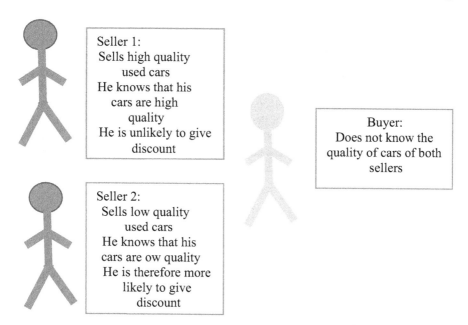

Fig. 6.1 Illustration of information asymmetry between the buyer and the sellers

legislation or any number of potential factors that could potentially influence the appropriate market price for a particular good. This theory in effect addresses the problem that in most systems, none of the parties have perfect information. Thus, what is then required is to simply do the best we can with the imperfect information available to us. Perfect information is complete and accurate, a situation which is not realistic in practice.

Information asymmetry can come about in a number of ways, most of them not as nefarious as the name suggests. While obviously foul play could result in insiders spilling secrets, or stolen information obtained through hacking or other means of industrial espionage, for the most part it is simply the result of one party being better informed than another. If a business owner spends more time speaking to his various suppliers, it is likely that he will know more than his more taciturn competitor.

If a party spends the resources to obtain and the time to learn from studies in an area, he will once again have more information than his competitor. Information asymmetry could also result quite easily from having misconceptions about how a particular asset is priced, something that could come about through misunder-standing or even by following differing, conflicting theories about how an asset is priced. Consider two securities traders, one trading based on fundamental analysis, and the other on technical graph-based analysis. Both are choosing to use all the information they can get, but processing it in wildly different ways that can often give contradictory conclusions. If the conclusions are contradictory, then only one party will be correct, and thus the net result is still asymmetry even though both parties have sought out all available information.

The efficiency of the market refers to information being absorbed by the marketplace, and then reflected in the prices of its offerings. If the effects of the information propagate through the market at a slower rate than new information modifies the marketplace, or through portions of the marketplace, considering the difference in the effects of information at various trading desks versus the same for a private investor, then the marketplace will never be completely efficient. Following on this, the degree of efficiency of the marketplace will be directly affected by the level of information asymmetry present in a given marketplace.

This chapter examines how these various concepts interact to create a full picture of what AI means for the marketplace with respect to information asymmetry.

6.2 Asymmetric Information

Information asymmetry is the study of decisions made by human beings where one agent has more information than another agent. Information asymmetry often leads to one party having an advantage over another. For example, when the Japanese Imperial Army attacked the United States in Pearl Harbour, Japan had the information on what will happen in Pearl Harbour which the Americans did not have. Due to this asymmetry of information between these two countries, American fleet was devastated and suffered a temporary setback. Technology could have prevented this setback by eliminating the information asymmetry. For example, satellite technology could have detected Japanese fleet and relevant American leaders could have planned a counterattack. Of course the victory of the Japanese in Pearl Harbour was just temporary and the Americans ultimately won the war. There are, therefore, cases were information asymmetry is not desirable, for example in an interview setting were one human agent, the potential employer, needs to know as much as possible about the potential employee and this problem was studied extensively by Nobel Laureate Michael Spence. In this case, the potential employer, who is interested in knowing as much information about the employee, signals to the employee to reveal as much information as possible. Likewise, the potential employee will signal to the potential employer information such as qualifications thus sending a message that he/she is skilled in the job. How does artificial intelligence help resolve such asymmetry of information through signaling? How do big data and deep learning resolve this asymmetrical dilemma? Of course these days, social networks which are often enabled by artificial intelligence are able to signal information much more accurately than a human agent is able to do. Therefore, artificial intelligence is able to help resolve the asymmetry of information.

The other issue with information asymmetry is that of screening, which was studied by Nobel Laureate Joseph Stiglitz in 1974 (Stiglitz 1974). Stiglitz introduced the concept of screening, where the human agent that knows less information, induces the human agent that knows more information to reveal some information. With the advent of artificial intelligence, it is no longer as necessary for one human agent to try to induce another human agent to reveal more about itself. One human agent can be able to use the internet to create a profile of the other human agent, which is more accurate and informative than the information that could have been extracted from the party in question. This is due to the fact that a human agent forgets facts very easily, and may even not be capable of revealing all the information for all sorts of reasons.

Regardless of the countermeasures, it is important to note the significant impact of information asymmetry in an economic system (Bojanc and Jerman-Blazic 2008). To this end, we shall consider an example of modelled trading amongst agents, where differing agents are created with varying levels of accuracy about the commodity being traded. This example utilises traded commodities, which for ease of understanding we will call "dimples", for simplicity's sake, ignoring the many other factors that would make a given asset have differing values to prospective buyers/sellers, assuming the simpler market value as its underlying true value. These agents have each undergone a series of 100 trades, randomly being assigned another trading partner. After these 100 trades, the net worth of each agent has been totalled up, to be compared to its accuracy in gauging the true value of dimples at this time. This accuracy is represented for ease of reference on a scale of 1–10, with 10 being the most accurate. Figure 6.2 below illustrates the relationship between knowledge and performance of these agents.

It is important to note that the agents themselves are not uniform in their skill at trading, representing the various dynamics at play involving bargaining power within any given market, which accounts for the disparity seen in the individual results. The aggregated results, however, show quite clearly that having more accurate information is a definite boon in the accumulation of wealth over time.

For another view, let us look at what tends to happen between two traders who have different levels of accuracy. In this case, we can analyse each of the ten thousand dimple trades to occur over the initial period in order to understand the

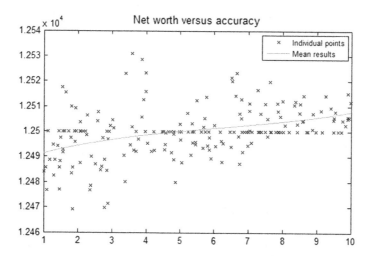

Fig. 6.2 Net worth versus accuracy for individuals

Fig. 6.3 Influence of trading
accuracy

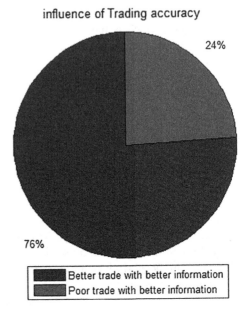

relationship. For all of these trades, the underlying true price of dimples has been set to 5 dollars. Figure 6.3 shows the proportion of individual trades that were in favour of the party with access to better information.

The conclusion from the above puts into stark relief just how significant an effect good information has on the ability to make good trades. With both fluctuations in the agent valuations and with varying levels of ability to make better deals, the agents who have better methods of evaluating the price, consistently, get the better deal from their less well-informed trading partners roughly three out of four times.

The conclusion is fairly simple, all the maths and all the modelling come down to one of the oldest maxims, namely that "knowledge is power", and in this case it represents the power to turn a profit.

6.3 Artificial Intelligence Makes Us Wiser

Artificial Intelligence is a computational approach, which is motivated by natural intelligence such as the functioning of the brain, the organization of animals as well as the evolution of physical and biological systems (Russell and Norvig 2010). Artificial intelligence is, therefore, capable of learning, adapting, optimizing and evolving (Marwala 2009, 2010, 2013, 2014, 2015). Some examples of artificial intelligence techniques are neural networks, which are capable of learning from data, genetic algorithm, which is capable of evolving and ant colony optimization, which is capable of optimizing. Artificial intelligence has been successfully used in decision making in a number of areas such as in engineering, missing data estimation, economics, political science as well as rational decision making. More recently, artificial intelligence has been applied in the markets for high frequency trading.

With the effects of information being established, the next question to answer (as is now becoming a pattern) is how precisely artificial intelligence affects the information available to both parties in a trading environment. As with most sources of information (and systems of understanding and interpreting data), not everyone will have access to the same systems, and by default some systems will be better than others. Similarly, some individuals will adopt systems quicker than others, all of which lead to a dynamic environment in which some level of information asymmetry will still exist as those with better systems exploit their advantage over those with lesser systems. The growing ease of access to such systems, however, means that all players in the market will likely have *better* quality of information than they had before, lowering their estimation error of whatever asset they happen to be trading. The result in this case is a net decrease in information asymmetry as the market gradually adopts better information sources within their respective price ranges.

6.4   Asymmetric Information and Market Efficiency

The Efficient Market hypothesis is a theory proposed by Nobel Laureate Eugene Fama which states that the market incorporates all the information such that it is impossible to beat the market (Fama 1965). Variations on the efficiency of the market (referred to colloquially as "hard" and "soft" forms of the efficient market hypothesis) allow for varying speeds of transmission of information within the market, which allows for some room to beat the market if you can find and exploit some inefficiency. Implicit in the efficient market hypothesis is the fact that the agents that participate in the market are rational. Of course we now know that human agents are not uniformly rational and, therefore, the markets cannot be completely rational (Kahneman and Tversky 1979). Theories such as prospect theory and bounded rationality have proven that at best human agents are not fully rational, but almost always are not rational. However, it has been surmised that artificial intelligent agents make markets more rational than human agents.

Another aspect that warrants close study is the relationship between asymmetric information and market efficiency. If a human agent A has smaller amount of information to make a decision than another human agent B, then the decision of human agent A is more rationally bounded than the decision of human agent B (Simon 1957). If a market is full of agents with the same characteristics as those of agents A and B, then such a market cannot be efficient because the decisions of significant players of the market are based on limited information. Therefore, even though asymmetric information promotes trading, it makes markets inefficient because they distort the markets. If human agents A and B are replaced by autonomous artificial intelligent agents A and B, then the information that each agent can be able to mine in the cyberspace will be similar, especially if their capabilities are assumed to be the same. This then means the information that is at the disposal of artificially intelligent agents A and B are symmetrical. If a market is full of agents such as the artificial intelligent agents A and B, then the market will have agents where information is more symmetrical and, therefore, it will be more rational. Moreover, these artificial intelligent agents will be able to analyse all the data at their disposal, estimate latent information and process all the information at their disposal better than a human being. Thus, the decisions of the artificial intelligent agents will be less rationally bounded than the decisions of the human agents. Therefore, the deployment of artificial intelligent agents makes information in the markets more symmetrical (or less asymmetrical) and this in turn makes the markets more efficient.

In order to understand this better, let us look back to our trading of dimples. The efficiency of the market can be measured by the lack of distance from the true price at which trades actually occur. In other words, the further the price is from the underlying value of 5 dollars for a price, the less efficient the market. In Fig. 6.4, we can see the results of analysing the combined understanding of the two parties versus the variance of all parties' trading prices.

What the bar chart readily shows is that as the average skill of the two trading parties gets higher, the variance of the trade price settled at becomes lesser. This reduction in trading variance can be viewed as the market being more efficient as the parties are better informed.

We learn more from observing what happens if the agents are allowed to learn over time, representing the marketplace adopting artificial intelligence technology over time. As happens with all technology, it is not adopted instantly but rather gradually over time as the technology proves itself to be effective. The more people see the technology to be effective, and the more accessible it becomes to smaller players, the more it is adopted. Figure 6.5 shows the reduction in variance, and thus reduction in market inefficiency over time.

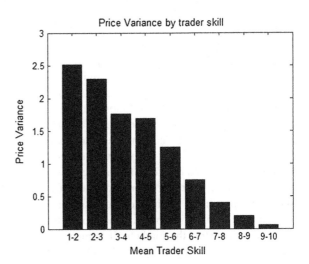

Fig. 6.4 Price variance versus trading skills

Fig. 6.5 Market efficiency
over time

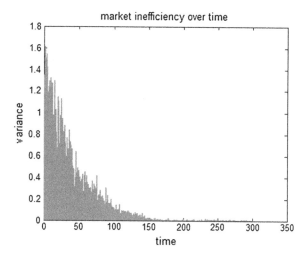

In this figure, the agents gain better and better accuracy over time as they start to adopt AI methods, and as a result of increased interest and competition, the AI methods themselves become better-hones and provide greater accuracy. Since the agents are more accurate, they make far smaller errors when evaluating the price of a dimple, allowing for far smaller arbitrage trades to take place. This in turn results in a much more efficient market as actors trade dimples much closer to the underlying value of 5 dollars now that they have better information. In other words, the drastic reduction in information asymmetry results in a much more efficient market.

6.5   Information Asymmetry and Trading Volumes

With the rise in acceptance of artificial intelligence techniques, and the consequent lessening of the degree of information asymmetry present in the marketplace, the result of trading volumes needs to be understood. In many cases, trade occurs because two parties have very different measures of value for a given asset, based on that party's own capabilities. Consider a merchant that processes and sells fish. This merchant buys fresh fish for a given amount, then debones the fish; separates the fish into three regular portions; seasons and cooks the fish; packages the fish and then delivers the fish to a customer that, for this example, will simply be a restaurant. To the merchant, the fish is worth what the restaurant will pay for the three portions of fish, after taking into account all of the costs of getting the fish from its raw state into a saleable state. To the supplier, the fish is worth what it cost him to get it to the merchant from the nearest fish farm (again for simplicity, let us assume the supplier is sourcing all his fish from one local trout farm). For both of these individuals, their valuations of the fish are entirely correct and yet they will likely come to very different values. In cases such as these, the reduction in information asymmetry resulting from the adoptions of artificial intelligence will have no effect on the volumes of fish traded.

This scenario, however, does not account for the entire market. In many cases, market players will *speculate* on commodities such as the value of a corn yield come harvest time, and to all those interested in such investments, one ear of corn is much the same as another (or at least is same by weight). It is in this case of traded commodities that the impact of artificial intelligence and its effect on information asymmetry is likely to be felt. In this case, the margins of profitability on speculative trades are likely to be squeezed, owing to the market having better information. This in turn will make it less attractive for many traders to speculate as their profit margin becomes more slight, and viable trades harder to find. The expectation is for artificial intelligence to lead to a reduction in trading volumes by making this type of trading more challenging and less lucrative.

Looking to the example of our agents trading dimples once more, we see that as they begin to adopt better analytics technology, and thus improve their level of accuracy, the number of arbitrage trades starts to decline quite steeply until it levels out at a point where all agents have similar access to the same information. The simulated results can be seen in Fig. 6.6.

Note that this simulation is only for traders who all have the same value proposition for dimples, and so are simply trying to turn a profit by buying dimples at a lower price and selling at a higher price. This analysis has little impact, if any, on actors in the marketplace who are adding value to dimples and then selling the modified product.

Fig. 6.6 Number of trades over time

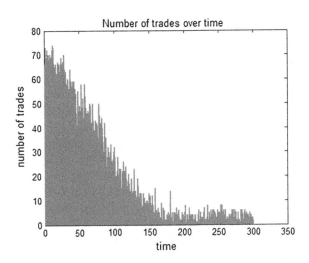

6.6 Conclusion

This chapter has proposed that the degree of asymmetry of information between two artificial intelligent agents is less than that between two human agents. As a result, it is also observed that the more artificial intelligence there is in the market, the less is the volume of trades in the market, and the overall efficiency of the market is likely to improve over time as the market becomes more saturated with intelligent trading and analysis agents.

References

Akerlof GA (1970) The market for 'Lemons': quality uncertainty and the market mechanism. Quart J Econ 84(3):488–500

Armstrong CS, Core JE, Taylor DJ, Verrachia RE (2010) When does information asymmetry affect the cost of capital? J Account Res 49(1):1–40

Bojanc R, Jerman-Blazic B (2008) An economic modeling approach to information security risk management. Int J Inf Manage 28(5):413–422

Chung KH, Kim J, Kim YS, Zhang H (2015) Information asymmetry and corporate cash holdings. J Bus Financ Acc 42(1):1341–1377

Fama E (1965) The behavior of stock market prices. J Bus 38:34–105

Kahneman D, Tversky A (1979) Prospect theory: an analysis of decision under risk. Econometrica 47(2):263

Marwala T (2009) Computational intelligence for missing data imputation, estimation, and management: knowledge optimization techniques. IGI Global, Pennsylvania. ISBN 978-1-60566-336-4

Marwala T (2010) Finite element model updating using computational intelligence techniques: applications to structural dynamics. Springer, Heidelberg. ISBN 978-1-84996-322-0

Marwala T (2012) Condition monitoring using computational intelligence methods. Springer, Heidelberg. ISBN 978-1-4471-2380-4

Marwala T (2013) Economic modeling using artificial intelligence methods. Springer, Heidelberg. ISBN 978-1-84996-323-7

Marwala T (2014) Artificial Intelligence techniques for rational decision making. Springer, Heidelberg. ISBN 978-3-319-11423-1

Marwala T (2015) Causality, correlation, and artificial intelligence for rational decision makING. World Scientific, Singapore. ISBN 978-9-814-63086-3

Marwala T, Lagazio M (2011) Militarized conflict modeling using computational intelligence. Springer, Heidelberg. ISBN 978-0-85729-789-1

Marwala T, Boulkaibet I, Adhikari S (2017) Probabilistic finite element model updating using bayesian statistics: applications to aeronautical and mechanical engineering. Wiley, NY

Russell SJ, Norvig P (2010) Artificial intelligence: a modern approach, 3rd edn. Prentice Hall, Upper Saddle River

Simon H (1957) Models of man, social and rational: mathematical essays on rational human behavior in a social setting. Wiley, New York

Spence M (1973) Job market signaling. Q J Econ (The MIT Press) 87(3):355–374

Stiglitz JE (1974) Incentives and risk sharing in sharecropping. Rev Econ Stud (Oxford Journals) 41(2):219–255

Stiglitz JE, Greenwald BC (1986) Externalities in economies with imperfect information and incomplete markets. Quart J Econ 101(2):229–264

Sun Y, Duong HN, Singh H (2014) Information asymmetry, trade size, and the dynamic volume-return relation: evidence from the Australian securities exchange. Financ Rev 49 (3):539–564

Chapter 7
Game Theory

Abstract Game theory has been used quite extensively in economics. In game theory agents with rules interact to obtain pay-off at some equilibrium point often called Nash equilibrium. The advent of artificial intelligence makes intelligent multi-agent games possible. This enriches the ability to simulate complex games. In this chapter, intelligent multi-agent system is applied to study the game of Lerpa.

7.1 Introduction

Game theory is one of those topics that people cannot help being drawn into, even if only in idle conversation. Everyone has played some form of game, and the notion that the lessons of those enjoyable diversions are applicable in other, more stressful areas of our lives is of course very appealing. The analogies are also intuitive—when one considers a real-world scenario, our available choices and constraints are quite easy to turn into game-like artefacts. The laws of society in general and of our specific surroundings, in particular, limit our available actions, our desires determine our goals, as well as the interactions and expectations determine the specific rules of the game. Take the example of our businessman producing and selling dimples. He wishes to sell his dimples for as much money as possible to the public, while keeping as much of the customer base as he can buying from his business rather than his competitor's. The laws of the country limit the options available to our businessman, defining the "moves" he can make. The laws of economics determine the effects of his actions, and his own desires determine his goals (unsurprisingly to maximise his profit). With these all established, game theory then enables us to analyse the best course of action for each player in order to reliably win the game. The task of game theory is thus to determine the best course of action for each player, given a defined game through which the players can interact. This theory has been applied to numerous different areas, from business dealings to interpersonal relationships, to international relations to name but a few (Ordeshook 1986; Webb 2007; van den Brink et al. 2008; Hui and Bao 2013; Laffont 1997; Fahrmeir and Tutz 1994).

T. Marwala and E. Hurwitz, *Artificial Intelligence and Economic Theory: Skynet in the Market*, Advanced Information and Knowledge Processing, DOI 10.1007/978-3-319-66104-9_7

7.2   Game-Theory Artefacts

Game theory consists of players, set of actions (strategy), and pay-off function, and the game is played until Nash equilibrium is reached (Ross 2006; Nash 1950a, b, 1951, 1953). Nash equilibrium is when no player can gain additional utility by playing further. When analysing a game, a number of factors determine the complexity of the analysis. The first of these would be the number of players. Single-player games are the simplest of all games analysed, effectively being optimisation problems viewed through a different lens. Far more common, are two-player games, in which two players interact through the game in order to maximise their own returns, measured by whatever measurement is appropriate to the particular game (so in a game involving a business venture, levels of success might be measured in dollars, while in a game involving influence, one might measure success in twitter re-tweets). In games where many players could have one of two approaches, the game is often simplified into a two-player game where all the players who ascribe to one strategy are treated as a single larger player, and the other players amalgamated similarly into the second player.

There are many types of games and the well-known one is the prisoner's dilemma. In this game, two players A and B are arrested for a crime and they are put in separate cells. They are given choices to either cooperate or defect, and this is represented in Table 7.1 (Rosenmüller 2000; Heap 2004; Marwala 2013).

Game theory can be used to solve this problem. If a player remains silent, he gets either 2 months in prison or serves 1 year in prison. If the player bargains, he gets either 6 months in prison or goes free. According to John von Neumann, the best strategy is the one that guarantees maximum possible outcome even if your opponent knew what choice you were going to make. In this case, the best strategy is to enter a plea bargain. The concept of Nash equilibrium states that the best strategy for each player is such that every player's move is a best response to the other players' move. Therefore, entering a plea bargain is a Nash equilibrium. All these assume that each player is rational and maximizes pay-off (Beed and Beed 1999). Figure 7.1 illustrates the means by which a large grouping of players can be viewed as a two-player game.

Some games will have multiple players, again increasing greatly in complexity with each added player. These multiplayer games can utilise the same principle of combining players when applicable, reducing down to the minimum number of

Table 7.1 Illustration of the prisoner's dilemma

	Prisoner B remains silent	Prisoner B plea bargains
Prisoner A remains silent	Each serves 2 months	Prisoner A serves 1 year Prisoner B goes free
Prisoner A plea bargains	Prisoner B serves 1 year Prisoner A goes free	Each serves 6 months

Fig. 7.1 Teams of similar players

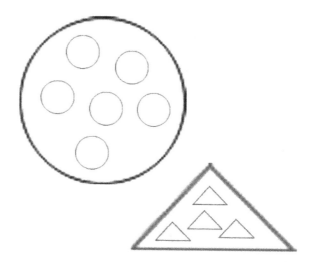

recognisably different players. Typically, multiple player games are referred to as *n-player* games, where *n* denotes the number of players present in the scenario.

The next issue to examine is the level of information available to each player. The simplest form of this variable is the scenario of *perfect information*, in which case all the players have full knowledge of the game, their own resources and their fellow players' resources, and all past moves made. In this form, it is easiest to evaluate all possible outcomes, and thus arrive at a strategy that reliably produces the best possible outcome. As with so many scenarios in both real-world examples and in typical games, the level of information available is often far more opaque than the perfect situation just described. Consider the popular game of poker: A player knows his/her own cards, and the communal cards shown on the table. Through elementary statistics, he/she can estimate the chances of the cards he/she needs being dealt over the remaining cards to come. He/she does not know his/her opponent's cards, which not only means he/she can only guess at his/her opponent's probability of drawing his/her needed cards, but there is also the chance that some of his/her desired cards are being held in his/her opponents' hands, which would cause his/her own statistical calculations to be in error. In this way, we can clearly see both the nature and effects of information being limited. Information can also be limited by the players having differing understanding of the rules of the game. Consider two investors with differing ideas on what drives the price of a particular commodity. Investor A believes dimples will become more expensive in times of drought, while investor B believes dimples will become cheaper in times of conflict. While both investors are players in this game, dealing with the dimple producer, they have different understandings of the rules, which can often be contradictory. Such cases can be viewed as inequitable information access, as players are not both privy to the same level of information, even though the basic information they are both presented with is the same.

In game theory, we refer to the rewards received as *payoffs*. These represent numerically the reward a player receives in a given situation. By making these payoffs numerical, we can compare the results of differing choices and easily identify the best choices. Speaking of choices, the act of consistently choosing a specific course of action is referred to as a *strategy*. Again, this should be fairly intuitive—if we consider a simple game of tennis, the choice to run to the centre of the back-line of the court after each shot would be a simple strategy. A more proficient tennis player would note that a better strategy would involve noting your opponent's position, and if that position was in a weak place, then a better move would be to approach the net. In such a way, a more complex strategy is developed, now contingent on both your own and your opponent's position. A strategy can further be modified statistically in order to avoid becoming predictable, which is often important in competitive games. Back to the same tennis game, a player might know that he is particularly proficient at a deep shot to the right hand corner of the court. A strategy that always hits the ball to that location would quickly become predictable, but the player could choose a strategy that chooses that shot 70% of the time, favouring the advantageous shot without allowing his opponent to beat him simply by predicting his next shot. While not completely deterministic, a probabilistic set of choices is still a valid (and often advantageous) strategy. The choice of payoffs when modelling a game must also reflect the end goal of the players. If we stick with tennis, the goal is to win a match. Payoffs in points won can easily obscure the end goal. As an example, consider the results of a tennis game in progress as shown in Table 7.2.

In this scenario, Jeffrey has won 11 points while Brian has won 9 points. If the game theory analysis used points as a payoff mechanism, the analysis would conclude that Jeffrey's strategy is a better strategy than Brian's. This is evidently false, however, as Brian has won 3 games to Jeffrey's 2, and as such is winning the current set. Clearly, the payoff structure for analyzing this game needs to be based on games won, and not the individual points that constitute the games. Similar issues crop up in games of all types. One very familiar to readers from the USA is that of the US general elections, wherein the winner-takes-all nature of the electoral college means that measuring the payoff of a candidate's campaigning strategy in votes is not very useful, since winning individual states will gain the victory regardless of the individual vote tally.

As with the tennis example, the bigger payoff is still made up of the smaller payoffs, and so it is not often that the counterintuitive case holds true. In the case of the US elections, only 5 times in the last 48 elections has a successful US

Table 7.2 Results of a tennis game in progress

Game #	Winner	Score
1	Brian	40–30
2	Jeffrey	0–40
3	Brian	40–15
4	Jeffrey	0–40
5	Brian	40–30

presidential candidate won while losing the "popular vote". Nonetheless, losing the presidency when more people supported you is a fairly embarrassing state of affairs, and the decision-makers in those campaigns would do well to pay more attention to appropriate payoffs, or in simpler terms to more relevant measures of success.

All of the examples mentioned previously make the assumption that each player values an outcome in the same way, but when examined using utility theory, one can transcend this limitation as well. First, we need to understand utility theory. Simply put, utility theory states that the same item or commodity may be worth more or less to different individuals based on the item's *utility*. Let us go back to our businessman manufacturing dimples. He has two potential customers, Darryl and Jonathan. Jonathan is a trader, and to him the dimples he buys are worth what he can sell them for. Darryl on the other hand manufactures pumples, and uses dimples in the manufacturing process. Darryl then values the dimples based on the proportion of his manufacturing cost of his pumples that they represent to him. As the two buyers have a different basis of valuing the dimples for sale, they are likely to arrive at different prices that they are prepared to pay for the dimples. There are times when this can lead to results that are at first glance counterintuitive, even when the same basis of value is used. Consider the valuation of this simple game: You have an option to draw a card from a full deck of cards. If you choose not to draw, you gain $5. If you draw a red card, you gain $10 and if you draw a black card you get nothing. The strategy of drawing nothing gives you a payoff of $5, and the strategy of drawing a card gives you a similar expected payoff of $5 (50% chance of $0, 50% chance of $10). Neither strategy is superior, and neither strategy is an obvious choice for us. Now we modify the game slightly. Let the prize for pulling a red card be $1,000,000, and the reward for choosing not to pull be $500,000. Once again, a statistical analysis shows that both strategies have the same payoff. Most of us, however, would choose to forego playing the game and walk home with the $500,000. The reason for this is that the first half a million has far more value to most of us than the second—you could pay off a house; repay loans; buy a car; take a vacation, perhaps even start up a small business. These options have a high amount of potential value to your life. The second half million has less obvious value once the higher priority items are dealt with, and as such holds far less to (most of) us. The act of playing would be risking the first half a million that we value highly for an equal chance to gain the second half a million that holds less value to us, which is clearly an irrational act.

The next issue to be considered is the degree of competition in a given game. This is understood through the game being zero-sum or not, and the degree of cooperation allowed between the players. A zero-sum game is one in which any gain made by one player amounts to a commensurate loss by the other player(s). This type of game represents a limited commodity that is being sought after, that all players desire to win. These are the simplest form of games to analyse, as they can always be analysed to give a clear-cut optimal strategy that maximises a player's payoff. Non-zero-sum games are better understood through cooperative theory which allows players to form binding agreements, a situation applicable to business dealings where a contract is in place, and through noncooperative theory which covers situations in which no enforceable agreement is in place. Consider two nations that make a deal. If one nation defaults, there is no governing body that can enforce the breached deal. Let us take a look at one of the most popular game-theory problems, the prisoner's dilemma. An attorney has two suspects accused of a crime, without enough evidence to convict either. He offers each accused the same deal. If the accused confesses to his crime and provides evidence, and his accomplice does not, then the accused who gave evidence will be pardoned while his accomplice will receive the maximum penalty. If both prisoners confess, they will both receive the minimum penalty for their crime. If they both remain silent, the attorney will use what information he has to convict them of a smaller, minor crime for which there is a light sentence. The dominant strategy for either prisoner is to rat out his accomplice, but the best result for the pair of them is to remain silent and both get the minor charge. If they are allowed to cooperate, they can achieve a better result than their dominant strategies would indicate. This problem has direct application in business, which in many cases indicates that competitors can achieve better results by cooperating with each other (a practice that in most cases falls under *price-fixing* and *collusion* legislation in many countries, despite its inherent appeal).

With an understanding of just what game-theory entails, we now look at what artificial intelligence (AI) brings to the table that impacts game-theory and its attendant financial and economic applications (Herbert 1982; Khosla and Dillon 1997; Hurwitz and Marwala 2007). The first of these is *multi-agent modelling* (MAM), sometimes referred to as *agent-based-modelling* (ABM), a simple concept enabled by the ever-growing power of modern computing (Wooldridge and Jennings 1994). In its simplest form, multi-agent modelling involves breaking a system up into its component features, and modelling those components in order to model the overall system. Central to this methodology is the notion of *emergent*

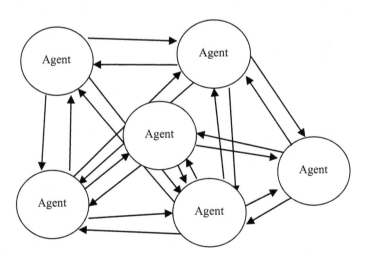

Fig. 7.2 Illustration of a multi-agent system

behaviour, that is, that the simple interactions between agents produce complex results. These results are often far more complex than the agents that gave rise to them. An illustration of a multi-agent system is shown in Fig. 7.2.

7.3   Multi-agent Modelling

Emergent behaviour is so pivotal to the understanding and utilisation of multi-agent modelling (MAM), that a brief elaboration becomes necessary. While it is not strictly speaking an instance of MAM, John Conway's *game of artificial life* provides an excellent illustration of emergent behaviour. In Conway's game, an MxN grid of squares (often infinite) each contains one binary value. A value of 1 is considered being *alive* while a zero is *dead*. With each iteration of the game, a *dead* square will become alive if exactly three adjacent squares are also alive, and a square that is alive will die if there are fewer than two adjacent living squares, or if there are more than three adjacent living squares, as depicted in Fig. 7.3.

In the next iteration, the two outermost living squares in Fig. 7.3a will die since each has only one living neighbour, and the two squares above and below the centre living square will come to life, as each has exactly three living neighbours, resulting in the situation depicted in Fig. 7.3b. As one can see, the rules are incredibly simple, but the consequences of these rules, i.e. the *Emergent Behaviour*, are far from simple. Figure 7.4 shows a simple-looking shape, commonly referred to as a *glider*.

This shape continues to propagate itself at a forty-five degree angle within the game, continuing until it hits the end of the grid (if the board is infinite, then it never terminates). In contrast, the even simpler-looking shape in Fig. 7.5, known as an *r-pentamino*, produces an explosion of shapes and patterns that continually change and mutate, only becoming predictable after 1103 iterations.

This emergent behaviour, complexity arising from the interaction of simple individuals following simple rules, allows multi-agent modelling to perform highly complex modelling tasks with relative simplicity.

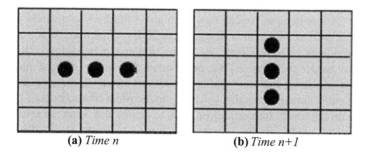

(a) *Time n*   (b) *Time n+1*

Fig. 7.3 A single iteration of Life

Fig. 7.4 Simple glider

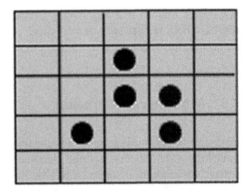

Fig. 7.5 R-Pentamino

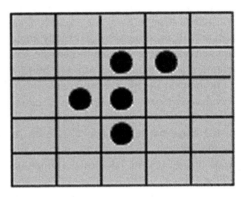

Multi-agent modelling is, simply put, the act of creating a number of computer-based models of individual actors in an environment, and putting them in a virtual environment that allows them to interact through environmental rules. By observing both their interactions and the emergent behaviour of the system as a whole, we are able to model the overarching system and better understand how the individuals and the system interact. As an example, we could model the flight of a flock of birds by coding in the rules of an individual (how close is it prepared to fly to its nearest neighbour, how far away from the flock is it prepared to fly, and similar) and then creating enough instances of this individual to constitute a flock. Observing the interactions, we can now learn about the flock as a whole while only having modelled individual birds (Engelbrecht 2002). While there is no requirement for all individuals to be identical, the more similar the individuals, the easier it becomes to model the system. We can extend this to the case of probabilistic systems, on which we can run what are known as *Monte-Carlo simulations*, simulating the environment many times (usually in the order of hundreds of thousands, depending on the level of accuracy you wish to attain) and using the result to build up a statistical model of the expected outcome (Marwala et al. 2017). As an example, consider trying to model a colony of ants whose individuals are characterised by the following rules:

(1) 90% chance to move forward
(2) 7% chance to turn right
(3) 3% chance to turn left.

While you know the expected movement of any individual, trying to predict where 100 individual ants are after 100 moves is analytically very challenging. Using the above approach, however, it is relatively easy to compile a statistical profile of where you expect that colony to be after 100 moves. These models can further be made to incorporate more complex (even intelligent) agents, agents that can adapt over time and learn to exploit their environments and even their fellow agents. An agent-based model holds many advantages over standard analytical techniques, which are traditionally mathematical or statistical in nature. Specifically, some of the advantages offered by an agent-based model are as follows:

- Agents are far simpler to model than the overall system they comprise, and hence, the system becomes easier to model.
- By exploiting the emergent behaviour property of agent-based models, one can tackle the modelling of highly complex systems while only performing much simpler individual modelling.
- Large systems with dissimilar agents can be easily handled within a multi-agent system, while this is incredibly difficult to cater for using traditional mathematics, which would make the often unrealistic demand that the components be identical.

While MAM has definite advantages, it is not without weaknesses. Since the emergent behaviour is arrived at empirically, and is not deterministic, it is difficult to state with any degree of certainty as to why a certain outcome has been arrived at. Similarly, since emergent behaviour is often unexpected, it can be difficult to ascertain whether the multi-agent system (MAS) is incorrectly modelling the system in question. Thus, validation of the model becomes an important aspect of any MAS (Granovetter 1978; Van Peach 2002). Multi-agent modelling lends itself to a number of applications and the following are some of the more common applications of multi-agent modelling.

7.3.1   Complexity Modelling

Multi-Agent modelling is well-suited to the task of *complexity modelling*. Complexity Modelling refers to modelling complex systems that are often too complex to be explicitly modelled. The usage of representative agents allows for the emergent behaviour of the MAM to model the complexity within the system, rather than said complexity being explicitly modelled by the analyst. Essentially, the complexity is contained by the *interactions* between the agents, and between the agents and the system, rather than the traditional, and often insufficient, mathematical models previously used (Tamas 2002).

7.3.2 Economics

Fundamentally an application of Complexity Modelling, Multi-Agent modelling can be applied to economic systems. This discipline, known as Applied Computational Economics (ACE), applies a bottom-up approach to modelling an economic system, rather than the traditional top-down approach, which requires full system specification and then component decomposition. In order to verify ACE system veracity, the ACE model is required to reproduce known results empirically. Once this has been accomplished, the same system can then be used to predict the results of unknown situations, allowing for better forecasting and policy decision-making (Gode and Sunder 1993; Marwala 2012).

7.3.3 Social Sciences

Many attempts have been made to model social phenomena, with varying degrees of success. Since social systems, by definition, involve the interaction of autonomous entities, multi-agent modelling offers an ideal methodology for modelling such systems. The foundations of such applications have already been laid, with the groundwork being solutions to such problems as the standing ovation problem. This particular problem is a fascinating look into applied psychology—if a show ends, and a certain number of people around you stand, at what point do you yourself stand? One step further, how many people, and in what groupings around the theatre, are required to stand in order to result in a standing ovation? Multi-agent modeling is one of many approaches used to answer this intriguing conundrum (Macy and Willer 2002).

7.4 Intelligent Agents

Intelligent agents add an extra layer of challenge and a greater level of modelling power to the analyst's arsenal. For an agent to be considered intelligent, it must be able to both learn from its surroundings and then to adapt based on changing circumstances. There are many techniques that can be used to achieve learning and adaptation and these include neural networks and evolutionary programming (Marwala and Lagazio 2011; Marwala 2012, 2014, 2015). A system with multiple intelligent agents is capable of producing emergent behavior that more closely represents the dynamics expected by human interaction, and can also mimic the expected responses to limited and/or misleading information. To understand this, consider the card game of *Lerpa*. This game is played with a standard deck of cards, with the exception that all of the 8, 9 and 10 s are removed from the deck. The cards are valued from greatest to least-valued from ace down to 2, with the exception that the 7 is valued higher than a king, but lower than an ace, making it the second most valuable card in a suit. At the end of dealing the hand, during which each player is dealt three cards, the dealer has the choice of *dealing himself in*—which entails flipping his last card over, unseen up until this point, which then declares which suit is the *trump suit*. Should he elect not to do this, he then flips the next card in the deck to determine the trump suit. Regardless, once trumps are determined, the players then take it in turns, going clockwise from the dealer's left, to elect whether or not to play the hand (to *knock*), or to drop out of the hand, referred to as *folding* (if the Dealer has *dealt himself in*, as described above, he is then automatically required to play the hand). Once all players have chosen, the players that have elected to play then play the hand, with the player to the dealer's left playing the first card. Once this card has been played, players must then play *in suit*—in other words, if a heart is played, they must play a heart if they have one. If they have none of the required suit, they may play a trump, which will win the trick unless another player plays a higher trump. The highest card played will win the trick (with all trumps valued higher than any other card) and the winner of the trick will lead the first card in the next trick. At any point in a hand, if a player has the Ace of trumps and can legally play it, he is then required to do so. The true risk in the game comes from the betting, which occurs as described below.

At the beginning of the round, the dealer pays the table whatever the basic betting denomination is (referred to usually as 'chips'). At the end of the hand, the chips are divided up proportionately between the winners, i.e. if you win two tricks, you will receive two thirds of whatever is in the pot. However, if you stayed in, but did not win any tricks, you are said to have been *Lerpa'd*, and are then required to match whatever was in the pot for the next hand, effectively costing you the pot. It is in the evaluation of this risk that most of the true skill in *Lerpa* lies.

The game is, for this model, going to be played by four players. Each of these players will interact with each other indirectly, by interacting directly with the *table*, which is their shared environment, as depicted in Fig. 7.6.

Over the course of a single hand, an agent will be required to make three decisions, once at each interactive stage of the game. These three decision-making stages are:

Fig. 7.6 System interactions

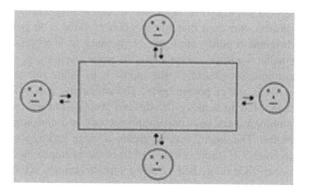

1. Whether to play the hand, or drop (*knock* or *fold*)
2. Which card to play first
3. Which card to play second.

Since there is no decision to be made at the final card, the hand can be said to be effectively finished from the agent's perspective after it has played its second card. Each player is designed to learn the probabilities of success based on the cards it holds and on the actions of the other players. This learning is constantly updated based on the results of the games as they are played. As a side note, an interesting trade-off occurs here of *exploitation* versus *exploration*—consider that you have a reasonably good hand in a weak position. You know that 60% of the time you had this hand, you lost but not badly. Statistically, you should fold your hand, but then you never learn if that hand is better than you first evaluated it, or if the nature of the players at the table has changed in such a way as to make it a more rewarding hand to play. When designing intelligent agents, you then need to designate a ratio of exploitation (playing the best move you have available) versus exploration (trying a different move in order to learn if another strategy is better than it appears).

Back to the game, over time, the agents all learned to play the game by playing against each other, becoming more proficient over time. Each agent was given a minor "personality trait", such as being slightly overconfident, or a bit cautious. A nice side-effect of intelligent agents is the ability to tweak their payoff functions in order to represent these personality traits. As the agents became more and more proficient, it emerged that players developed the technique of bluffing as a natural extension of understanding the game and the players at the table. The result is that by using intelligent multi-agent modelling, it was shown that bluffing is in fact a natural extension of the strategy of a card game with limited information that conveys information through betting.

7.5 The Road Ahead

Clearly, multi-agent modelling is a technique that has great potential to advance game-theory. The ability to model large numbers of non-identical agents in a system expands the range of situations that can be analysed using game-theory greatly. One area that shows great promise is in policy analysis. When an entity develops a policy (this can be as large as a proposed government legislation, or smaller such as a company-wide policy statement, or even as focused as a sales commission structure), the intent is to guide human behaviour through a set of rewards and/or punishments. Unfortunately, it is often the case that such induce-ments fail to achieve the desired results. For an easy example of this, consider prohibition-era laws preventing the sale and consumption of alcohol in the United States. The intent was to create a more moral society through the banning of alcohol. The desire for alcohol from the average citizen meant that the underground booze trade flourished, creating a much stronger criminal class and endangering the general populace in the process. None of the latter was intended, but the results were undeniable.

Through use of intelligent agents, it is very soon going to be possible to evaluate the effects of proposed policies, greatly lessening the risk of falling afoul of such unintended consequences. This could well mean more effective laws governing labour without stifling growth; better trading controls at exchanges; better HR incentives that improve both productivity and worker satisfaction, all by virtue of being able to test the policy on virtual agents rather than implementing them on human beings and simply hoping that they achieve their intended outcomes.

7.6 Conclusions

This chapter described game theory where agents with rules interact to obtain pay-off at some equilibrium point often called Nash equilibrium. The advent of artificial intelligence makes the multi-agents game theory much more effective. The applications of intelligent multi-agent systems to study a game of Lerpa is conducted.

References

Beed C, Beed C (1999) Intellectual progress and academic economics: rational choice and game theory. J Post Keynesian Econ 22:163–185
Engelbrecht AP (2002) Computational intelligence: an introduction. Wiley, London
Fahrmeir L, Tutz G (1994) Multivariate statistical modelling based on generalised linear models. Springer, Berlin
Gode DK, Sunder S (1993) allocative efficiency of markets with zero intelligence traders: market as a partial substitute for individual rationality. J Polit Econ 101:119
Granovetter M (1978) Threshold models of collective behavior. Am J Sociol 83(6):1420–1443
Heap, S. H. (2004). Game theory: A Critical Introduction. Routledge
Herbert S (1982) The architecture of complexity. The sciences of the artificial. MIT Press, Cambridge
Hui ECM, Bao H (2013) The logic behind conflicts in land acquisitions in contemporary China: a framework based upon game theory. Land Use Policy 30:373–380
Hurwitz E, Marwala T (2007) "Learning to bluff: a multiagent approach". IEEE International Conference on Systems, Man and Cybernetics. Montreal, Canada, pp 1188–1193
Khosla R, Dillon T (1997) Engineering intelligent hybrid multi-agent systems. Kluver Academic Publishers, Dordrecht
Laffont J-J (1997) Game theory and empirical economics: the case of auction data. Europ Econ Rev 41:1–35
Macy MW, Willer R (2002) From Factors to actors: computational sociology and agent-based modelling. Ann Rev Sociol, pp 143
Marwala T (2012) Condition monitoring using computational intelligence methods. Springer, Heidelberg
Marwala T (2013) Economic modeling using artificial intelligence methods. Springer, Heidelberg

Marwala T (2014) artificial intelligence techniques for rational decision making. Springer, Heidelberg

Marwala T (2015) Causality, correlation, and artificial intelligence for rational decision making. World Scientific, Singapore

Marwala T, Lagazio M (2011) militarized conflict modeling using computational intelligence. Springer, Heidelberg

Marwala T, Boulkaibet I, Adhikari S (2017) Probabilistic finite element model updating using bayesian statistics: applications to aeronautical and mechanical engineering. Wiley, London

Nash JF (1950a) Non-cooperative games PhD thesis. Princeton University, Princeton

Nash JF (1950b) Equilibrium points in n-person games. Proc Natl Acad Sci 36(1):48–49

Nash JF (1951) Non-cooperative games. Ann Math 54(2):286–295

Nash JF (1953) Two-person cooperative games. Econometrica 21(1):128–140

Ordeshook PC (1986) Game theory and political theory: an introduction. Cambridge University Press, Cambridge

Rosenmüller J (2000) Game theory: stochastics, information, strategies and cooperation. Springer, Berlin

Ross D (2006) Evolutionary game theory and the normative theory of institutional design: binmore and behavioral economics. Polit Philos Econ 5:51–79

Tamas V (2002) Complexity: the bigger picture. Nature 418(6894):131

van den Brink R, van der Laan G, Vasil'ev V (2008) Extreme points of two digraph polytopes: description and applications in economics and game theory. J of Math Econom. 44:1114–1125

Van Peach H (2002) Complexity and ecosystem management: the theory and practice of multi-agent systems. Edward Elgar Publishing Limited, Cheltenham

Webb JN (2007) Game theory: decisions, interaction and evolution. Springer, Berlin

Wooldridge M, Jennings NR (1994) Intelligent agents: theory and practice. knowledge engineering review, 1994, Revised January 1995

Chapter 8
Pricing

Abstract Pricing theory is a well-established mechanism that illustrates the constant push-and-pull of buyers versus consumers and the final semi-stable price that is found for a given good. Embedded in the theory of pricing is the theory of value. This chapter studies various pricing models and, in particular, how they are changed by the advances in artificial intelligence (AI). The first pricing model studied is game theory based pricing where agents interact with each other until they reach a Nash equilibrium price. Multi-agent systems are found to enhance this pricing model. The second is rational pricing and here when pricing the amount of arbitrage is minimized and AI is found to improve this model. The third is capital asset pricing model, which is also improved by the advent of evolutionary programming. Then the fourth is the Black-Scholes pricing model, which is impacted by the use of fuzzy logic to model volatility. The last one is the law of demand and supply, and it is found that the advent of AI within the context of online shopping infrastructure results in individualized pricing model.

8.1 Introduction

Pricing is one of the fundamental aspects of business transactions. Pricing is the process of assigning a price to a particular asset. Price is also a measure of a value of an asset. Prices are arrived at using the cost of production. For example, if a business entity produces a particular set of goods, at say $5 per item, then the seller is not incentivized to sell it at a price lower than the cost of production. In fact, if the seller sells it at $5, he will just break even. So the sensible price will be to sell it at a profit, which will mean at a price higher than $5. If the seller is a rational agent, he will sell it a price that maximizes profit. The question is how does he identify that price that maximizes profit? If he decides to sell this at $100, no one will buy it because it is too expensive. So pricing also has to take into account the customer's willingness to buy the good. This depends on how the customer values that particular good and, therefore, understanding the concept of value becomes important. Just because something is valuable does not mean that it has economic value. For example, the air we breathe has value but this value cannot be priced because it

© Springer International Publishing AG 2017 89
T. Marwala and E. Hurwitz, *Artificial Intelligence and Economic Theory: Skynet in the Market*, Advanced Information and Knowledge Processing,
DOI 10.1007/978-3-319-66104-9_8

does not have economic value. It is evident that the value of the air we breathe is higher than the value of the cars we drive but we can price the latter because of its economic value rather than the former. The price of a good is determined by the forces of demand and supply. The point at which the demand meets the supply is called equilibrium and has a price associated with it. Goods and services that have economic value can be tangible e.g. a car or intangible e.g. an insurance contract. Some of the objects that can be priced include options and derivatives, which are mainly insurance products and, cars which are physical assets.

8.2   Pricing

Pricing is the process of assigning a monitory value to goods and services. There are various strategies that have been pursued to assign prices to goods and services and these can be grouped into three or four broad areas i.e. behavioral economics, rational theory, strategic advantages and regulatory arguments (Irvin 1978; Neumeier 2008; Brennan et al. 2011; Dibb et al. 2013; Nagle et al. 2016). The rational approach to pricing seeks to maximize profit and is based on the theory of rational choice. The maximization of profits can be achieved in various ways and these include maximizing operational efficiencies or number of customers.

Behavioral type of pricing includes customer based pricing, which includes premium prices for premium brands, or relationship based pricing where pricing is done to maintain relationships with customers. Social oriented pricing uses pricing as a mechanism to either encourage or discourage behaviors. One example of this type of pricing includes penalties for drunk driving. Another emerging type of pricing is dynamic pricing that has emerged as a result of social networks and online market places. In this model, technology which is powered by artificial intelligence (AI) creates behavioral profiles of customers in platforms such as Amazon and is, therefore, able to create demand and supply curves of individuals. This allows for individualized pricing. Individual pricing is inherently unfair because the same good or service can be sold to different people at different prices at the same time. Moving trades to online platforms results in a higher density of differential pricing.

8.3   Value Theory

One fundamental principle of pricing is that it must have value (Dewey 1939; Debreu 1972). Value can be loosely defined as a measure of how desirable the object is. For example, a car has value because it is useful for transportation. So when one is using this car, one is exhausting its utility and as a result, a one year old simple car has more utility than a ten year old car. As described before, just because an object has value does not mean that it can be priced. For example, air is valuable but it is not economically valuable because for us to use it we do not have to pay for it. What differentiates value from economic value is scarcity. How does one measure how valuable an object is? In the social network media such as Facebook and LinkedIn, postings can be valued by how many people like them. An example, which is shown in Fig. 8.1, from LinkedIn shows an article which was viewed by 1744 people and liked by 28 people. With the widespread of social media it is now possible to easily quantify value of artefacts. The process of evaluating whether goods and services can be priced is shown in Fig. 8.2.

Fig. 8.1 The article posted on LinkedIn

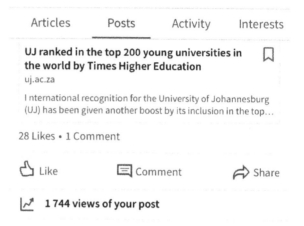

Fig. 8.2 A process that determines whether goods and services can be priced

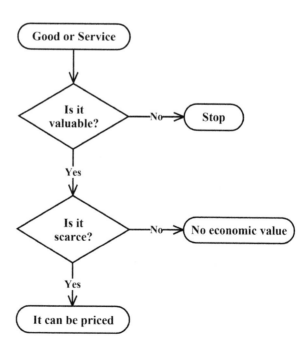

To evaluate whether a good e.g. a car, can be priced or not, one needs to ask whether the car is valuable and the answer is affirmative since it can still drive and, therefore, still has residual utility. Then the next question to ask is whether it is scarce or not and the answer is affirmative and therefore it can be priced. If we consider another commodity, e.g. air, the first question on whether air is valuable, has the answer which is affirmative. The second question which is whether it is scarce has the answer which is negative and, therefore, air cannot be priced.

8.4 Game Theory

Suppose Mbali goes to buy a Rolex watch in a market in New Delhi from a shopkeeper Vinod. Vinod informs Mbali that the watch costs Rs. 1000 then Mbali says she is prepared to pay Rs. 500, then Vinod says no he can only accept Rs. 900 and they keep on negotiating until they agree on the price of Rs. 700. Here, Vinod knows how much profit he is willing to take whereas Mbali has a vague idea of the utility of the watch. This is called information asymmetry and it so happens that the seller almost always has more information on the product they are selling than a buyer (Stigler 1961; Akerlof 1970; Stiglitz and Greenwald 1986). Because of this reason, sellers tend to extract more utility than buyers. The interaction between Vinod and Mbali can be summarized in Table 8.1.

Here, the Rs. 700 is a Nash equilibrium because Mbali and Vinod will not be able to increase their utility by further engaging each other. The process of reaching this conclusion of a sale price of Rs. 700 is called game theory. Game theory was first proposed by John von Neumann and advanced by John Nash who invented the concept of the Nash equilibrium (Nash 1950, 1951, 1953; Kuhn and Tucker 1958). Two players in this game of purchasing the watch are Mbali and Vinod and there are some rules of this engagement and they interact until they reach a Nash equilibrium (Rosenmüller 2000; Webb 2007).

The other factor that is worth noting is that this price is individualized and another customer can possibly come to buy the same watch and end up paying Rs. 800. These individualized markets are common in many parts of Asia and Africa and the advancement in online shopping, using platforms such as Alibaba and Amazon, make individualized pricing a possibility. Of course in these

Table 8.1 Interaction between Mbali and Vinod on the purchase of a Rolex watch (Rs. stands for Rupees)

Mbali (Rs.)	Vinod (Rs.)
500	1000
600	900
700	850
700	800
700	750
700	700

individualized markets a Nash equilibrium is never really reached and as a result, one player, which is normally the seller, extracts more utility than the buyer.

8.5 Rational Pricing

Rational pricing is a theory that assumes that pricing is free from arbitrage. Arbitrage is a situation when there is an imbalance in the markets because of geographical location (Fischer 2014). For example, suppose Peter is selling pota-toes in Johannesburg at Rs. 30 per kilogram and Sarah is selling the same potatoes in Cape Town at Rs. 200 per kilogram. Then John realizing this imbalance in the market can establish a business in which he simply buys potatoes in Johannesburg and sells them in Cape Town. In time, both Sarah and Peter will realize this imbalance and will cut the middle man, John, and in the long run the prices between Johannesburg and Cape Town will converge to some equilibrium position. In this case, the difference in prices between Johannesburg and Cape Town is said to be arbitraged. The reason for this arbitrage is the lack of or slow flow of information between the two positions. With advent of big data analytics, internet and AI, it is now possible for information including that which is hidden to flow much more efficiently between geographical locations than before the advent of these tech-nologies. This, therefore, implies that pricing is more and more becoming rational than before because of the advent of these technologies.

8.6 Capital Asset Pricing Model

CAPM (Capital Asset Pricing Model) modelling is a process designed to obtain a given value of risk from a composite portfolio often significantly lower in value than the lowest efficient portfolio in the universe of portfolios (Jiang 2011). To achieve this, an *optimal portfolio* is first found along the efficient horizon. This portfolio is then combined in a linear fashion with a *zero-risk* portfolio in a pro-portional manner to create a new portfolio, which meets the required specifications.

A *zero-risk* asset is an asset so safe that it has a variance of zero (Jiang 2011). Such commonly used assets are treasury bonds and other government-backed securities that are assumed never to default. This obviously does not account for political risk, or the possibility of a state collapsing like what happened in Zimbabwe or Libya or Somalia. In this way, the system is analogous to a feed-forward control system, that aims to control the targeted variable (return or risk) while, at the same time, optimizing the secondary variable. With the advent of artificial intelligence, it is now possible to use evolutionary techniques, such as genetic algorithm and particle swarm optimization, to optimally price CAPM and this was conducted successfully by Hurwitz and Marwala (2012).

8.7 Black-Scholes Equation

An option is a financial derivative of a different financial security such as stock, credit, interest rate or exchange rate and any of these instruments are the primary asset of an option. Options are called derivatives for the reason that they are derived from other financial securities (Hull 2003). An option provides for the right, but not an obligation to the owner of the option, to buy or sell the asset at a later time called the maturity date by entering into a contract that specifies a price for the underlying asset now. This agreed price is known as the strike price. Because of their high value, options are treasured and organizations pay a premium known as the price of the option to possess them. There are two types of options and these are call and put options. A call option is when a person intends to buy the underlying asset, while a put option is when the individual intends to sell the underlying asset.

Options are utilized daily by organizations to hedge their financial risk. For example, consider a firm with an exposure to foreign trade. This company's financial risk is governed by the exchange rate and, if the rate changes dramatically, the company may not be able to meet its financial obligations. A firm can normally use an option to protect itself by purchasing a call option and thus giving the firm the option of a fixed exchange rate.

This practice is called hedging and makes options very treasured and, therefore, organizations pay a premium called the price of the option. Other financial mechanisms that can be used for hedging include forwards and futures. There are two types of options and these are European and American options. European options only permit the option owner to exercise them on the expiry date of the contract, while American options permit the owners to exercise the option on any date between accepting and the end date of the contract. American options are more valuable and introduce a second random process into the model because of their flexibility on the date they can be exercised.

Black, Scholes and Merton presented the Black-Scholes model for option pricing (Black and Scholes 1973; Merton, 1973) and proposed the option pricing formula for European options. The Black-Scholes model is premised on the following assumptions (Black and Scholes 1973; Merton 1973):

- Absence of arbitrage.
- Cash can be borrowed and lent at a known constant risk-free interest rate.
- Stock can be bought and sold.
- Transactions have fees or costs.
- The stock price is described by a geometric Brownian motion with constant drift and volatility.
- The underlying security does declare dividend.

The Black-Scholes model offers a mechanism of approximating the underlying asset's volatility which can be predicted using the Black-Scholes equation. The Black-Scholes model depends on the following parameters: volatility of the returns of the underlying assets, risk free annual rate, the strike price, the spot price of the underlying asset, the time to maturity and the cumulative distribution function which is normally a Gaussian distribution. With the advent of AI, it is now possible to model a property of the Black-Scholes model i.e. volatility which is fuzzy using fuzzy logic. Fuzzy logic is an AI procedure that is used to model linguistic variables mathematically (Sugeno 1985).

8.8 Demand and Supply

The demand and supply curves show the relationship between the supplier and the customer and is shown in Fig. 8.3. The supplier produces goods and services with economic value and, therefore, can be priced and his intention is to maximize utility and in this case this is the return on his investment. The customer with money estimates the value of the goods and services he wants to buy, and he prices these goods and services to maximize utility. This transaction proceeds if the supplier's perception of value of the price offered by the customer is higher than the value he places on the good. Furthermore, the customer buys the good if his perception of the value of the good is higher than the value of the money he needs to buy the goods.

   This is what is called the asymmetry of information with regards to perception of value. The point at which the demand and supply curves meet is called equilibrium and it has a corresponding equilibrium price. When one goes to a big department shop to buy a particular good, it is priced using the equilibrium price which is derived from the aggregate demand and supply curves. Nowadays, people are no longer just going to the big physical stores but are shopping online and are profiled. This allows for their buying patterns as well as demand curves to be much more known and, therefore, can now be subjected to their own individual demand curve as illustrated in Fig. 8.4. This is due to the fact that these online shopping platforms are powered with technologies such as artificial intelligence, which is able to perform complicated data analytics and, consequently, estimate an individualized

Fig. 8.3 The demand and supply curve

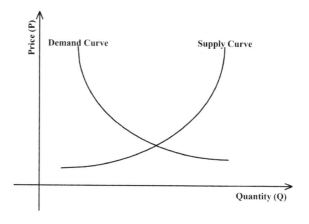

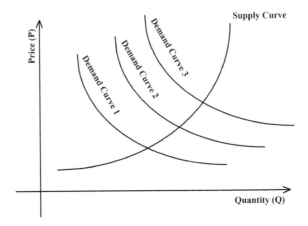

Fig. 8.4 Demand curves for different users for a particular good

demand curve. One such example, is the online shopping platform Amazon which is illustrated in Fig. 8.5. In this Figure, there are two books from the same publisher and these are taken from the same user profile and were taken on May 2, 2017 and

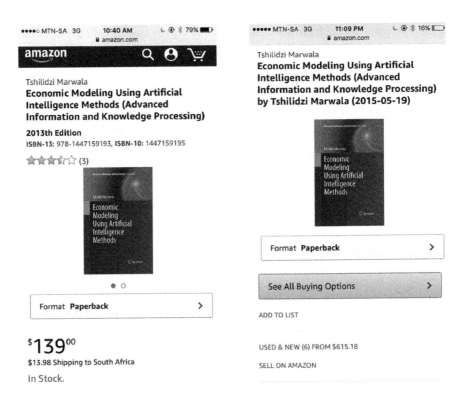

Fig. 8.5 Book sales on Amazon

May 3, 2017 showing different prices. It is, therefore, now possible to offer differential prices for one type of good to different people buying at the same time because they have individual demand curves. The questions that remain are: Is it fair to offer differential prices for the same good to different customers? How will these different prices impact on the market? Will this adversely distort the character of the market? Do these online shopping platforms increase or decrease the levels of arbitrage in the market? At the superficial level it seems that online shopping decreases the levels of arbitrage in the markets but studies should be made in this regard.

Figure 8.6 is a diagram showing how these transactions are conducted. On the one hand, we have the supplier who has some inputs into the making of goods and services. Given all these, one can create some artificial intelligence model which takes the factors that influence the production of goods and services and generates the supply curve. On the other hand, there are a group of customers and here, AI can be used to generate the demand curve. It should be noted that these demand and supply curves can be individualized, segmented into group of individuals or aggregated. The detector takes the AI demand and supply curve generators and comes up with some equilibrium price which can be individualized or segmented over groups of people or aggregated. The way this detector works can be by using game theory, where the demand and supply curve generators can be viewed as

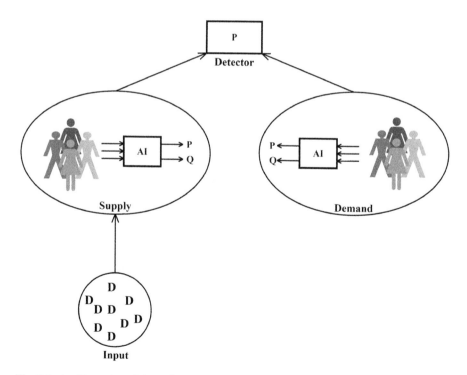

Fig. 8.6 An illustration of the online shopping model

players in a game with rules and this game is played until Nash equilibrium is reached. The advantage of this procedure is that one can be able to reach Nash equilibrium, a state which is not necessarily achievable in the traditional marketplace.

8.9 Conclusions

This chapter studied the theory of value, which is linked to pricing and observed that online social networks, such as facebook, offer a unique opportunity to estimate value of goods and services by counting the number of 'likes' and 'views' in a particular page. Various pricing models were considered and these were game theory, rational pricing model, capital asset pricing model, Black-Scholes model and the law of demand and supply. Game theory was found to be enhanced by the advent of multi-agent systems, whereas artificial intelligence was found to improve the rational pricing model. The capital asset pricing model was found to be improved by the advent of evolutionary programming whereas the Black-Scholes pricing model was impacted by the use of fuzzy logic to model volatility. For the law of demand and supply, it was found that the advent of artificial intelligence within the context of online shopping infrastructure results in individualized pricing models.

References

Akerlof GA (1970) The market for 'Lemons': quality uncertainty and the market mechanism. Quart J Econ 84(3):488–500
Black F, Scholes M (1973) The pricing of options and corporate liabilities. J Polit Econ 81: 637–654
Brennan R, Canning L, McDowell R (2011) Business-to-business marketing, 2nd edn. London, Sage
Dewey J (1939) Theory of valuation. University of Chicago, USA
Debreu G (1972) Theory of value: an axiomatic analysis of economic equilibrium. Cowles Foundation—Yale University, USA
Dibb S, Simkin L, Pride WC, Ferrell OC (2013) Marketing: concepts and strategies, Cengage
Fischer T (2014) No-arbitradge pricing under systematic risk: accounting for cross-ownership. Math Finance 24(1):97–124
Hurwitz E, Marwala T (2012) Optimising a targeted fund of strategies using genetic algorithms. IEEE International Conference on Systems, Man, and Cybernetics, pp 2139–2143
Hull JC (2003) Options, futures and other derivatives. Prentice Hall, New Jersey
Irvin G (1978) Modern cost-benefit methods. Macmillan, UK
Jiang P (2011) Corporate finance and portfolio management. CFA Institute Report, CFA Institute, Virginia
Kuhn HW, Tucker AW (1958) John von Neumann's work in the theory of games and mathematical economics. Bull Amer Math Soc 64 (Part 2)(3):100–122. doi:10.1090/s0002-9904-1958-10209-8. MR 0096572

Merton RC (1973) Theory of rational option pricing. Bell J of Econ Manage Sci 4:141–183

Nagle T, Hogan J, Zale J (2016) The strategy and tactics of pricing: a guide to growing more profitably. Routledge, Oxon

Nash JF (1950) Equilibrium points in N-person games. Proc Natl Acad Sci 36(1):48–49

Nash JF (1951) Non-cooperative games. Ann Math 54(2):286–295

Nash JF (1953) Two-person cooperative games. Econometrica 21(1):128–140

Neumeier M (2008) The brand flip: why customers now run companies and how to profit from it (voices that matter)

Rosenmüller J (2000) Game theory: stochastics, information, strategies and cooperation. Springer, Berlin

Stigler GJ (1961) The economics of information. J Polit Econ 69(3):213–225

Stiglitz JE, Greenwald BC (1986) Externalities in economies with imperfect information and incomplete markets. Quart J Econ 101(2):229–264

Sugeno M (1985) Industrial applications of fuzzy control. Elsevier Science Publication Company, Amsterdam

Webb JN (2007) Game theory: decisions, interaction and evolution. Springer, Berlin

Chapter 9
Efficient Market Hypothesis

Abstract The efficient market hypothesis (in its varying forms) has allowed for the creation of financial models based on share price movements ever since its inception. This chapter explores the impact of artificial intelligence (AI) on the efficient market hypothesis. Furthermore, it studies theories that influence market efficiency and how they are changed by the advances in AI and how they impact on market efficiency. It surmises that advances in AI and its applications in financial markets make markets more efficient.

9.1 Introduction

Market efficiency hypothesis is one of the most controversial theories in economics. It prescribes that markets are efficient because they reflect all the information that impact on them. Embedded in this theory is the assertion that markets are rational. Markets cannot be both irrational and efficient. How do we measure whether markets are efficient or not? One way to measure whether the markets are efficient is to measure the aggregate amount of profits that can be derived from the markets. This is because efficient markets have little or no free money (i.e. profits) to be made. The only amount of money that can be made in the efficient markets is due to the growth in the company. For example in market A, company X invents a new product and this results in an increase in the profit margins of company X. Then the money that the investors make in this market is due to an expansion in productive forces by company X. In an irrational market, money can be unduly made. For example, company X is sold to company Y at less than the normal market rate and investors unduly profit from this transaction because X was underpriced. One of the powerful assertions around the efficient market hypothesis is that the inefficiencies in the market are quickly corrected and that inefficiencies are fundamentally temporal in the markets. This is thought to be reinforced by the principles of free trade which are thought to be underpinned by the law of survival of the fittest which is

T. Marwala and E. Hurwitz, *Artificial Intelligence and Economic Theory: Skynet in the Market*, Advanced Information and Knowledge Processing,
DOI 10.1007/978-3-319-66104-9_9

inspired by the principles of Darwinism. In this explanation, it is said that inefficient companies and players in the markets are driven out of the markets by the principles of competition.

To understand the markets, it is important to understand what constitutes the markets. One element of the markets is people who make decisions that influence the markets, what we also call customers. Of course, much of the decision making in the markets are more and more being made by artificial intelligent (AI) machines with serious consequences for the character of the markets. The second aspect of the markets are assets in the markets that form part of production. Here, again, this is changing as more and more products are being made by machines. The other aspect of the markets that requires attention is the regulatory framework, which can impede or expand the markets. For example, the anti-trust regulations in the USA has a huge impact on how far companies can grow and how they should interact with one another.

In this chapter, we study how some of the big ideas in the field of economics influence the character of the markets. These ideas are the theories of rational expectations, rational choice, bounded rationality, information asymmetry, behavioral economics, pricing and demand and supply.

9.2 Efficient Market Hypothesis

The efficient market hypothesis is a theory that was developed by Nobel Laureate Eugene Fama, which basically states that markets reflect all the information and, therefore, cannot be outperformed (Fama 1970). In this regard, Fama observed that stock market movement can be approximated by a random walk and, therefore, are not predictable. He furthermore, observed that it is not possible to reject market efficiency without rejecting the notion of market equilibrium. The only time markets can be beaten is if they are inefficient, thereby, exploiting the inefficiency of the markets. Furthermore, he classified market efficiency into three types and these are weak-form efficiency, semi-strong-form efficiency and strong-form efficiency. In weak-form efficiency, future prices of stocks cannot be predicted from past values. Predicting future prices of stocks from its past values is called adaptive expectations and has been found to give biased results and, therefore, cannot be used consistently with success. In this regard, technical analysis, i.e. the use of available data analysis, cannot give consistent results while there is a room for fundamental analysis to give good results. Semi-strong-form efficiency states that markets incorporate newly available public information so quickly that there is no opportunity to use that information for any form of meaningful gain. This implies that neither technical nor fundamental analysis consistently return results. Strong-form efficiency reflects all information both private and public and there is no form of analysis that can consistently beat the markets. Any growth in earnings will be as a consequence of organic growth of the companies involved.

Fig. 9.1 Illustrations of the factors that impact on various aspects of efficient market hypothesis

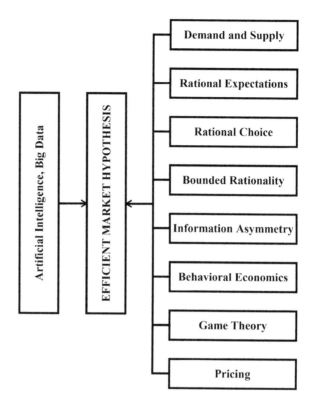

The efficient market is influenced by various economic theories and some of them are rational expectations, rational choice, bounded rationality, behavioral economics, information asymmetry, game theory, pricing as well as demand and supply. On the other hand, new paradigms such as artificial intelligence are having an impact on this theory and this is illustrated in Fig. 9.1.

9.3   Rational Expectations

Rational expectations is a theory that states that agents cannot systematically make mistakes on prediction of the future because they are able to use all available information at their disposal. It turns out that people trading in stock markets can make lots of mistakes because they have different biases, experiences, risk appetites and other exogenous characteristics. Because of this, markets are full of people who faced financial ruin for no other reason than the fact that they just could not systematically predict the future or, differently stated, systematically made errors of judgment. What is the implication of this in the market as far as the efficient market hypothesis is concerned? The impact of this is that such people who are making systematic errors in predicting the future prices of stocks actually contribute towards making the markets inefficient. Why would such people make systematic errors if they have all the information at their disposal? They make such systematic errors because human beings cannot process efficiently and effectively all the information that is at their disposal and such information is often incomplete, imperfect and imprecise. How do the advent of artificial intelligence and the related topics of big data and signal processing change the market inefficiency resulting from human behavior on analyzing the data? Firstly, artificial intelligence is a better predictor of the future price of stocks than a human being. Consequently, AI discounts the effect of a human beings inability to predict the future leading to market inefficiency and, thereby, resulting in markets becoming more efficient when compared to markets with human traders.

9.4   Rational Choice

The theory of rational choice prescribes that rational agents choose that option that maximizes utility (Green and Shapiro 1994; Friedman 1996; Irons and Hepburn 2007; Hedström and Stern 2008; Grüne-Yanoff 2012). Normally to achieve this, the agents will evaluate information available and put this information into some causal model giving different outcomes, and then choosing that outcome that maximizes utility. Again, there are a number of problems with the theory of rational choice and these include that the information used to make the decision is imperfect, incomplete and imprecise, that not all the options are accessible, that calculating utility might not be easy and often it is subjective. Because of these reasons, very few agents manage to maximize utility. Given this problem, what is the impact of this on the efficient market hypothesis? Can agents that do not maximize utility but dominate the market-place give rise to an efficient market? The answer seems to be obvious and that these agents that are not rational cannot result in an efficient market.

9.5   Bounded Rationality

The idea of rational choice is limited because information is often imprecise, missing and imperfect. Additionally, the process of utilization of such information is also limited due to processing speed and capability of the human brain. Furthermore, it is not always possible to evaluate all options required to be considered for making a decision. Because of these reasons, it is not always possible to identify optimally the best possible decision and this concept is called bounded rationality (Simon 1957, 1990 and 1991). The idea of optimality has two consequences, and these are local optimality and global optimality. Local optimality implies inefficiency and because of this reason, even an optimized decision is not globally optimized, thereby, truncating rationality. Because of this reason, the process of evaluating utility is compromised. Bounded rationality essentially implies that rationality is limited. Since rationality is directly linked to the efficiency of the market, therefore, bounded rationality implies that the efficient market hypothesis is bounded. The advances of artificial intelligence have been observed to improve the utilization of information and also to account for hidden information and, thereby, moving the bounds of rationality for better decision making. Because of this reason, AI makes markets more efficient and, thereby, making the efficient market hypothesis more valid.

9.6 Information Asymmetry

Information asymmetry is the theory about the impact of imbalance between two parties on access to information (Akerlof 1970; Spence 1973; Stiglitz 1974; Aboody and Lev 2000). The classical example of this is the situation where there are two car salesmen, one selling good cars and another selling bad cars but the buyers do not know who is selling which cars. The used car salesman that sells good cars will ultimately be driven out of the market because he is less likely to give a discount than the one who sells bad cars. Therefore, information asymmetry distorts the market negatively. There are various classes of information asymmetry and these include adverse selection models and moral hazard. In the adverse selection model, the ignorant agent lacks information when the agent is negotiating a contract of the transaction. Moral hazard is when the ignorant agent does not have information on the performance of the agreed contract.

The advent of artificial intelligence in trading makes information much more accessible through extensive data mining procedures that use analytics to identify similar cases in the past. Therefore, trading artificial intelligent agents have lower asymmetric information than trading human beings. The consequence of this is that trading becomes more rational and the volume of trade decreases because people exchange goods because their individual perception of values differ. For example, consider a situation where Taku has an orange and Vule has an apple. For Taku to give his orange to Vule, he must think that an apple is more valuable than an orange. Conversely, for Vule to agree to this transaction he must think an orange is more valuable than an apple. This transaction can only happen if there is an asymmetrical perception of value. If this information asymmetry is reduced, then the probability of such transaction happening is reduced.

The market is full of such transactions where information asymmetry is a norm and this contributes towards making the markets inefficient. When the human agents in the market are replaced by artificial intelligent trading machines, the contribution of the effects of information asymmetry towards market inefficiency is greatly reduced thus making the efficient market hypothesis more valid.

9.7 Behavioral Economics

Behavioral economics is based on the fact that human beings are decision makers in the markets (Kahneman 2011; Kahneman and Tversky 1979; Tversky and Kahneman 1973). Consequently, issues that have to do with human behavior such as mood swings, biases and prejudices are an integral part of human decision making and often contribute towards making markets inefficient. There have been many theories that have been proposed to understand human beings making decisions and key among these is what is called prospect theory. In fact, the theory of bounded rationality can be interpreted within the context of behavioural economics where the human behavior serves as the bound that limits the degree of rationality in decision making. Behavioral economics can be viewed as a fusion of psychology and economics where the concepts from psychology are used to understand economics. Behavioral economics has found that people make decisions based on the rule of thumb rather than on firm logic. Prospect theory is an exampe of behavioral economics which states that human beings are more averse to loss than attracted to gain, that human beings depend on some reference point when making decisions, that people overweigh small probabilities and underweigh large probabilities as well as that they have diminishing sensitivity to gain and losses. These behavioural traits that dominate human decision making make the markets that are dominated by human beings irrational, and thus contribute towards the reduction of the relevance of the efficient market hypothesis.

As stated before, more and more trading robots that are powered by artificial intelligence are being used in the market. These robots do not exhibit behaviors observed in prospect theory. They are not averse to losses than they are attracted to gain. They do not overvalue small probabilities and undervalue large probabilities. They do not depend on some reference point as a basis of their decision making nor do they have diminishing sensitivity to gains and losses. They do not use rules of thumb to make decisions but they use logic. Consequently, the presence of these trading robots make the markets more efficient and limit the applicability of behavioral economics.

9.8 Game Theory

Game theory is a mathematical technique that is used for making rational decisions that are optimized through what is called a Nash equilibrium (Heap 2004; Laffont 1997). Much of big decisions in the market such as negotiations about mergers of large companies are done using game theory. If there are two companies, A and B, that are bidding for a third company, C, then the shareholders of C will interact with shareholders of A and B until further interactions do not result in A, B and C gaining further utilities. The way the framework of game theory works is that there are players in a game and here, the players are companies A, B and C, and then

Table 9.1 A game of war

Zimbabwe	Malawi	
	Defend	Attack
Defend	4,4	1,5
Attack	5,1	3,3

there is a game and in this case, for A or B to acquire C and this is a zero sum game because a win for A is a loss for B and vice versa. Then these two players A and B bid to acquire C, and this is repeated until a Nash equilibrium is achieved. An example of an application of game theory that has been discussed commonly by many researchers is between countries e.g. Malawi and Zimbabwe where if both defend, they get equal utilities of 4, if they both attack they both get a utility of 3 and if Zimbabwe attacks while Malawi defends then Zimbabwe gets a utility of 5 while Malawi gets 1. If Malawi attacks while Zimbabwe defends then Malawi gets a utility of 5 while Zimbabwe gets 1. This is shown in Table 9.1 and the best strategy is to attack while the opponent defends and this is a Nash equilibrium.

If all the negotiations in the markets were done logically with Nash equilibrium solutions, then the markets will be more rational. This will, therefore, add towards making the efficient market hypothesis more valid. Unfortunately, this is not the case and many negotiations even for big organizations result in catastrophic failures, thereby, making markets more irrational. This, therefore, discounts from the validity of the efficient market hypothesis. However, with the rise of artificial intelligence in the markets, this becomes more and more valid, thereby, rendering the markets more efficient and, therefore, rendering the efficient market hypothesis more valid.

9.9   Demand and Supply

The law of demand and supply is one of the fundamental principles that defines trade and economics (Marshall 1920; Mankiw and Taylor 2011). Demand curve is negatively sloped as the more expensive a good is, the less the quantity of that good is demanded. Conversely, the less expensive the good is, the more quatity of that good is demanded. This of course assumes that it is a valuable good. The supply curve is positively sloped in the sense that the higher the price of a good, the more quantity of that good the suppliers are willing to produce. The point at which the demand and the supply meet is called equilibrium and the associated price is called the equilibrium price. It is the equilibrium price that is normally used as an anchor for fair pricing. In essence, the equilibrium price is the price at which all the economic forces that influence the production, distribution and selling of the good are balanced. In the normal market, the market price of a good is not necessarily the equilibrium price and this imbalance the economic forces that are at play in the production, distribution and selling of that good. This is what is called mispricing and it has serious ramifications on the rationality of the markets and, consequently, it contributes towards the inefficiency of the markets. Because of the inability to get the accurate demand and supply curves, there is always an overproduction of goods and services and, consequently, there is always wastage which ends up making the market not to be efficient and, therefore, irrational.

The advances in AI have had serious consequences on the principle of demand and supply. For example, it is now possible to have a seamless model that is powered by AI and is able to search for vasts amounts of information, which may be data, pictures and texts to predict the demand of a particular good as well as the required supply of that particular good. The advances of production which is based on the just-in-time principles, with more accurate robots that are powered by AI and better prediction capabilities of demand and supply, result in a more efficient market. These, therefore, render the theory of efficient market hypothesis more valid.

9.10 Pricing

Pricing is an important aspect of the exchange of goods and services (Dewey 1939; Debreu 1972; Fischer 2014). As described above, the most efficient strategy of pricing is to use the law of demand and supply which gives an equilibrium price, which is a point where demand and supply intersect. However, the practical reality is that many pricing models take into account other factors such as price discounting, market positioning and market sengmentation as well as other factors which are not necessarily rational. These result in prices that are far from the equilibrium price. Furthermore, aggregate demand and aggregate supply of a particular good or service result in aggregate equilibrium price. This, however, does not necessarily result in the optimum individualized price and this compromises the realization of maximization of utilities by both customers and buyers. Furthermore, information asymmetry between the buyers and the sellers results in the mispricing of goods or services, where the informed party extracts value from the uninformed party. All these factors described result in a pricing regime that contributes towards the inefficiency of the markets and, thereby, renders the efficient market hypothesis less valid.

With the advent of AI, it is now possible to reduce information asymmetry and, thereby, contribute towards rational pricing, which consequently improves the validity of the efficient market hypothesis. Furthermore, the increasing use of online buying platforms such as Amazon makes it possible to individualize demand and supply curves and consequently individualize equilibrium pricing. This makes pricing rational and, thereby, contributes towards improving the validity of the efficient market hypothesis.

9.11 Artificial Intelligence

Artificial intelligence is a computational paradigm where high level cognitive and organizational skills usually observed in biological and physical systems are codified to solve practical problems (Marwala 2007, 2009, 2010, 2012, 2013, 2014; Marwala and Lagazio 2011). This chapter is on the use of artificial intelligence to improve the validity of the efficient market hypothesis. What elements of artificial intelligence are relevant for improving the efficiency of the market? There are two main types of artificial intelligence techniques and these are learning methods, such as neural networks, as well as optimization methods, such as genetic algorithm. In this chapter, it is observed how several ideas in economics impact on efficient market hypothesis and how the influence of artificial intelligence on these ideas in turn change the efficient market hypothesis.

In the theory of rational expectations, learning methods such as neural networks can be used as a model to predict expectations of the future. The theory of rational choice uses the theory of rational expectations to predict different expected scenarios given the data and different choices. So, rational choice requires the use of both learning methods to predict future expected scenarios and optimization methods such as genetic algorithm to optimally choose a rational scenario. The theories of demand and supply as well as pricing require both learning and optimization techniques. To individualize demand and supply requires learning methods to learn the behavioral profiles of the individuals as well as learning and optimization methods to improve the efficiency of the production and distribution of goods and services. Information asymmetry requires both learning and optimization as information will have to be searched from the internet and optimized to reduce asymmetry. Bounded rationality requires both learning and optimization to automate decision making and thus relax the bounds of rationality. Human beings in behavioral economics are replaced by learning machines. In game theory, agent based modelling which optimizes and learns is used to improve the attainment of the Nash equilibrium.

9.12 Conclusions

This chapter studied the impact of artificial intelligence on the efficient market hypothesis. It studied concepts that influence market efficiency and how these concepts are changed by the advances in artificial intelligence and in turn how these concepts then impact on market efficiency. The concepts that were studied are demand and supply, rational expectations, rational choice, bounded rationality, behavioural economics, information asymmetry, pricing and game theory. It is surmised that advances in artificial intelligence result in making markets more efficient.

References

Aboody D, Lev B (2000) Information asymmetry, R&D, and insider gains. J Financ 55(6): 2747–2766

Akerlof GA (1970) The market for "lemons": quality uncertainty and the market mechanism. Quart J Econ 84(3):488–500

Debreu G (1972) Theory of value: an axiomatic analysis of economic equilibrium. Cowles Foundation – Yale University, New Haven

Dewey, J. (1939). Theory of valuation. University of Chicago, USA

Fama E (1970) Efficient capital markets: a review of theory and empirical work. J Financ 25 (2):383–417

Fischer T (2014) No-arbitradge pricing under systematic risk: accounting for cross-ownership. Math Financ 24(1):97–124

Friedman J (1996) The rational choice controversy. Yale University Press, New Haven

Green DP, Shapiro I (1994) Pathologies of rational choice theory: a critique of applications in political science. Yale University Press, New Haven

Grüne-Yanoff T (2012) "Paradoxes of Rational Choice Theory". In: Sabine R, Rafaela H, Per S, Martin P (Hrsg) Handbook of Risk Theory, pp. 499–516. doi:10.1007/978-94-007-1433-5_19

Heap SH (2004) Game theory: a critical introduction. Routledge, Abingdon

Hedström P, Stern C (2008) Rational choice and sociology. The New Palgrave Dictionary of Economics, 2nd Edition. Abstract

Irons B, Hepburn C (2007) Regret theory and the tyranny of choice. Econ Rec 83(261):191–203

Kahneman K (2011) Thinking, fast and slow. Macmillan, New York

Kahneman D, Tversky A (1979) Prospect theory: an analysis of decision under risk. Econometrica 47(2):263

Laffont J-J (1997) Game theory and empirical economics: the case of auction data. Europ Econom Rev 41:1–35

Mankiw NG, Taylor MP (2011) Economics (2nd ed., revised ed.). Cengage Learning, Andover

Marshall A (1920) Principles of economics. Library of economics and liberty. ISBN 0-256-01547-3

Marwala T (2013) Economic modeling using artificial intelligence methods. Springer, Heidelberg

Marwala T (2012) Condition monitoring using computational intelligence methods. Springer, Heidelberg

Marwala T, Lagazio M (2011) Militarized conflict modeling using computational intelligence. Springer, Heidelberg

Marwala T (2010) Finite element model updating using computational intelligence techniques: applications to structural dynamics. Springer, Heidelberg

Marwala T (2009) Computational intelligence for missing data imputation, estimation, and management: knowledge optimization techniques. IGI Global, Pennsylvania

Marwala T (2007) Computational Intelligence for Modelling Complex Systems. Research India Publications, Delhi

Marwala T (2014) Artificial intelligence techniques for rational decision making. Springer, Heidelberg

Simon H (1957) A behavioral model of rational choice. In: Models of man, social and rational: mathematical essays on rational human behavior in a social setting. Wiley, New York

Simon H (1990) A mechanism for social selection and successful altruism. Science 250 (4988):1665–1668

Simon H (1991) Bounded rationality and organizational learning. Organ Sci 2(1):125–134

Spence M (1973) Job market signaling. Q J Econ (The MIT Press). 87(3):355–374

Stiglitz JE (1974) Incentives and risk sharing in sharecropping. Rev Econ Stud (Oxford Journals). 41(2):219–255

Tversky A, Kahneman D (1973) Availability: a heuristic for judging frequency and probability. Cogn Psychol 5(2):207–232

Chapter 10
Mechanism Design

Abstract In game theory, players have rules and pay-off and they interact until some point of equilibrium is achieved. This way, we are able to see how a game with sets of rules and a pay-off reaches equilibrium. Mechanism design is the inverse of that, we know what the end-state should look like and our task is to identify the rules and pay-off function which will ensure that the desired end-state is achieved. This is done by assuming that the agents in this setting act rationally. However, these agents are bounded rationally because the degree of rationality is limited. This chapter also discusses how artificial intelligence impacts mechanism design.

10.1 Introduction

A fascinating offshoot of Game Theory is *Mechanism Design* (Myerson 1981, 1983; Harris and Raviv 1981). Concerned primarily with situations in which players have imperfect knowledge (that is to say, limited knowledge about either the system or about the other players), mechanism design focuses on designing a system such that specific outcomes are achieved. If we consider our own lives, this is the equivalent of those bleary moments when we daydream that we could rewrite the rules of a situation to suit our own needs (That lunch break really should be a full hour! Who says the ball is dead after two bounces on the squash court? I absolutely should be allowed to drive in the emergency lane!). Of course, everything I have just said would be an abuse of the rules to benefit myself, a player, which is why the formulation of mechanism design is such that the game designer is not an active player in the game, but instead, attempting to achieve some other outcome (Your boss decides your lunch break duration. The world squash federation decides how many times the ball may bounce on the floor before being dead. Your local roads agency determines who may drive in the emergency lane and under what circumstances those individuals may do so).

Mechanism Design was first postulated by the Economist Leonid Hurwicz (1917–2008), who received recognition for his contribution to the discipline in the

© Springer International Publishing AG 2017

T. Marwala and E. Hurwitz, *Artificial Intelligence and Economic Theory: Skynet in the Market*, Advanced Information and Knowledge Processing,
DOI 10.1007/978-3-319-66104-9_10

form of a Nobel Prize for economics in 2007, becoming the oldest recipient of the Nobel Prize to date at the ripe old age of 90 years old (Hurwicz 1960). As a side-note, the Nobel Prize is not permitted to be awarded posthumously, and having passed away the next year it seems Hurwicz (no relation to the co-author of this book) managed to pick up the accolade at the absolute last possible moment.

If we return to our running thread of the man selling dimples, he now has some stock of dimples that he wishes to sell, but does not know at what price the market will buy them. How should he go about selling them? Should he make public all the offers he receives? Should he allow for multiple stages of bidding? Should he only inform the market of the highest bid? Should he let bidders know who has the highest bid? Mechanism design attempts to determine the optimal way in which he can go about offering his dimples to the market in such a way that gets him a fair price while still being fair to the buyers (since if the mechanism is not fair to the buyers, they will simply elect not to bother bidding). In effect, mechanism design involves the design of the marketplace itself in which the dimple salesman will interact.

10.2 The Players

In order to begin this task, one first needs to set the stage. The very first things on the stage are the players themselves, and the attributes that describe them. Our first assumption is that of *individual rationality*. This is essentially the *bounded rationality* referred to earlier in this book, although we can take a quick scenic tour to remind ourselves of the concept and what it means for our intrepid dimple magnate. A rational agent is one that always acts so as to achieve the greatest personal benefit for themselves in a given situation. In the field of game theory, the expected return of a given *strategy* (i.e. a proposed set of actions/reactions linked to specific situations within a given game) is modelled, and it can be assumed that the player will take such an action as to gain the maximum benefit from within that model. Keep in mind that this might not always mean choosing the optimal move in every situation for various reasons (consider the possibility that a player in a competitive game may have a greater return by choosing a given option, but if that play is known by his opponent then his own predictability will cause him to lose. He may then choose, for example, to favour that option 70% of the time, in order not to lose his own advantage to predictability. This means that 30% of the time his optimal strategy will involve him choosing what is a sub-optimal move when scrutinised under the microscope). For the case of mechanism design, we assume that all players will behave in a manner so as to maximise their own expected reward *according to their own limited information*. These limitations need not be uniform amongst players either—some buyers of dimples may have intimate knowledge of the dimple market in foreign countries; while others directly on-sell to retail stores; while others still are speculative day-traders looking to turn a quick profit from the dimple futures market. These differing levels of information can lead to significant levels of information inequality. Two types of information uncertainty are recognised in this case. One is that of *Preference uncertainty*, in which one is uncertain of the particular predilections of the other players in the game. Consider the bidding at an art gallery—one may have excellent information of the worth and likely growth of a particular sculpture of horses mid-gallop, but due to personal tastes, another bidder may value that piece significantly higher due to his own personal infatuation with the equine form. The other form is that of *quality uncertainty*, in which one is uncertain of the genuine value of the offered item. Regardless of the level of information available, it can be assumed that each individual player will then act in such a way as to maximise his/her expected reward given both his/her own information and whatever information can be inferred about his/her fellow players.

The means by which the players interact form the *mechanism* of mechanism design. Hurwicz posited the mechanism as a means of communication—the mechanism receives the instructions from the various players in the game and then follows specified rules in order to adjudicate the result. This is illustrated below in Fig. 10.1.

These rules can be as complex or simple as can be imagined, in real terms often representing the various interests of the parties and the meeting of required legislation (and of course the application of such analysis could easily aid in the crafting of appropriate legislation). The efficiency of such trades has long been established by economists under only the strictest of conditions, but with the advent of mechanism design, such systems could be analysed under far less stringent conditions, in particular the conditions involving access to information. Furthermore, instead of merely analysing such systems, the theory could now be applied to

Fig. 10.1 Unspecified mechanism receiving player messages

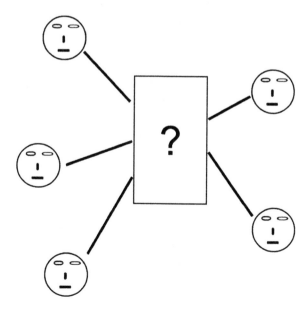

design mechanisms that produce intended results, taking the process one step further than merely predicting expected behaviour.

10.3 Efficiency and Equilibria

Before going any further, two important concepts within the field of economics need to be understood. These are the concepts of *efficiency* and of an *equilibrium* (Abreu and Sen 1991; Fudenberg and Tirole 1993). In economic terms, a situation is deemed to be *efficient* if no further gain can be achieved without incurring an additional cost. There are two primary forms of efficiency that are referred to in this case. In terms of production, one talks of *productive efficiency*, which is to say that nothing further can be gained without paying an additional cost. If our dimple magnate is producing 20 dimples per hour in his factory, but can through revising his work-flow (maybe moving two subsequent construction benches closer together) improve the production rate to 23 dimples per hour, then his system is not productively efficient. If, on the other hand, the only way to produce more than his current 20 dimples per hour is to buy a more expensive dimple processing machine then his system can be said to be productively efficient since he cannot improve his output without taking on an extra cost.

The other form of efficiency, which is a more common reference with respect to mechanism design, is *pareto efficiency* (also known as allocative efficiency). This refers to a system that involves many agents engaged in an interrelated task. The task is said to be Pareto efficient if any changes that aid one or more agents would result in harm to one or more different agents. If we again examine our dimple magnate, let us assume he is dealing with three suppliers of raw materials, A B and C, required in specific quantities for each dimple (One of A, One of B and two of C). In the above example, he produces 20 dimples per hour, and so in an eight-hour working day produces 160 dimples. The situation then of him purchasing 160 of A, 160 of B and 320 of C is then Pareto efficient as it is precisely the situation that benefits everyone. If he were to purchase 200 of A, he would have excess of A to his own detriment, and thus the situation would be less efficient. The same holds true for any modification of the purchase amounts, given that holding excess raw materials is an unwanted cost. Achieving a state of market efficiency is considered to be the goal of most economic planning—to be able to allocate resources such that every person pays according to the appropriate worth of a good with no wastage in the transaction.

The next concept to understand is that of an *equilibrium*. In economic terms, an equilibrium is a stable state in which multiple parties find a stable state of negotiation. In order for a system to be considered in a state of equilibrium, it must be in a stable state (i.e. no longer changing); it must be the result of a dynamic process (so some form of negotiation) and the behaviour of the players must be consistent (and so be repeatable). We can consider an equilibrium to be the end-state of any economic negotiation, the point at which the deal is set and hands are shaken. One form of equilibrium encountered swiftly in economics is that of a competitive equilibrium. This equilibrium occurs when two competing forces balance each other out. The most commonly encountered example of this is the classic supply versus demand curve explained earlier in Chap. 2. The conflicting forces of the supply curve and the demand curve meet at a given crossover point to establish a price, and that price is the stable equilibrium price that determines the sales price to suit the needs of both parties (buyer and seller). The next type of equilibrium is the so-called *Nash equilibrium*, named after the economist J. F. Nash, the subject of the movie *a beautiful mind* (though his resemblance to Russel Crowe thankfully stops there). Applied primarily to game-theory (and by extension to mechanism design), this particular form of equilibrium applies when all players, knowing the strategies of the other players in a particular game, cannot improve their expected gains by changing their own strategy. The key difference in this case being that the players are effectively treating their opponents' strategies as a part of the game, and thus should their opponents' strategies change for any reason, then the game itself will have changed, and a new set of analyses must be performed. The underlying principle of a Nash equilibrium is that it is futile to analyse only ones best personal choices without taking into account the proclivities of the other players in the game. Consider a game of poker—it is a relatively trivial task to calculate the percentage chance of winning given a particular opening hand. If one were to devise a betting strategy purely on that, however, without taking into account the information implied by the other players' bets, then one would surely lose a hefty sum of money before realising the error of your ways.

10.4 Incentive Compatibility and the Revelation Principle

In order to extend the theory he posited in 1960, Hurwicz (still no relation) proposed the idea of *incentive compatibility* in 1972. This idea states that if a player's dominant strategy (i.e. the strategy that garners the highest expected return for the player regardless of the choices of the other players) is to represent his private information honestly, then the system can be said to be incentive compatible. Using this formulation, he was then able to show the (mildly distressing) result that hidden information makes it impossible to achieve Pareto efficiency in a standard exchange economy. The next questions that needed to be addressed were then "how large are the inefficiencies?"; "Can less stringent efficiency measures be used?"; "Can efficiency be obtained using less stringent mechanisms?". The biggest stride in tackling these questions came in the form of the *revelation Principle*.

The revelation principle states (and proves, using maths that in a fit of mercy is not being printed in this book) that any function representing player choices (either dominant or Nash variants) can be implemented in an incentive compatible formulation. In other words, it proved that for modelling purposes any set of choices can be represented such that the players have no incentive to lie, making modelling a much more attainable task. Myerson's work showed that this applies even in situations when players take actions unseen by the other players, and in multi-stage mechanisms, greatly expanding the realm of possibilities for applying mechanism design to practical scenarios (Myerson 1979).

The revelation principle allows a researcher to generalize results despite the full potential search space of mechanisms being unmanageably large, since the revelation principle shows that the optimal solution can always be found within the much smaller (and thus more manageable) sub-set of solution found within direct mechanisms (a direct mechanism being a system in which the only options available to a player are those in which the player states its intentions directly). This principle applies to both systems involving dominant strategies, and to systems with more uncertainty that are governed by statistical models.

10.5   Goalposts

Amidst all of these definitions, it matters that we not lose sight of our goal. In this case, we are attempting to design a system in which the greatest number of dimple customers are served and the greatest number of dimple suppliers sell off their wares, with as little money as possible "wasted" in market inefficiencies. Despite the public's persistent view of those working in the world of finance (a view that has gotten significantly dimmer since the 2008 market crash), this goal is at the heart of most economic thought.

The typical framing of this problem is that of *auction design* (Chatterjee and Samuelson 1983; Bulow and Klemperer 1996, 2004). This is a means of evaluating the dynamics of multiple individuals attempting to find individually optimal prices for the buying of an object. This analysis is primarily concerned with the selling of a single item, so in our case the dimple manufacturer has a single batch of dimples for sale, and will sell the lot to one of his many customers. He would obviously like to get as high a price as possible, but also must be wary of the price becoming so high that he does not sell his wares at all. While there are a large number of potential auctions (as large as ones imagination could conjure up), there are four primary forms of auction considered for the sale of a single item. The first of these is the First-price sealed bid auction (also referred to as the "blind auction"). In this form of auction, all bidders privately submit their bid to the auctioneer, and the item is sold to the highest bidder at the highest price. This type of auction is a typical mechanism of government tenders, where only one bid is accepted without any form of revision available to the players. The next is a more theoretical auction, the second-price sealed bid auction (also known as a Vickrey auction). This is also a blind auction, but the winner pays not the amount he has bid, but rather the second-highest bid received. This type of auction is incentive-compatible, and so it pays each bidder to bid the honest value that they place upon the item. While not used much practically, this form of auction has started gaining some traction in automated bidding systems for online advertising. It is studied extensively in game theory and mechanism design literature owing to its highly appealing properties.

One of the problems with this form of auction is that it does not allow for price discovery (bidders who are unsure of their valuations can form an approximate valuation through consecutive bidding if the bidding system is open. This clearly cannot happen under the single-bid, sealed format of the Vickrey auction). The third form of auction is the one that most people are familiar with, having been popularised throughout so much of our popular culture, the English auction. In this form, prospective buyers continuously bid in ascending price until the price is too high for an individual and that individual ceases to bid. When no players are prepared to bid, the item is sold to the highest bidder at the bid price. Unlike the first two auctions, this auction is both open (all players can see the bids of other players) and is multi-stage (each player can bid multiple times). This method allows for price discovery as the bidders keep imparting information into the system with each bid. An interesting effect occurs that theoretically both the English and the Vickrey auction award the item to the player that places the highest value on the item at a price equal to that of the second-highest valuation, even though the mechanism used to get to the solution is wildly different. The final class of auction examined is that of the *Dutch* auction—this can be considered the inverse of the English auction, in that a price is initially declared by the auctioneer that is clearly too high for any player to buy the item. The price is iteratively reduced by the auctioneer until one of the players elects to buy the item at the announced price, ending the auction. Even though the players get to interact only minimally with this form of auction, it still involves open information and a form of price discovery. Dutch auctions are considerably faster than English auctions, and tend to favour the seller as they guarantee the highest reasonable price is set, as opposed to English auctions which favour the buyer. If there are more than one items for sale, then this auction will continue until all of the available offerings can be sold. This method of auction is popular for public offerings such as bonds and treasury bills, with the auction favouring the issuer (to the surprise of precisely nobody).

One particular form of this is the problem of so-called *public goods*, goods that are available to all, and the consumption of which does not reduce the availability of the good to others. Consider the use of a public road—it is available to all, and yet the use of it by one party does not meaningfully (excluding extreme situations of traffic) preclude its use by another party. How should we fund the road? Should everyone pay for it equally? Should those closest to it pay more than those farther away? What about the dimple producer whose factory is far from the road, but regularly uses the road to deliver to his largest customer? These questions are fairly commonplace when any public works or infrastructure-building task is posited, and often results in lengthy (and heated) debates in public forums. Before the advent of mechanism design, the perceived wisdom was that one could not efficiently fund public goods because of the incentive to lie about ones valuation of the good in question. Clarke and Groves found through mechanism design a means by which an efficient funding mechanism could be achieved (Clarke 1971; Groves 1973). It did have a flaw, namely that for a given system, there was a strong likelihood that the project would not be funded. In this regard, the mechanism required that the project not be undertaken if the projected funds raised were insufficient to complete the project so we should not be celebrating the solving of public financing quite yet, but progress is progress and as such, needs to be respected. Clarke and Groves focused primarily on dominant-strategy mechanisms, which eventually showed that only undesirable mechanisms, such as a dictatorial mechanism in which one preferred player is always favoured, was greatly advanced by taking a more statistical approach and loosening the equilibrium criterion to that of a Nash equilibrium. Still, in a move that, depending on your outlook, is either endlessly depressing or oddly inspiring, Myerson and Satterthwaite (1983) did manage to show that there is no way for two entities to trade a single good that they both have hidden knowledge/ opinions about without a risk of one entity trading at a loss. While economists may view this as a negative result, the silver lining is that quality research is likely to be rewarded in the marketplace, since it means you have access to theoretically better information.

10.6 So What?

So with all of that covered, where exactly are we currently seeing mechanism design? This is the polite form of the question "so why should we care?". While the examples scattered throughout this chapter have hinted at the answers, it is worth looking explicitly at where and why mechanism design is being used to influence the lives we lead. Understanding this is also essential in order to understand what the advent of artificial intelligence (AI) means to us in this context. While there is no time to fully detail all of the applications of mechanism design, some general categories of the applications will be highlighted in order to grasp the general feeling of where and why this branch of seemingly abstract economics impacts our lives.

The first of these applications is the most obvious, namely buying and selling. The principle of course is simple, in that an entity has an object to sell but is not certain what individuals are prepared to pay for the item. The various auctions described earlier show that multiple different types of sales (with different desired outcomes) can be catered to through use of mechanism design. This principle can be extended beyond simple private transactions, to transactions that are often maximised not for the single trade but for some other, social benefit (in effect still allowing the good to be sold to the player that values it the most, meeting the desired outcome of mechanism design). One initial thought was that if a good is inappropriately allocated through an imperfect mechanism (so it ended up being sold to a party that valued it less than another party), then that item would be on-sold to the party that valued it higher after the initial distribution. This turns out to be false, however, as the nature of private information precludes the two parties from realising the mis-allocation and acting on it. Consider if our dimple salesman sold his dimple container to Joe for $100, while Geoff actually values the dimple container at $130. In theory, Joe should be happy to sell the lot to Geoff for $120, with both parties walking away smiling. In practice, however, the fact that neither party is aware of the other's valuation means they are unlikely to ever make a plan to perform this secondary trade. We see the results of the theory in the functioning of typical auctions, in private pricing of goods, in pricing of public goods and funding of public schemes. The results of such applications affect us in almost every financial transaction we enter into, and so should not be taken lightly.

Another common application is in that of regulations. This is particularly important in order to curtail the emergence and impact of monopolies (a single entity that wholly controls a specific market) and oligopolies (a typically small group of companies that collaborate to jointly control a specific market) on the economy. It is well-established economic doctrine that monopolistic actions are to the detriment of both consumers and to society as a whole. Mechanism design has been applied to ascertain optimal frameworks for regulation that prevents monopolistic behaviour while still incentivising the bigger fish in the pond to remain in the market. This would typically involve the government regulator making a trade-off in its own desire to extract rents (in the form of taxes) from the big fish. This type of analysis also applies to social outcomes resulting from regulation, which can be of crucial importance. As an example, consider a regulation aimed at improving the lot of the workers in our producer's dimple plant. The proposed regulation would lift the minimum wage by 15% of its current level. The intent is to have workers bring home a greater income for various social needs, but will the legislation achieve this? At what point does the business owner decide to further mechanise, retrenching half his work-force? What level of price elasticity does the dimple market have (in other words, how much of a price change can it bear)? Will this regulation simply force our businessman to close up shop, and all local dimple demand will then be met by imported dimples? Answering these questions with reasonable certainty is clearly a key concern in establishing if regulations can in fact achieve their intended outcomes, and again mechanism design is an integral tool in answering these questions. This same principle can also be extended to a more intimate setting, in determining HR policies in the workplace, or even abstracted to appropriate rules for children in a classroom. Any time a rule is introduced in order to induce some desired behaviour, this tool jumps up and down shouting "me! Me! Pick me!", and we would be foolish to ignore it.

10.7   Through the Looking Glass

Now we look to the effects of AI on all of the above. The machines are rising up, getting more intelligent, but (thankfully) not sentient (yet). There are two primary aspects in which AI affects mechanism design. The first means by which mechanism design is likely to be impacted is in the modelling side, as AI is applied by mechanism design researchers in order to find better answers. The second way it affects mechanism design is by impacting the very systems that are being modelled, effectively changing the nature of the players as AI becomes more widespread and is gradually adopted by a growing portion of the marketplace.

A number of the techniques and capabilities of AI that have been covered in previous chapters of this book are potentially relevant to mechanism design. In terms of modelled players, the ability to model players that learn can easily expand the scope of mechanism application. That learning can make for more complex, more realistic probabilistic estimation of the various player estimations and reactions. The use of intelligent agents can also be used to examine the effects of varying degrees of both preference uncertainty and quality uncertainty in the players. Furthermore, the effects of misconceptions in the marketplace can be introduced quite easily into a system involving intelligent agents, with mechanisms then being designed to take into account what is effectively "user error". Consider a group of individuals that consider the value of a good to be higher on a Monday than on a Wednesday. Clearly, the belief is nonsensical, but if a significant portion of the market believes it to be true then the mechanisms need to account for this belief else they will not achieve their desired outcomes. Incidentally, the example chosen is less ridiculous than it seems, as many trades for institutional investors are put through on a Monday, and thus if a particular share is expecting good news, it is likely to be priced in on the Monday of that week. As discussed previously, the finding of equilibria within various games is very much doable through multi-agent modelling, and as such can extend the realm of games that can be modelled significantly. It would similarly be doable to test for Pareto efficiency using an agent-based model populated with intelligent agents. Furthermore, when it comes to implementation, yet another of the available tools within the AI Engineer's arsenal comes to the fore, namely the optimisation tools discussed in previous chapters. As a quick reminder, these tools allow the system to make optimal choices from within very large search spaces, a tool that is very well-suited to implementing a mechanism for a specific purpose. Say for example you wish to design a mechanism by which preferred smaller shop-owners could get access to dimple stock (possibly because the dimple manufacturer has cousins he wishes to supply on account of being family) without buying in large lots, without prejudicing his larger, bread-and-butter customers. The designer could input all of the conceivable mechanism components into an optimisation system [let us say a genetic algorithm (GA)], and use the desired results as a measurement of effectiveness (fitness). The GA would then assemble as close a fitting mechanism as possible to achieve the desired outcome. Of course, if the demands are too stringent, then the results may be very unsatisfactory—we are talking about an optimisation system, not a magic wand. If something is unfeasible, then the optimisation system will indicate precisely that. The same applies to the use of mechanism design in order to induce some social result—the modelling of human agents with varying and less predictable desires will aid in crafting more robust regulations that achieve their desired outcomes more reliably and with fewer adverse side-effects.

The other arena in which AI will disrupt the market is in the actual players themselves. It is all very well to model a player with a statistical spread of preferences, but how good is that estimate when 40% of the market is using AI to do their estimating for them? The mechanism design agent models will have to adapt to account for these more intelligent players. The speed of trading and the learning done whilst trading is similarly going to affect the expected outcomes. Already, today, automated traders are quickly changing the landscape of share trading. Agent-based modelling is capable of analysing adaptive agents, and the introduction of adaptive models is going to be crucial to creating mechanisms fit for efficiently handling trading done by these automated agents. Regulatory frameworks will similarly need to be reworked through a new lens that incorporates these intelligent agents in order to prevent them adapting to and quickly exploiting any loopholes prevalent in an existing framework. In terms of both public goods and socially uplifting legislation, a more efficient means of crafting legislation that attempts to promote certain behaviour can be both optimally found and robustly examined through the above AI methods, as opposed to the often haphazard crafting of legislation that is commonly seen throughout the world. Feel free to chalk that one up to an academic dreaming of a world where politicians let slack the reins of power by a fraction in order to do things right, to do things better, but I am allowed to dream as well.

10.8 Application to Market Design

The mechanism design has been applied to the design of the kidney exchange market by Nobel Laureate Alvin Roth. The kidney exchange market is a matching problem where the kidneys have to match (Roth and Peranson 1999; Roth 2015). Furthermore, the exchanged kidney does not have a price because it is illegal to trade kidneys. Furthermore, the contract to exchange a kidney is not binding and, therefore, a potential kidney donor can change his/her mind. An illustration of a matching kidney exchange example is illustrated in Fig. 10.2. In this figure, we have John and his wife Denga as well as Khathu and his wife Jane. John requires a kidney and is a group B blood type and his wife Denga is willing to give him one of her kidneys but she is of blood type A so there is no match. However, Khathu also needs a kidney and is of blood group A whereas Jane is willing to give him one of her kidneys but is of group B blood type. The two couples decide that they will exchange the kidneys, with John receiving from Jane and Khathu receiving from Denga. This exchange should be conducted simultaneously to avoid one or more parties deciding to change their minds and cannot be forced due to legislation.

The other way in which kidney transplant is conducted is through a waiting list. Here is an example of a graphical user interface (GUI) system that was originally designed by Golding et al. (2008) which is in Fig. 10.3. In this system the planner and the doctor input information of the patient and all infrastructure required such as the operation rooms into the system and the system using artificial intelligence techniques (genetic algorithm, reinforcerment learning and fuzzy inference system) generates a queing table (q-table).

The systems in Figs. 10.2 and 10.3 can then be combined such that the general kidney donations (to the kidney bank) is combined with the specific kidney donation (to a relative or friend). This forms a chain which ultimately has been found to increase kidney transplants. This is illustrated in Fig. 10.4.

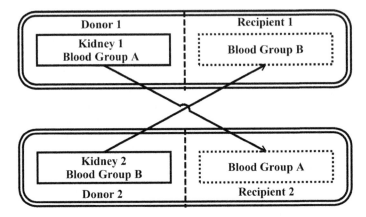

Fig. 10.2 An illustration of the exchange of kidneys amongst four people

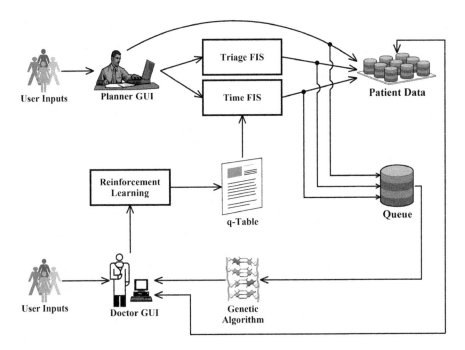

Fig. 10.3 A scheduling procedure

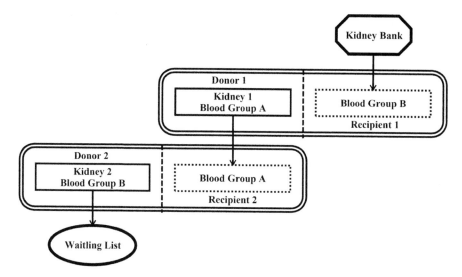

Fig. 10.4 An illustration of the kidney exchange amongst relatives, kidney bank and the waiting list

10.9   Conclusions

In game theory, players have rules and pay-off and they interact until some point of equilibrium is achieved. This chapter described mechanism design, which is the reverse game theory which can be used to design sets of rules which give rise to a particular outcome. The implications of AI on the theory of mechanism design were also outlined. Examples on how mechanism design has been applied to the creation of a kidney exchange market was discussed.

References

Abreu D, Sen A (1991) Virtual implementation in Nash equilibria. Econometrica 59:997–1022
Bulow J, Klemperer P (1996) Auctions versus negotiations. Am Econ Rev 86:180–194
Chatterjee K, Samuelson W (1983) Bargaining under incomplete information. Oper Res 31:835–851
Clarke EH (1971) Multipart pricing of public goods. Public Choice 11:17–33
Fudenberg D, Tirole J (1993) Game theory. MIT Press, Cambridge
Golding D, Wilson L, Marwala T (2008) Emergency centre organization and automated triage system. ArXiv:0810.3671. Last accessed 1 June 2017
Groves T (1973) Incentives in teams. Econometrica 41(4):617–631
Harris M, Raviv A (1981) Allocation mechanisms and the design of auctions. Econometrica 49:1477–1499

Hurwicz L (1960) Optimality and informational efficiency in resource allocation processes. In: Arrow KJ, Karlin S, Suppes P (eds) Mathematical methods in the social sciences. Stanford University Press, California

Klemperer P (2004) Auctions: theory and practice. Princeton University Press, Princeton, p 2004

Myerson R (1979) Incentive compatibility and the bargaining problem. Econometrica. 47:61–73

Myerson R (1981) Optimal auction design. Math Oper Res 6:58–73

Myerson R (1983) Mechanism design by an informed principal. Econometrica 52:461–487

Myerson R, Satterthwaite M (1983) Efficient mechanisms for bilateral trading. J Econ Theor 28:265–281

Roth AE (2015) Who gets what and why. Eamon Dolan/Houghton Mifflin Harcourt

Roth AE, Peranson E (1999) The redesign of the matching market for american physicians: some engineering aspects of economic design. Am Econ Rev Am Econ Assoc 89(4):748–780

Chapter 11
Portfolio Theory

Abstract The basis of portfolio theory is rooted in statistical models based on Brownian motion. These models are surprisingly naïve in their assumptions and resultant application within the trading community. The application of artificial intelligence (AI) to portfolio theory and management have broad and far-reaching consequences. AI techniques allow us to model price movements with much greater accuracy than the random-walk nature of the original Markowitz model. Additionally, the job of optimizing a portfolio can be performed with greater optimality and efficiency using evolutionary computation while still staying true to the original goals and conceptions of portfolio theory. A particular method of price movement modelling is shown that models price movements with only simplistic inputs and still produces useful predictive results. A portfolio rebalancing method is also described, illustrating the use of evolutionary computing for the portfolio rebalancing problem in order to achieve the results demanded by investors within the framework of portfolio theory.

11.1 Introduction

Modern portfolio theory begins its life with the theories of Markowitz (Markowitz 1952). In particular, he posited that any investment destination can be characterised by its *risk* σ, and its *return* R (Markowitz 1952). The return of an investment is simply the percentage of the original invested capital that the investment provides (or in the case of modelled system is predicted or expected to provide), while risk is simply the variance of the return on an investment (Markowitz 1952), representing the likelihood that actual return deviates from the expected return, and to what extent it deviates. While seeming arbitrary, these values of measurement define the core of what one needs to evaluate in the management of any investment.

The most obvious of these is the return R—this simply measures the relative return an investment makes on the invested resources. Consider the case of an investor wanting to put some money towards a dimple factory. If he invests $1000 in the factory for a 10% shareholding, which then goes on to manufacture and sell

© Springer International Publishing AG 2017   125
T. Marwala and E. Hurwitz, *Artificial Intelligence and Economic Theory: Skynet in the Market*, Advanced Information and Knowledge Processing,
DOI 10.1007/978-3-319-66104-9_11

dimples over time, and after a number of years he then sells his portion of the factory for $1500, he will have made a profit of $500 off of an investment of $1000, making his return R 50%, in other words reaping a profit of half of the invested amount (after recouping his initial investment). This is the first concept that investors learn, and in many cases they stop there, a bridge too soon.

The second of these, risk σ, is a measurement of how likely you are to receive the expected return. If we go back to the dimple factory, our investor does not know what return he is going to get when he invests. He does, however, do a thorough investigation into the factory, and finds that over the past five years the factory has produced a profit of $4000; $5000; $6000; $5000; and $5000 respectively for each year. Averaging these returns out using a simple average, he expects the factory to produce a profit of $5000 per year, which means his potential purchase of 10% of the company can be expected to produce a return of $500 per year. By evaluating the fluctuations in the yearly returns, you come to a statistical measure of uncertainty or risk, typically measured as *variance* σ^2. This measure represents how reliable the expected return is. This allows investors to compare the riskiness of potential investments, and then choose to invest according to their particular requirements. As an example of these differing desires, consider Joe Sixpack, who is investing a bonus he received into the market for his daughter when she graduates from high school in ten years. He has no particular use in mind for this gift, and so can accept a relatively high level of risk, favouring the return heavily. In contrast, Bethany is a professional investor for Wellbeing medical aid, and she knows that each year, a minimum of 90% of the invested funds will need to be drawn in order to pay out member claims. She knows that she needs to choose investments with a far lower risk profile than those of Joe in order to meet the requirements of her business, and will thus pay far more attention to the risk measurements of the various investments than Joe will.

While the theory is applicable to investments of all sorts, it is applied most often to investment portfolios that rely on highly liquid assets (an asset's liquidity refers to the ease with which it can be sold) such as stocks, bonds and similarly liquid derivatives (Rupper 2004). By characterizing all investments in this manner, it becomes possible to compare various investments objectively using these measurements. It is worth noting that these measurements themselves can be somewhat arbitrary, as the values of both risk and return can change dramatically for different sampling periods, especially if a particular investment target undergoes periods of upheaval (A yearly calculation may yield very different results than a monthly calculation, especially when it comes to a calculation of variance). An investment is said to be *efficient* if it achieves a higher value of return than any other investment that has a similar level of risk (Markowitz 1952). The limit of these efficient investments within a given universe of investments is said to constitute the *efficient horizon* (Markowitz 1952). This principle is illustrated in Fig. 11.1 (Duma 2013; Hurwitz and Marwala 2011, 2012; Hurwitz 2014), in which the x values denote various investment opportunities plotted on a common set of axes, plotting them by risk versus return.

Fig. 11.1 The efficient
horizon

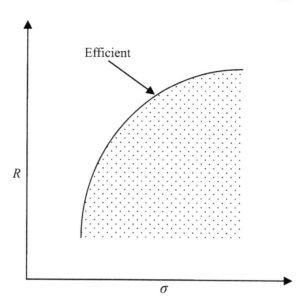

By finding investments that suit a client's needs in terms of risk or reward, and remaining as close to the efficient horizon as possible, the investment manager ensures the most efficient use of funds to suit a client's purpose. The result of an investor choosing a portfolio on the efficient horizon is that, depending on the desire of the investor, they will have achieved either the highest possible return for a given level of risk or have achieved the lowest exposure to risk for a given expected return.

This technique can be extended further, in order to cater for the possibility that a desired risk value is in fact lower than that of any point within the efficient horizon. By utilising *zero-risk assets* (this denotes assets, such as government bonds/treasury bills) that have a σ of zero, a portfolio can be constructed using a linear combination of the zero-risk asset and the optimal portfolio to efficiently achieve the desired risk-reward portfolio (Jiang 2011). This methodology is illustrated in Fig. 11.2.

As can be seen in Fig. 11.2, the desired risk σ_d is decidedly outside of the bounds of the efficient horizon.

By linearly combining the risk-free asset represented on the Cartesian y-axis with the investment tools tangential to the linear extension of the risk-free asset at the efficient horizon, a combinational portfolio is created that allows the financial engineer to create a portfolio that meets his client's, otherwise, unattainable needs (Rupper 2004). The purpose of this is to meet required levels of risk that lie to the left of the efficient horizon, a desired risk that is lower than those of the investments available. If we consider risk as a gamble (an imprecise analogy, but one that serves to illustrate the point), and an investor is comfortable with a one-in-ten chance of losing but only has at best a one-in-two chance of losing in the available

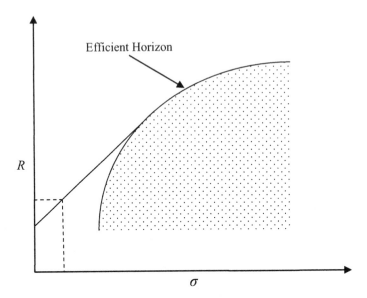

Fig. 11.2 CAPM optimization

investments, he can then use this mechanism to create his own portfolio that meets his stringent, highly risk-averse needs.

A more recent move by many portfolio managers is to consider the valuation of risk not as a pure mathematical variance, but rather as only a downside variance. This means considering only variance from instances that are below the mean return (Jiang 2011). The argument in this case is that neither they nor their clients consider making abnormal profits to be particularly risky, and only consider unpredictable losses to be truly risky (Jiang 2011). This issue is still being debated today in both professional and academic circles, since mathematically abnormal profits do represent risk, but practically many players in the market feel otherwise.

11.2 Assumptions and Limitations

The description of market instruments by Markowitz as explained previously has a number of assumptions inherent in its formulation, and as a result creates complications and imposes limitations on any individual looking to utilise these theories and methodologies in order to safeguard his financial future. These problems can easily be the undoing of any individual unaware of them or their implications, and it is in order to create tools useful in dealing with these limitations that artificial intelligence becomes useful. The assumptions that are inherent in the Markowitz formulation are as follows (Mendelbrot 2004):

1. Market instruments adhere to a stochastic, random-walk process.
2. Market instruments are governed by a Gaussian distribution.
3. Historical performance is a strong indicator of future performance.
4. Market instruments are stationary in nature.

The first of these assumptions, the random-walk nature of the market, assumes that all market fluctuations can be thought of as random movements from period to period, with no correlation between these movements. This assumption presupposes that no model can accurately predict any price movements owing to their inherently random nature. While this assumption is a useful shorthand for modelling a larger system, it does not hold up when looked at in more detail, as quickly illustrated by the reliable success of many fund managers who would be unable to produce reliable returns were the instruments that they are trading truly random.

The second of these assumptions governs the nature of the randomness from the first assumption. The Gaussian distribution is commonly known by the more descriptive name of the "bell curve" as illustrated in Fig. 11.3.

This distribution represents the likelihood of any event occurring that is greater than or less than the most likely outcome, which is the top of the "bell". This is a commonly used distribution that is pervasive in much of statistical analysis, and it was the application of this statistical concept in particular to finance and portfolio theory that earned Markowitz a Nobel prize. The concept here is that the likelihood of a particular event occurring decreases the farther removed it is from the most likely event. The danger in this is that the events that throw markets into turmoil, dubbed in 2007 by Nicholas Taleb as "black swan" events, get ignored owing to their low probability (Taleb 2007). This is precisely how market crashes catch us all by surprise—the professionals trading on a daily basis cater for the events that occur daily, and do not (understandably) take into account events that happen once every decade or so. Nonetheless, the impact of these black swan events is so

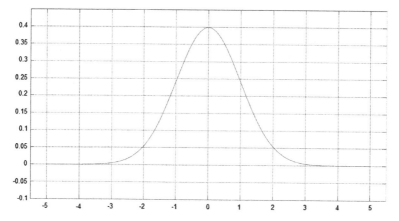

Fig. 11.3 Normal Distribution Curve

pronounced that a more complex model is certainly required in order to prevent such market shocks from throwing lives and livelihoods into turmoil.

The fourth assumption governs the optimization of a portfolio. Considering how even a simple calculation of risk or return can be heavily influenced by the duration and specific time-period evaluated, it should be abundantly clear that we cannot rely on any long-term stationarity of the instrument. Stationarity is a measure of how consistent a given phenomenon is over time. If we witness that high traffic in a commercial area is strongly correlated with high sales, we can create a model that links the two. This model may be valid for a long time, until something changes the dynamics. Enter the age of online shopping, and suddenly the model becomes invalid as the correlation between heavy traffic and strong sales becomes weakened. The net result of this is that not only must one engage in the often challenging task of optimizing a portfolio, but that this optimization must be continually re-evaluated or even re-formulated as the dynamics and relationships within the portfolio change over time.

Despite their inherent limitations, these assumptions are extremely useful when planning a portfolio of investments. By quantifying an instrument's risk-return profile, we are to gain an insight into the future performance of the instrument. The problem with this is a simple calculation of risk and return are only accurate over the time period of their calculation—in order to better model an instrument's likely performance, more detailed, nuanced approaches are required (Atsalakis and Valavanis 2002).

11.3 The Trading Machine

We have now begun to see the advent of automated trading. This is currently being utilized by large institutions such as banks and investment houses, owing to the complexity and expense of such mechanisms, but of course this can be expected to be adopted more and more by smaller trading entities as the barriers to entry become progressively lowered, as is inevitable when it is expertise and computing power that hinders usage, both of which can be automated once firmly established. Yes, you read that right—expertise is indeed fairly easy to automate once the technology is firmly understood. For an obvious example, consider today's cars: The vast majority of the driving population of the world have either minimal or zero understanding of any of the following concepts:

- Torque.
- Laws of motion.
- Gearing.
- Electronics.
- Vibrations.
- Hydraulics.

We will stop there, but that is certainly not a complete list of the concepts, let alone designs, required to build a car. Consider how many of those concepts you yourself are familiar with, enough to describe superficially, and then consider if you could apply it with enough detail to actually design a car. We have not even touched on fully-designed sub-components that need to be understood (or redesigned) such as a braking system; an airbag safety system or the internal combustion engine. Yet, despite this vast ignorance regarding the working of a vehicle, so very many of us drive with remarkable competence considering our overwhelming ignorance about its workings. The reason is fairly obvious, of course. We learn to use the machine, and not to build it. This same principle applies to the financial instruments becoming available—the expertise we develop is centered on the use of a tool, rather than the inner workings of the tool itself. Once the technology behind the automated trading tools are relatively stable (consider that the car has evolved a great deal over the last century, but yet the basic principles governing the car are still the same), then a piece of software can be written for public use, making the technology available to all those who wish to learn to use it.

The advantages of the trading machine are varied. In the simplest of cases, the simple speed of trading is a tangible advantage—if an opportunity is noticed, then the fastest actor to both notice the opportunity and then act upon it will obtain the greatest rewards. More complex systems can model the market, and attempt to exploit the knowledge in order to trade to better advantage. Keep in mind that it is not a zero-sum game (a system in which for one actor to gain, another must lose) as different actors will value performance differently owing to their varying risk appetites. In other words, two different investors could potentially both make an informed trade, and still both benefit. Consider two businessmen, one is a farmer growing wheat, while the other manages a wheat distribution center. Owing to differing financial demands (the wheat farmer requires a large regular payment in order to replant his fields, while the distributor can handle more uncertainty since he is storing the wheat in his storage facilities until such a time as he can sell), the farmer places a much higher premium on guaranteeing a sale than the distributor, and so the two sign a contract for the sale to be guaranteed at a small discount to the market price. This is a direct translation of two traders pricing based on their varying risk appetites, with the distributor accepting a higher risk owing to having a better ability to manage said risk.

11.4   The Emerging Trading Machine

The trading machine is, developmentally speaking, still in its infancy. This means there will emerge varying incarnations of trading machines in the coming years, of differing value in both efficacy and efficiency, where an efficacious trading machine either trades to good advantage or models the market accurately, while an efficient machine does the same task as other machines with greater accuracy or speed. As these machines evolve in a competitive marketplace, weaker variants will give way to superior alternatives within a similar price bracket. While the end-point is reasonably clear, in that fund managers are going to be able to tailor products more precisely to individual clients' requirements, the dynamics of the upcoming growth period are much murkier.

One can reasonably expect that there will be a number of failures of the system as users of less successful machines find their flaws the hard way. This is inevitable, as all financial models have implicit assumptions that govern their functionality. While a flawed assumption will often be caught in testing and simulation, some assumptions may simply cease to be valid over time, or simply be unfortunately missed during testing. As trading machines become more complex, some may base their own function on predicting the activities of other agents, which of course could be disastrous if that other agent then changes its own behavior (perhaps by adopting a new trading machine algorithm itself?). It is similarly inevitable that at least one, maybe more of these failures will be high profile, and are likely to gain a fair amount of public and potentially even legislative scrutiny. This is likely to be an issue even without a public blowout or scandal, as regulators are going to have to scramble to put in place safeguards against systems that are by definition non-deterministic. A system that constantly learns and updates itself is one that the designer cannot realistically predict the behavior of. The net result is that a designer of a trading machine cannot reliably tell a regulator precisely how it is going to be making its decisions.

For smaller traders, such as individual investors, the advent of affordable automated traders could herald many opportunities. The ability to customize a portfolio to specific needs would allow individuals to plan for their own financial needs in a way that is currently only available to the wealthy. Conceivably, working people could plan for medium and long term goals such as children's schooling or college fees or retirement without the need for expensive financial planning services who in many cases cannot justify their time on lower-earning clients. This is not to say that all barriers will fall, but certainly they will be lowered, and the broader access to financial planning and market understanding is something that enables those smaller investors to trade with greater focus on their investment goals, while also lowering barriers to entry that could easily expand the pool of people willing to engage with the marketplace. For the larger investors, the opportunities afforded by the advent of the trading machine represent an opportunity to be both more precise in servicing specific client needs and a potential to ward off market-shaking events before it is too late. The path ahead will not be smooth, but it is inexorable and I believe worth the journey. These trading machines must have several characteristics and the most important ones are intelligence and adaptability through evolution.

11.5   Intelligence

These trading machines should be intelligent, which is an attribute associated with biological systems like human beings. Artificial intelligence research has made progress on making machines intelligent. There are many intelligent techniques that have been proposed but key amongst these are neural networks. Neural networks were inspired by the manner in which the human brain functions. They have several attributes that have been inspired by attributes in the human brain and these include neurons, dendrites, cell body, axons and synapses. The neuron is (human being inspired) the processing element in a neural network, dendrite inspired the combining function, cell body the transfer function, axons the element output and the weights the synapses. The transfer function is an element in the neural network that determines the extent of nonlinearity. The network weights are extracted from the data through a process called learning and, mathematically, this is done through optimization.

The optimization process can be deterministic or stochastic, and the advantage of stochastic optimization techniques is that they allow for a probabilistic interpretation of a neural network whereas deterministic optimization just gives a snapshot albeit optimized state of the probability distribution. The neural network is a powerful learning machine that has found successful applications in a number of areas such as crowdfunding (Xing and Marwala 2017a), maintenance (Xing and Marwala 2017b), aerospace structural monitoring (Marwala et al. 2017), rational decision making (Marwala 2014, 2015), economic modelling (Marwala 2013), electrical engineering (Marwala 2012), interstate conflict prediction (Marwala and Lagazio 2011), mechanical engineering (Marwala 2010), missing data imputation (Marwala 2009) and for modelling complex systems (Marwala 2007).

11.6 Evolutionary Programming

The main aspect about portfolio optimization is that different stocks are combined to reduce risk. The manner in which stocks are combined is done such that the return on investment is maximized. Because of the dynamic nature of the financial markets, the optimal basket of stocks is not necessarily the optimal basket of stocks in the future. This basket should be evolved dynamically to be in line with the changing environment to maintain optimal returns (this should include transactional costs). Now, how can this be achieved? In nature, there is a concept called evolution that ensures that a group of species (portfolio) maximizes its survival. This process of evolution is driven by three concepts and these are mutation, crossover and reproduction. Mutation brings into the population genes that are not already present, and crossover mixes genes that are present, and reproduction happens in order to maximize survival. From this mechanism, a computational technique which can be used to optimize a portfolio called genetic algorithm is derived. In this context, genetic algorithm takes a portfolio and creates different baskets (i.e. ways of making a portfolio), crossover the different baskets, then mutates some baskets and reproduces the results to maximize the return. Genetic algorithm has been used quite extensively in many different areas such as in HIV problem (Crossingham and Marwala 2008), design of aero-structures (Marwala 2002) and damage detection in structures (Marwala and Chakraverty 2006).

11.7 Results Analysis

The set of portfolios looked at targeted risk as the control variable. The targeting of the variable is a hard target, desiring an exact controlled match. This first portfolio was designed to obtain the minimum possible risk that the component strategies allowed. The results shown in Fig. 11.4 indicate that the portfolio achieved the desired risk, or better, for the vast majority of the time period. Spikes of poor performance are inevitable, owing to the lack of any feedback in the system, and the unreliable nature of the component strategies themselves.

When studying the strategy choices made by genetic algorithm when optimizing the portfolio, it was observed that there was the heavy dependence (as expected) on

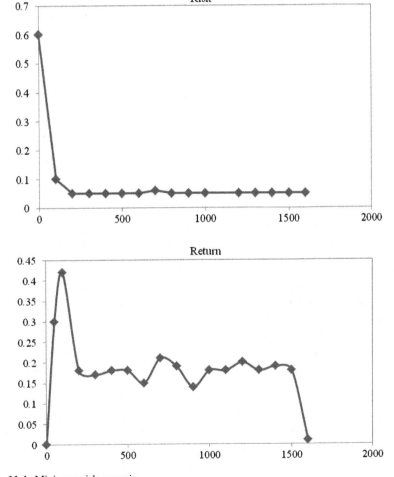

Fig. 11.4 Minimum-risk scenario

the *zero-risk* portfolio. The rest of the portfolios were generated in a similar manner, with the various parameters changing. Of particular interest is the fact that as the targeted risk is relaxed (i.e., set to a higher value), the returns achieved by the portfolio become greater, matching the expectations of modern portfolio theory. The achievement of a mean variance within the targeted risk bounds indicates the usefulness of the technique to successfully balance (and rebalance) a portfolio. Of further interest is the difference between portfolios with the same targeted risk, but where one is allowed for the risk to be merely an upper bound, while the other targets the exact value. The freedom to not specifically target a given risk value actually allows for a greater return, while the mean risk still remains within the controlled bounds.

11.8 Conclusion

The idea of creating a dynamic portfilio that adapts to the changing environment is a natural extension of Markowitz's portfolio theory. It is even more appropriate particularly when decisions are being made by intelligent machines which are enabled by neural networks. The adaptation to the environment is enabled by a group of methods called evolutionary optimization and in our case genetic algorithm. Artificial intelligence is used to create an automated portfolio optimization technique that is able to adapt to the environment by learning from the data to improve its performance.

References

Atsalakis GS, Valavanis KP (2009) Surveying stock market forecasting techniques—Part II: Soft computing methods. Expert Syst Appl 36(3):5932–5941

Crossingham B, Marwala T (2008) Using genetic algorithms to optimise rough set partition sizes for HIV data analysis. Adv Intell Distrib Comput Stud Comput Intell 78:245–250. doi:10.1007/978-3-540-74930-1_25

Duma M (2013) Predicting insurance risk using incomplete data. University of Johannesburg Doctoral Thesis

Hurwitz E (2014) Efficient portfolio optimization by hybridized machine learning. University of Johannesburg Doctoral Thesis

Hurwitz E, Marwala T (2011) Suitability of using technical indicators as potential strategies within intelligent trading systems. IEEE International Conference on Systems, Man, and Cybernetics, pp 80–84

Hurwitz E, Marwala T (2012) Optimising a targeted fund of strategies using genetic algorithms. IEEE International Conference on Systems, Man, and Cybernetics, pp 2139–2143

Jiang P (2011) Corporate finance and portfolio management. CFA Institute

Mandelbrot BB (2004) The (mis)behavior of market. Basic Books, London

Markowitz HM (1952) Portfolio selection. J Finance 7(1):77–91

Marwala T (2002) Finite element updating using wavelet data and genetic algorithm. American Institute of Aeronautics and Astronautics. J Aircr 39:709–711

Marwala T (2007) Computational intelligence for modelling complex systems. Research India Publications, Delhi

Marwala T (2009) computational intelligence for missing data imputation, estimation, and management: knowledge optimization techniques. IGI Global, Pennsylvania

Marwala T (2010) Finite element model updating using computational intelligence techniques: applications to structural dynamics. Springer, Heidelberg

Marwala T (2012) Condition monitoring using computational intelligence methods. Springer, Heidelberg

Marwala T (2013) Economic modeling using artificial intelligence methods. Springer, Heidelberg

Marwala T (2014) Artificial intelligence techniques for rational decision making. Springer, Heidelberg

Marwala T (2015) Causality, correlation, and artificial intelligence for rational decision making. World Scientific, Singapore

Marwala T, Chakraverty S (2006) Fault classification in structures with incomplete measured data using autoassociative neural networks and genetic algorithm. Curr Sci 90(4):542–548

Marwala T, Lagazio M (2011) Militarized conflict modeling using computational intelligence. Springer, Heidelberg. ISBN 978-0-85729-789-1. Translated into Chinese by the National Defence Industry Press

Marwala T, Boulkaibet I, Adhikari S (2017) Probabilistic finite element model updating using bayesian statistics: applications to aeronautical and mechanical engineering. Wiley, London

Rupper D (2004) Statistics and finance: an introduction. Springer, Berlin

Taleb NN (2007) The black swan: the impact of the highly improbable. Random House, New York

Xing B, Marwala T (2017a) Smart computing applications in crowdfunding. CRC Press, Boca Raton (accepted)

Xing B, Marwala T (2017b) Smart maintenance. Springer, Berlin (accepted)

Chapter 12
Counterfactuals

Abstract The concept of rational counterfactuals is an idea of identifying a counterfactual from the factual (whether perceived or real), and knowledge of the laws that govern the relationships between the antecedent and the consequent, that maximizes the attainment of the desired consequent. In counterfactual thinking, factual statements like: 'Greece was not financially prudent and consequently its finances are in tatters', and with its counterfactual being: 'Greece was financially prudent and consequently its finances are in good shape'. In order to build rational counterfactuals, artificial intelligence (AI) techniques are applied. The interstate conflict example considered uses AI to create counterfactuals that are able to maximize the attainment of peace.

12.1 Introduction

Rational decision making is important for many areas including economics, political science and engineering. Rational decision making involves choosing a course of action which maximizes utility. This concept of make a rational choice that maximizes utility is called the theory of rational choice (Muth 1961). It has been observed by Herbert Simon that rationality is bounded due to imperfect and imprecise information, inaccessible complete decision options and imperfect processing capabilities (Simon 1991). Behavioral economics is a special type of bounded rationality where the margins of decision making are far from the bounds of rationality and in fact to the levels of irrationality (Kahneman 2011; Kahneman and Tversky 1979). The implications of these findings are far reaching on the efficiency of the markets.

This chapter studies the counterfactual thinking, in particular, the theory of rational counterfactuals for rational decision making. The idea of using counterfactual thinking for decision making is an old concept that has been explored extensively by many researchers before (Lewis 1973, 1979; Marwala 2014, 2015).

In counterfactual thinking, factual statements like: 'Saddam Hussein invaded Kuwait, consequently, George Bush declared war on Iraq', has a counterfactual: 'If

T. Marwala and E. Hurwitz, *Artificial Intelligence and Economic Theory: Skynet in the Market*, Advanced Information and Knowledge Processing,
DOI 10.1007/978-3-319-66104-9_12

Saddam Hussein did not invade Kuwait and George Bush would not have declared war on Iraq'. If Saddam Hussein did not invade Kuwait then George Bush would not have declared war on Iraq, then there would not have been a causal relation between Saddam invading Kuwait and Bush declaring war on Iraq. Counterfactual thinking has been applied for decision making and is essentially a process of comparing a real and hypothetical thinking and using the difference between these to make decisions. Counterfactual tool of analysis is a powerful framework that can be used to prevent future catastrophes. For example, there is a factual that Adolf Hitler took over power in Germany and, consequently, there was a terrible war that resulted in millions of innocent people dying. We can identify conditions that could have led to the prevention of the rise of Hitler and the Second World War and use this information to prevent future similar conflicts.

A framework called a rational counterfactual machine was developed by Marwala (2014) which is a computational tool which takes in a factual and gives a counterfactual that is based on optimizing for the desired consequent by identifying an appropriate antecedent. This counterfactual was based on the learning machine called the neuro-fuzzy network (Montazer et al. 2010; Talei et al. 2010) and simulated annealing optimization (De Vicente et al. 2003; Dafflon et al. 2009). The rational counterfactual machine was applied to identify the antecedent that gave the consequent which is different from the consequent of the factual, and the example that is used in this chapter is a problem of interstate conflict (Marwala and Lagazio 2011). The rational counterfactual machine was applied to identify the values of antecedent variables *Allies*, *Contingency*, *Distance*, *Major Power*, *Capability*, *Democracy*, as well as *Economic Interdependency* that will give the consequent *Peace* given the factual statement.

12.2 Counterfactuals

Counterfactual thinking has been around for a very long time. Some of the thinkers who have dealt with the concept of counterfactuals include Hume (1748), Mill (1843), Hegel's dialectic concept of thesis (i.e. factual), antithesis (i.e. counterfactual) and synthesis (Hegel 1874) and Marx's concept of the unity of opposites also called the principle of contradiction (Marx 1873). Counterfactual can be understood by breaking this word into two parts *counter* and *factual*. As described by Marwala (2014) the factual is an event that has happened, for example: *Saddam Hussein invaded Kuwait and, consequently, George Bush declared war on Iraq*. *Counter* means the opposite of, and in the light of the factual above: *If Saddam Hussein did not invade Kuwait, George Bush would not have declared war on Iraq*. Of course, counterfactual can be an imaginary concept and, therefore, the fundamental question that needs to be asked is: How do we know what would have happened if something did not happen? There are classes of problems where it is possible to estimate what might have happened, and this procedure is a rational counterfactual machine in the form of structural equation models which can be implemented using artificial intelligence (AI) techniques.

There are different types of counterfactuals and these include self/other as well as additive/subtractive. Additive and subtractive counterfactual is the case where the antecedent is either increased or decreased. One example of such will include: *He drank alcohol moderately and consequently he did not fall sick.* The counterfactual of this statement might be: *He drank a lot of alcohol and consequently he fell sick.* The 'a lot' adds to the antecedent in the counterfactual.

There are a number of theories that have been proposed to understand counterfactuals and these include norm and functional theories (Birke et al. 2011; Roese 1997). Kahneman and Miller (1986) described norm theory as comprising of a pairwise evaluation between a cognitive standard and an experiential outcome. Functional theory entails looking at how a counterfactual theory and its processes benefit people. Rational counterfactuals can be viewed as an example of the functional theory of counterfactuals.

Figure 12.1 indicates a factual and its transformation into a counterfactual. It indicates that in the universe of counterfactuals that correspond to the factual, there are many if not infinite number of counterfactuals. Suppose we have a factual: *Mandela opposed apartheid and consequently he went to jail for 27 years.* Its counterfactual can be: *If Mandela did not oppose apartheid then he would not have gone to jail* or *If Mandela opposed apartheid gently he would not have gone to jail* or *If Mandela opposed apartheid peacefully he would not have gone to jail.* It is clear that there are multiple ways in which one can formulate counterfactuals for a given factual.

There are a number of ways in which counterfactuals can be stated and this involves structural equations (Woodward 2003; Woodward and Hitchcock 2003). Figure 12.1 shows that within the counterfactual universe, there are a group of

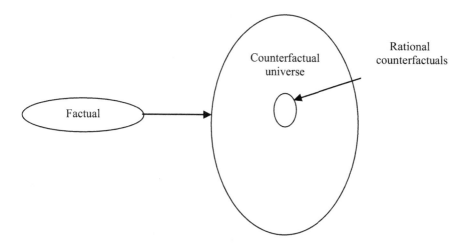

Fig. 12.1 An illustration of a transformation of a factual into a counterfactual

counterfactuals that are called rational counterfactuals which are counterfactuals that are designed to maximize the attainment of particular consequences and are the subject of the next section.

12.3   Rational Counterfactuals

Now that we have discussed the concept of counterfactual, this section describes the concept of rational counterfactual and the corresponding machine for creating this concept (Marwala 2014). As shown in Fig. 12.1, rational counterfactuals are those counterfactuals in the counterfactual universe corresponding to a given factual that maximizes a particular utility and in this regard, are deemed to be rational in line with the theory of rational choice. Of course, the attainment of this maximum utility is not perfect, as a result, rational counterfactuals are in fact bounded in line with the theory of bounded rationality.

There is a statement attributed to Karl Marx that states: *"The aim of a revolutionary is not merely to understand the world but to actually change it"*. In this chapter we, therefore, use counterfactual theory to solve practical problems and this is called the functional theory to counterfactual thinking. In this chapter, we also build what is known as a counterfactual machine, which is a computational system which gives a rational counterfactual whenever it is presented with a factual and a given problem domain. An illustration of a rational counterfactual machine is given in Fig. 12.2 (Marwala 2015). This figure shows that there are three objects in a rational counterfactual machine and these are the factual which is the antecedent leading to the rational counterfactual machine to give a rational counterfactual.

The rational counterfactual machine consists of a model that describes the structure and rules that define the problem at hand and a feedback which links the consequent (outcome) of the model and the antecedent. This model is shown in Fig. 12.3 (Marwala 2015).

In this chapter, we apply the problem of interstate conflict to illustrate the concept of rational counterfactuals. In this regard, we use a neuro-fuzzy model to construct a factual relationship between the antecedent and the consequent. Then to identify the antecedent given the desired consequent, an optimization method is used (Marwala and Lagazio 2011).

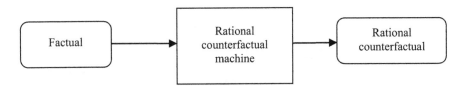

Fig. 12.2 An illustration of a rational counterfactual machine

Fig. 12.3 An illustration of a rational counterfactual machine

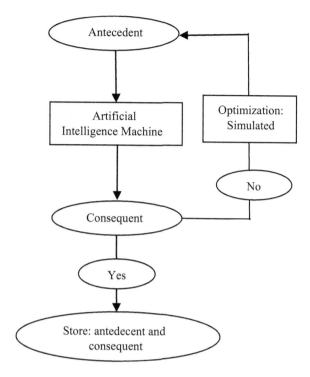

12.4   Counterfactuals and Causality

One use of a counterfactual is to define causality. Hume in 1896 proposed the following principles of causality:

1. The cause and effect are connected in space and time.
2. The cause must happen before the effect.
3. There should be a continuous connectivity between the cause and effect.
4. The specific cause must at all times give the identical effect, and the same effect should not be obtained from any other event but from the same cause.
5. Where a number of different objects give the same effect, it ought to be because of some quality which is the same amongst them.
6. The difference in the effects of two similar events must come from that they are different.
7. When an object changes its dimensions with the change of its cause it is a compounded effect from the combination of a number of different effects, which originate from a number of different parts of the cause.
8. An object which occurs for any time in its full exactness without any effect, is not the only cause of that effect, but needs to be aided by some other norm which may advance its effect and action.

The concept of causality is probabilistic. For example, if there is a probabilistic causal relationship between *A* and *B* then whenever *A* happens then *B* occurs with a probability that is higher than chance. Counterfactuals can be used to define causality. For example, if one wanted to find out if *A* causes *B* then one can perform a number of experiments and one of these is to find out if *B was* caused by another phenomenon e.g. *C* other than *A*. The general counterfactual view of causality can be expressed as follows as it was done by Menzies (2017): "Where *c* and *e* are distinct actual events, *e causally depends* on *c* if and only if, if *c* had not occurred, the chance of *e* occurring would be much less than its actual chance."

In this regard, "if *c* had not occurred…" is a counterfactual.

12.5   Counterfactuals and Opportunity Cost

The other aspect of counterfactual is its relations to the economic principle of opportunity cost (Buchanan 2008). The opportunity cost is an opportunity forgone when one makes a choice. For example, a young man, Khathu, obtains two scholarships, one to go and study a degree in mechanical engineering at Case Western Reserve University in the USA and another to go and study mechanical engineering at the University of Cambridge in the UK. If he chooses to go and study mechanical engineering at Case Western Reserve University, then Cambridge University becomes his opportunity cost. So the opportunity cost is in effect a counterfactual. This scenario is symmetrical to choosing Cambridge University over Case Western Reserve University and then this leaves Case Western Reserve University as an opportunity cost. The concept of opportunity cost is so influential that other economics concepts such as the theory of comparative advantage which is the basis of international trade hinges on the theory of opportunity costs.

Suppose there is a lawyer named Mpho who can do legal work at a rate of $200 per hour. He can also do secretarial work at the rate of $20 per hour. He has a secretary named Shoni who cannot do legal work but can do secretarial work at the rate of $15 per hour because she is less competent in typing than Mpho. Suppose each can work for 7 h a day, how should they distribute their work? This problem is what David Ricardo called the comparative advantage problem and it is represented in Table 12.1 (Ricardo 2017).

Mpho has an absolute advantage on both legal and secretarial work than Shoni. However, the opportunity costs for Mpho on typing is higher than the opportunity costs for Shoni. Therefore, Mpho should only do legal work whereas Shoni should only do secretarial work. This principle of comparative advantage can be extended

Table 12.1 An illustration of the work distribution between Mpho and Shoni

	Legal work	Secretarial work
Mpho	$1400	$140
Shoni	0	$105

to other areas such as the reason why certain countries should specialize in certain industries.

How does artificial intelligence assist us in evaluating opportunity costs? The problems that can be handled using AI are problems that can be modelled using structural equation models.

12.6   Counterfactuals and Artificial Intelligence

Suppose we intend to model the relationship between the interest rates and the economic growth. Suppose we have a simple structural equation model which relates interest rate to economic growth. The model should ideally be a learning model that is able to adapt as the economic situation in a given country changes. There are many techniques that can be used to learn and adapt and these include artificial intelligence techniques such as neural networks and fuzzy logic (Marwala 2013, 2012, 2014). Now we can add an additional layer to this model that will imagine various counterfactuals and their respective utilities. For example, one can assume that supposing the interest rate is 5%, then what will be the economic growth, and, the model will be able to give an economic growth say 3%. Then one can imagine another counterfactual, say supposing the interest rate is 4.5% and the model then gives an economic growth of 3.5%. This process can be repeated until a desired economic growth is achieved with each iteration a different counterfactual. In fact, these iterations can be achieved using an artificial intelligence optimization method such as particle swarm optimization or genetic algorithm (Marwala 2007, 2009, 2010). The counterfactual that maximizes economic growth here is deemed a rational counterfactual.

12.7   Interstate Conflict

This chapter implements artificial intelligence methods (i.e. neuro-fuzzy model and simulated annealing) to build a rational counterfactual machine which is described in Fig. 12.3 and follows the work conducted by Marwala and Lagazio (2011). This model is used in the problem of militarized interstate dispute (MID). We use four variables associated with realist analysis and three "Kantian" variables and four "realistic" variables. *Allies* is a Kantian variable which is a binary measure coded 1 if the members of a dyad (pairs of countries) are linked by any form of military alliance, and 0 in the absence of military alliance. *Contingency* is a realist variable which is binary, and is coded 1 if both states share a common boundary and 0 if they do not, and *Distance* is a realist variable which is the distance between the two states' capitals. *Major Power* is a realist binary variable, coded 1 if either or both states in the dyad is a major power and 0 if neither are super powers. *Capability* is a realist variable which is the ratio of the total population plus the number of people in urban areas plus industrial energy consumption plus iron and steel production plus the number of military personnel in active duty plus military expenditure in dollars in the last 5 years measured on stronger country to weak country. The variable *Democracy* is a Kantian variable which is measured on a scale where the value of 10 is an extreme democracy and a value of −10 is an extreme autocracy. The variable *Dependency* is Kantian variable which is measured as the sum of the countries import and export with its partner divided by the Gross Domestic Product of the stronger country. It is a continuous variable measuring the level of economic interdependence (dyadic trade as a portion of a state's gross domestic product) of the less economically dependent state in the dyad. These measures are derived from conceptualizations and measurements conducted by the Correlates of War (COW) project (Anonymous 2010).

Politically relevant population, which are all dyads containing a major power, are selected for the reason that it sets a hard test for prediction. Neglecting all distant dyads composed of weak states means that we ignore much of the influence of variables that are not very responsive to policy intervention (distance and national power). This exclusion makes the task difficult by decreasing the extrapolative power of such variables. Using the training and validation sampling procedure, it is revealed that a strong performance is realized even when the analysis is circumscribed to the politically relevant group. By concentrating only on dyads that either encompass major powers or are contiguous, the discriminative power of artificial intelligence is tested on a difficult set of cases. The artificial intelligence learning machine is trained with only highly informative data because every dyad can be considered to be at risk of experiencing a dispute, hitherto it is harder for the AI machine to discriminate between the two classes (dyad-years with disputes and those without disputes) for the reason that the politically relevant group is more homogeneous (e.g., closer, more inter-dependent) than the all-dyad data set.

As in Marwala and Lagazio (2011), the training data set consisted of 500 conflict- and 500 non-conflict cases, and the test data consisted of 392 conflict data and 392 peace data. A balanced training set, with a randomly selected equal number of conflict- and non-conflict cases was chosen to yield robust classification and stronger comprehensions on the explanation of conflicts. The data were normalized to fall between 0 and 1. The antecedent variables were *Distance (D1), Contiguity (C), Major Power (MJ), Allies (A), Democracy (D2), Economic Interdependency (EI)*, and *Capability (C)* and the consequent was either peace or war. In this regard, and due to normalization, two countries with the largest distance between their capitals were assigned a Distance value of 1 while the two countries with the shortest distance between their capitals were assigned a Distance of 0. If both countries were superpowers, then they were assigned a Major Power value of 1 while if none were a major power, of 0. If two countries were not allies, they were assigned a value of 0 while if they were allies, a value of 1. If the two countries share a border, they were assigned a Contiguity value of 1 while if they did not share a border a contiguity of 0. If the two countries had no economic interdependency, the variable economic interdependency was 0 while if they had maximum economic interdependency recorded, they were assigned a value of 1. For the maximum military capability, the value was 1 while minimum was 0. The results obtained for modelling the relationship between the antecedent and consequent demonstrate that detection rate of conflict was 77% and for peace was 73% whereas the overall detection rate of a correct outcome was 75%.

Artificial intelligence methods were implemented to model militarized interstate dispute data. When these data were used in the modelling process, a factual below is obtained:

If it is the case that D1 = 0, C = 1, MJ = 0.4, A = 0.1, D2 = 0.3, EI = 0.1, Cap = 0.6, then it will be the case that Consequent = War.

Optimization was used in a manner described in Fig. 12.3 to identify the antecedent that would turn this factual into a counterfactual. In this regard, the following rational counterfactual was identified that achieved a peaceful outcome:

If it were the case that D1 = 0.7, C = 1, MJ = 0.4, A = 0.8, D2 = 0.3, EI = 0.1, Cap = 0.7, then it will be the case that Consequent = Peace.

This counterfactual was deemed a rational counterfactual because it was formulated by identifying the antecedent which maximized the attainment of a particular desired consequent (utilitarianism), and this is a peaceful outcome.

12.8   Conclusions

This chapter introduced rational counterfactuals which are counterfactuals that maximize the attainment of the desired consequent. The theory of rational counterfactuals was applied to identify the antecedent that gave the desired consequent. The results obtained demonstrated the viability of a method of identifying rational counterfactuals.

References

Anonymous (2010) Correlates of war project, http://www.correlatesofwar.org/. Last accessed: 20 Sept 2010

Birke D, Butter M, Koppe T (eds) (2011) Counterfactual thinking—counterfactual writing. de Gruyter, Berlin

Buchanan JM (2008) Opportunity cost. The New Palgrave Dictionary of Economics Online (Second ed). Retrieved 18 Sept 2010

Dafflon B, Irving J, Holliger K (2009) Simulated-annealing-based conditional simulation for the local-scale characterization of heterogeneous aquifers. J Appl Geophys 68:60–70

De Vicente J, Lanchares J, Hermida R (2003) Placement by thermodynamic simulated annealing. Phys Lett A 317:415–423

Hegel GWF (1874) The logic. encyclopaedia of the philosophical sciences, 2nd edn. Oxford University Press, London

Hume D (1748) An enquiry concerning human understanding. Hackett Publishing Company, USA

Hume D (1896) (Selby-Bigge, ed) A treatise of human nature. Clarendon Press, Oxford

Kahneman K (2011) Thinking, fast and slow. Macmillan, UK

Kahneman D, Miller D (1986) Norm theory: comparing reality to its alternatives. Psychol Rev 93 (2):136–153

Kahneman D, Tversky A (1979) Prospect theory: an analysis of decision under risk. Econometrica 47(2):263

Lewis D (1973) Counterfactuals. Blackwell, Oxford

Lewis D (1979) Counterfactual dependence and time's arrow. Noûs 13:455–476

Marwala T (2007) Computational intelligence for modelling complex systems. Research India Publications, Delhi

Marwala T (2009) Computational intelligence for missing data imputation, estimation, and management: knowledge optimization techniques. IGI Global, Pennsylvania. ISBN 978-1-60566-336-4

Marwala T (2010) Finite element model updating using computational intelligence techniques: applications to structural dynamics. Springer, Heidelberg

Marwala T (2012) Condition monitoring using computational intelligence methods. Springer, Heidelberg

Marwala T (2013) Economic modeling using artificial intelligence methods. Springer, Heidelberg

Marwala T (2014) Artificial intelligence techniques for rational decision making. Springer, Heidelberg

Marwala T (2015) Causality, correlation, and artificial intelligence for rational decision making. World Scientific, Singapore

Marwala T, Lagazio M (2011) Militarized conflict modeling using computational intelligence. Springer, London

Marx K (1873) Capital afterword to the second German Edition, vol I

Menzies P (2017) https://plato.stanford.edu/entries/causation-counterfactual/ Last accessed: 3 May 2017

Mill JS (1843) A system of logic. University Press of the Pacific

Montazer GA, Saremi HQ, Khatibi V (2010) A neuro-fuzzy inference engine for farsi numeral characters recognition. Expert Syst Appl 37:6327–6337

Muth JF (1961) "Rational expectations and the theory of price movements" reprinted in The new classical macroeconomics. Volume 1. (1992): 3–23 (International Library of Critical Writings in Economics, vol 19. Aldershot, Elgar, UK)

Ricardo D (2017) The principles of political economy and http://socserv2.socsci.mcmaster.ca/~econ/ugcm/3ll3/ricardo/prin/index.html. Last accessed 1 May 2017

Roese N (1997) Counterfactual thinking. Psychol Bull 121(1):133–148

Simon H (1991) Bounded rationality and organizational learning. Organ Sci 2(1):125–134

Talei A, Hock L, Chua C, Quek C (2010) A novel application of a neuro-fuzzy computational technique in event-based rainfall-runoff modeling. Expert Syst Appl 37:7456–7468

Woodward J (2003) Making things happen: a theory of causal explanation. Oxford University Press, Oxford

Woodward J, Hitchcock C (2003) Explanatory generalizations. Part I: a counterfactual account. Noûs 37:1–24

Chapter 13
Financial Engineering

Abstract Financial engineering has grown with the advent of computing and this growth has accelerated in the last decade with the advances in artificial intelligence (AI). This chapter explores how subjects such as evolution, deep learning and big data are changing the effectiveness of quantitative finance. This chapter explores the problem of estimating HIV risk, simulating the stock market using multi-agent systems, applying control systems for inflation targeting and factor analysis. The results demonstrate that AI improves the estimation of HIV risk, makes stock markets homogeneous and efficient, is a good basis for building models that target inflation and enhances the identification of factors that drive inflation.

13.1 Introduction

Financial engineering is a discipline that uses engineering principles to solve financial problems (Beder and Marshall 2011; Akansu and Torun 2015). It is closely linked to the discipline of quantitative finance and financial mathematics. Unlike econometrics which studies economic variables and their interrelationships, financial engineering takes engineering principles and use these to create new instruments. For example, one can take the underlying price of stocks and the resulting volatility and create a derivative instrument. Financial mathematics normally uses applied mathematics, usually in the form of partial differential equations to create financial instruments. The classical example of this is the Black-Scholes equation which is a linear and second order differential equation along the same lines as the heat equation in mechanical engineering (Pires 2005; Pires and Marwala 2004, 2005). Quantitative finance uses statistics and applied mathematics to analyze financial problems.

With the advent of the market crash of 2007, a great deal of blame was apportioned to financial engineers who were creating financial instruments which interwove debts, derivatives, portfolios and other factors to the extent that the resulting instruments became intractable. This chapter deals with financial engineering and some areas are addressed. These are how to use financial engineering techniques to handle risk, how to predict and understand the stock markets, and

© Springer International Publishing AG 2017   147
T. Marwala and E. Hurwitz, *Artificial Intelligence and Economic Theory: Skynet in the Market*, Advanced Information and Knowledge Processing,
DOI 10.1007/978-3-319-66104-9_13

how to control economic outcomes. How to manage portfolios and how to price derivatives which is also an important part of financial engineering is not covered here because it was covered in early chapters. In particular, these analyses are understood within the context of the recent advances in artificial intelligence (AI), big data analytics and other related technologies.

13.2   Risk

Suppose you enter a quarantined area called Duthuni where there is a deadly flu that has killed half of the population. Now, what is your risk of entering such a place without any protective garments? The risk of entering this place is defined as the probability of getting this deadly flu and here it is 50%. Now, how does one mitigate/manage this risk? Mitigation of a risk is achieved by putting processes that will reduce this risk. Here, wearing protective clothing is a method for mitigating this risk. Suppose the manufacturers of this garment performed an experiment where they put 100 people into an area where there is this deadly virus, wearing protective clothing and found out that 20 people were infected by this virus despite the fact that they were wearing protective clothing. Then the risk of contracting the virus given the fact that he/she is wearing protective clothing is 20 of 100 which is 20%. The combined risk of entering Duthuni wearing protective clothing is 10%.

In South Africa, when customers apply for a mortgage, they are required to take an HIV test. This is primarily because South Africa has the highest burden of HIV and insurance companies have not yet discovered a method for assessing the risk of HIV. Several attempts have been made in this regard to use antenatal data and artificial intelligence to assess the risk of HIV. Marivate et al. (2008), Mistry et al. (2008) as well as Marwala and Crossingham (2008) used AI to relate the demographic characteristics to HIV risk.

The HIV risk estimation method is shown in Fig. 13.1 and here the demographic characteristics which are race, age of mother, education, parity which is the number of times a person has given birth, gravidity which is the number of pregnancies, age of the father and income which were discussed in detail by Tim and Marwala (2006) and Leke et al. (2006) are used to predict the risk of HIV. When this framework was implemented to estimate the HIV risk from demographic data, an accuracy of 62% was obtained. How do we contextualize these results within the context of economic theory? The theory is based on rational expectations where the expectations of the HIV risk are based on a wide range of existing data. However, not all the information that are relevant to the estimation of HIV risk are necessarily accessible and, therefore, this procedure is subjected to the theory of bounded rationality. The fact that the insurance companies do not have access to information on the risky behavior of the customers, which the customers are fully aware of raises the issue of information asymmetry and how this can distort the nature of the insurance market.

Fig. 13.1 A process for
using demographic data to
diagnose HIV

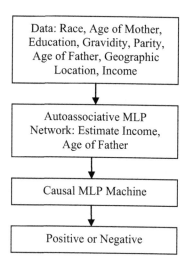

13.3   Stock Markets

Another area that has emerged as computers improved their processing power due
to Moore's law is multi-agent systems. The area of multi-agent systems is closely
associated with the area of software engineering. Multi-agent system basically
builds an ecosystem, say of interacting community of people, and studies their
collective behaviour, and has found much use in finance and economics. This
section describes how multi-agent systems are used to understand economic phenomenon. It is called the multi-agent system because it is a system of multiple
agents. An agent is an object that is autonomous, perceives its environment, acts on
its environment (is intelligent), and operates autonomously in that environment.
Much work on multi-agent systems can be found in the works of Russell and
Norvig (2003), Franklin and Graesser (1996) as well as Kasabov (1998). Agents are
flexible, reactive, proactive, social and have control capability.

An illustration of the functioning of a multi-agent system, a well-known swarm
intelligence theory, can be used as was done by Marwala (2013). In the case of
swarm of birds, agents or birds operate using two simple rules. These are that, in
seeking the next move, a bird considers the best position it has encountered and the
best position the entire flock has encountered (where other birds are going). Using
these simple rules, the swarm is able to solve very complex problems. More details
on the workings of the swarm of birds are found in the work by Marwala (2009,
2010, 2012), Marwala and Lagazio (2011), as well as Marwala (2013). An example
of the use of the multi-agent systems is the work by Teweldemedhin et al. (2004)
who used multi-agent systems, to develop a bottom-up model that simulated the
spread of the human immunodeficiency virus (HIV) in a given population.

Another celebrated work which was widely covered by the magazine "The New
Scientist" is the work by Hurwitz and Marwala (2007) who studied bluffing, a

human characteristic which has puzzled game designers. This work found that, the very act of bluffing was even open for debate, introducing additional difficulty to the procedure of producing intelligent virtual players that can bluff, and, therefore, play truthfully. Through the application of intelligent, learning agents, and carefully designed multi-agents, agents were found to learn to predict their opponents' reactions based on their own cards and actions of other agents. It was observed that, agents can learn to bluff their opponents, with the action not indicating an "irrational" action, as bluffing is usually regarded, but as an act of maximizing returns by an actual statistical optimization, thereby, making them rational. By using the principles of reinforcement learning to adapt a neural network based agent's intelligence, they demonstrated that agents were able to learn to bluff without outside encouragement.

This section uses a multi-agent system to simulate the stock market as was done by Marwala et al. (2001), and the agent architecture used is shown in Fig. 13.2 whereas the multi-agent system is shown in Fig. 13.3.

This agent has diverse intelligence capability which is enabled by a combination of multiple networks of various sizes and architectures. Diversity is an important principle as it is a better reflection of the stock brokers observed in real stock markets.

These agents were made to be able to adapt using genetic programming, by adapting their structure e.g. size and type of neural networks. Neural networks were applied to enable the agents to be intelligent. Each agent is a player in the stock market and the simulation framework consists of a population of these players and they compete for a fixed number of stocks. The agents learn through the use of neural networks. The structure of each agent evolves using genetic algorithm such that its contribution to the overall function of an agent adapts to the evolutionary time-varying nature of the problem. Each agent, known as a player, trades stocks with other agents and when prices of stocks are announced, the players trade by following these rules (Marwala 2000; Marwala et al. 2001):

Fig. 13.2 Illustration of an agent (Marwala 2013)

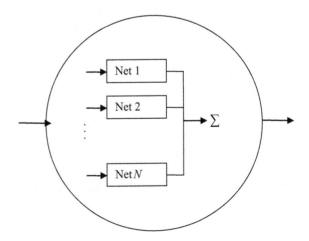

Fig. 13.3 Illustration of a multi-agent system (Marwala 2013)

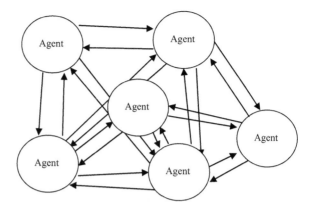

- Once a price is announced, the agent looks at the current price and the future price of stocks. The future price is determined from the agents that learn using neural networks. For a player, the predicted price is the average of the prediction of each agent within that particular player.
- If the predicted price of a stock is lower than the current price, then the player tries to sell the stock. If the predicted price for the stock is higher than the current price, then the agent tries to buy the stock.
- At any given stage, the agent is only prepared to sell the maximum of 40% of the volume of stocks it has.
- The amount of stocks that an agent buys or sells depends on, amongst other factors, the predicted price. If the predicted price of a particular stock is x% higher than the current price, the agent tries to acquire x% of the volume available on the market of that particular stock. This simulation is started by choosing the number of players that participate in the trading of stocks, together with the number of agents that form a player. Then the agents are trained by randomly assigning different number of hidden units and assigning weighting functions to the agent. The agents are trained using the data from the previous 50 trading days. The trained agents are grouped into their respective players and are then used to predict the next price, given the current price. The simulation followed in this chapter is shown in Fig. 13.4.

After 50 days of trading have elapsed, the performance of each agent and the weighting functions are evaluated and these are transformed into 8 bits, and each player exchanges bits with other players, a process called crossover. Thereafter, the agents mutate at low probability. The successful agents are duplicated, while the less successful ones are eliminated. Then the networks are retrained again and the whole process is repeated. This is to enable the stock market to evolve to the changing dynamics of the market. When a price is announced, trading of stocks is conducted until the consensus is reached. At this state, the overall wealth of the agents does not increase as a result of trading.

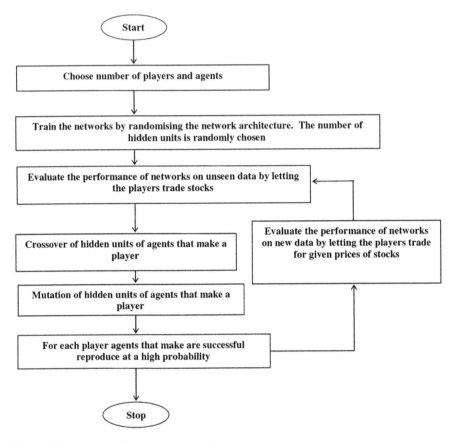

Fig. 13.4 Illustration of the simulation of the stock market

The example that is considered is the trading of three stocks, namely: (1) the Dow Jones; (2) NASDAQ; and (3) S&P 500. The time-histories of the stocks were downloaded from the Internet and used to train agents. For a given set of price of these stocks, the agent predicts the future prices of stocks. It should be noted that, on implementing this procedure, the total number of stocks available is kept constant. The results indicate that sometimes, the players with successful strategies do not necessarily dominate indefinitely. This is due to the fact that, strategies that are successful in one time frame are not necessarily successful at a later time.

When the scalability of the simulations was studied, it was found that the method proposed was scalable. However, it was observed that the computational time increased with the increase in the number of agents and players. A linear relationship existed between the average computational time taken to run the complete simulation and the number of players, as well as the number of agents that form a player.

The complexity of the populations of agents that make players of the game was studied and defined as the measure of a degree of variation in a population of agents. Each species of agents form a dimension in space. Each dimension has a variation indicating the level of complexity of a population of that species. The results indicated that, as the system evolved, the agents became more homogenous and that no player had a monopolistic advantage on the prediction of the stock market. The results obtained indicate that the use of AI in the stock market makes the players in the stock market more homogenous and this, therefore, reduces the opportunity for arbitrage in the market and, thus, makes the market more efficient.

13.4   Control Systems

Another area that is closely related to engineering is the area of control systems, which is a procedure by which a system is designed to have a particular outcome. Control system is a form of mechanism design, although mechanism design is normally defined as reverse game theory. Control systems have been applied to the problem of inflation targeting, a task that bedevils reserve banks around the world. Inflation is essentially a non-stationary phenomenon and, therefore, its characteristics are always changing and, therefore, making it difficult to model. Predictive control systems with non-stationary environment require that the predictive model be dynamic enough to be able to evolve with the predictive model in line with the evolution of non-stationarity. The advent of AI makes this problem relatively easy to handle.

Artificial intelligence has been able to offer models that are sufficiently flexible to be adaptive and evolve. The control system that is able to deal with the problem of non-stationarity is shown in Fig. 13.5 (Marwala 2013). In this figure, the predictive model receives the input data which can be categorized into the controllable and uncontrollable input variables. The predictive model then transforms these input variables into the output. This output is compared to a reference signal, which is the desired output. If the desired predicted output is not sufficiently close to the reference output, then a controller identifies appropriate controllable variables and the process is repeated. As this scheme is being implemented, the predictive model senses its changing environment to improve its predictive capacity in line with the sensed environment. The next section explains the multi-layered perceptron, which is adaptable to account for non-linear control.

The next section implements a method for a predictive model, which is a multi-layered neural network. The inflation rate scheme proposed in this chapter is based on the premise that there is a relationship between the inflation rate and the interest rate. The input variables are mining output; transport, storage and communication output; financial intermediation, insurance, real estate and business services output; community, social and personal services output; gross value added at basic prices; taxes less subsidies on products; affordability; economic growth; repo rate; GDP growth; household consumption; as well as investment, and output

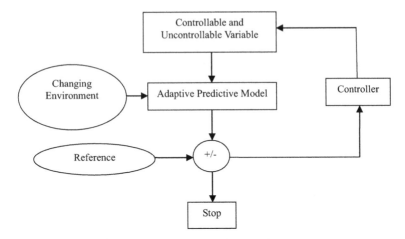

Fig. 13.5 Illustration of the control system for non-stationary environment

variable inflation rate. These data were obtained from the Reserve Bank of South Africa.

The actual observed inflation rates were assumed to be the targeted inflation rate. The measure of how well the inflation targeting strategy is, is how well the targeted inflation rate is to what was actually observed and, at the same time, how close the corresponding interest rate was to the actual one. This is the best we can do because it is costly to implement this technique in real life because of the associated cost of testing a new method on a real economy.

For the optimization procedure, a genetic algorithm was used and simple cross-over, simple mutations, and Roulette wheel reproduction were used. The results obtained when these methods were employed are shown in Fig. 13.6 (Marwala 2013).

Fig. 13.6 Achieved versus targeted inflation rate (Marwala 2013)

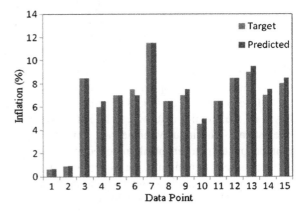

The results obtained indicate that inflation targeting seems to work. Of course this model can be improved by using more robust predictive models as well as optimization methods.

13.5   Factor Analysis

Another important area in financial engineering is factor analysis. Suppose one needs to understand what caused the Gulf War. There are many factors that were at play during that time such as the Israeli-Palestinian issue, the fight for Oil etc. Factor analysis is a procedure that is intended to identify the factors that caused a particular outcome and in this regard the Gulf War. Artificial intelligence has been used for financial forecasting for some time and can also be used to identify variables that drive a particular phenomenon. The reason why AI has attracted followers of economic and financial forecasting is because of its ability to fuse different data such as images i.e. weather patterns, voice i.e. speeches by politicians, texts e.g. reports and market sentiments in addition to traditional data. One form of AI that has proven useful is the automatic relevance determination (ARD) algorithm that identifies variables that drive a particular outcome and in our example the Gulf War and the inflation rate. Inflation is measured using a concept called Consumer Price Index (CPI). Artificial intelligence has been used above to model inflation. The CPI is a measure of inflation in an economy. It measures the changes in prices of a fixed pre-selected basket of goods. A basket of goods which is used for calculating the CPI in South Africa is as follows:

1. Food and non-alcoholic beverages: bread and cereals, meat, fish, milk, cheese, eggs, oils, fats, fruit, vegetables, sugar, sweets, desserts, and other foods.
2. Alcoholic beverages and tobacco.
3. Clothing and footwear.
4. Housing and utilities: rents, maintenance, water, electricity, and others.
5. Household contents, equipment, and maintenance.
6. Health: medical equipment, outpatient, and medical service.
7. Transport.
8. Communication.
9. Recreation and culture.
10. Education.
11. Restaurants and hotels.
12. Miscellaneous goods and services: personal care, insurance, and financial services.

This basket is weighed and the variation of prices of these goods are tracked from month to month and this is the basis for calculating inflation. It must be noted that there is normally a debate as to whether this basket of goods is appropriate. For example, in South Africa where there are two economies, one developed and formal and another informal and under-developed, there is always a debate on the validity of the CPI. This is even more important because the salary negotiations are based on the CPI.

In this chapter, we use the CPI data from 1992 to 2011 to model the relationship between economic variables and the CPI, and then identify variables that drive the CPI. These economic variables are listed in Table 13.1. They represent the performance of various aspects of the economy represented by 23 variables in agriculture, manufacturing, mining, energy, construction, etc. A multi-layered perceptron neural network was used and the results indicating the relevance of each variable is indicated in Table 13.1 (Marwala 2013).

From Table 13.1, the following variables are deemed to be essential for modelling the CPI and these are: mining, transport, storage and communication, financial intermediation, insurance, real estate and business services, community, social and personal services, gross value added at basic prices, taxes less subsidies on products, affordability, economic growth, repo rate, gross domestic product, household consumption, and investment.

Table 13.1 Automatic relevance in inflation modelling

Variable	Alpha	Inverse alpha	Relative weights
Agriculture fish forestry	14.4832	0.0690	1.79
Mining	5.7440	0.1741	4.51
Manufacturing	24.2071	0.0413	1.07
Electricity gas water	6.8551	0.1459	3.78
Construction	7.3717	0.1357	3.51
Retail and trade	15.0679	0.0664	1.72
Transport, storage and communication	2.3174	0.4315	11.18
Financial intermediation, insurance, real estate, and business services	0.9391	1.0648	27.59
Community, social, and personal services	0.4626	2.1616	56.00
Government services	7.2632	0.1377	3.57
Gross value added at basic prices	4.7935	0.2086	5.40
Taxes less subsidies on products	0.6467	1.5462	40.06
Affordability	1.0664	0.9377	24.29
Economic growth	4.0215	0.2487	6.44
Rand/USD exchange	25.8858	0.0386	1.00
Prime interest	5.5639	0.1797	4.66
Repo rate	5.5639	0.1797	4.66
Gross domestic product	0.2545	3.9287	101.78
Household consumption	0.4407	2.2692	58.79
Investment	0.5909	1.6924	43.84
Government consumption	7.5703	0.1321	3.42
Exports	20.8664	0.0479	1.24
Imports	5.9678	0.0386	1.00

13.6 Conclusions

This chapter studied various methods in financial engineering. The methods studied are risk, multi-agent systems, control systems and factor analysis. On studying risk, AI was used to estimate the risk of a person having HIV given his/her demographic characteristics. This problem of estimating the HIV risk is important in the insurance industry in countries such as South Africa. The second financial engineering problem studied is in the area of simulation of the stock market. In this regard, the multi-agent systems were used and it was observed that AI makes the markets more homogeneous, more rational and reduces the opportunities for arbitrage. The third financial engineering technique studied is in the area of control systems and this was used to study the problem of inflation targeting. AI was found to work well on inflation targeting particularly given the non-stationary characteristics of inflation. The final financial engineering problem studied is factor analysis which is useful in identifying factors that drive a particular economic or financial phenomenon. In this regard, factors that drive inflation were identified using automatic relevance determination artificial neural network.

References

Akansu AN, Torun MU (2015) A primer for financial engineering: financial signal processing and electronic trading. Academic Press, Boston

Beder TS, Marshall CM (2011) Financial engineering: the evolution of a profession. Wiley, London

Franklin S, Graesser A (1996) Is it an agent, or just a program? A taxonomy for autonomous agents. In: Proceedings of the third international workshop on agent theories, architectures, and languages, pp 21–35

Hurwitz E, Marwala T (2007) Learning to bluff. Arxiv 0705.0693. Last accessed 1 May 2017

Kasabov N (1998) Introduction: hybrid intelligent adaptive systems. Int J Intell Syst 6:453–454

Leke BB, Marwala T, Tettey T (2006) Autoencoder networks for HIV classification. Curr Sci 9 (11):1467–1473

Marivate VN, Nelwamondo VF, Marwala T (2008) Investigation into the use of autoencoder neural networks, principal component analysis and support vector regression in estimating missing HIV data. In: Proceedings of the 17th World Congress of The International Federation of Automatic Control, Seoul, Korea, July 6–11, pp 682–689

Marwala T (2000) On damage identification using a committee of neural networks. J Eng Mech 126:43–50

Marwala T (2009) Computational intelligence for missing data imputation, estimation and management: knowledge optimization techniques. IGI Global Publications, New York

Marwala T (2010) Finite element model updating using computational intelligence techniques. Springer, London

Marwala T (2012) Condition monitoring using computational intelligence methods. Springer, London

Marwala T (2013) Economic modeling using artificial intelligence methods. Springer, Heidelberg

Marwala T, Crossingham B (2008) Neuro-rough models for modelling HIV. In: Proceedings of the IEEE International Conference on Man, Systems and Cybernetics, pp 3089–3095

Marwala T, Lagazio M (2011) Militarized conflict modeling using computational intelligence techniques. Springer, London

Marwala T, De Wilde P, Correia L, Mariano P, Ribeiro R, Abramov V, Szirbik N, Goossenaerts J (2001) Scalability and optimisation of a committee of agents using genetic algorithm. In: Proceedings of the 2001 international symposium on soft comput and intelligent systems for industry: Arxiv 0705.1757 Last accessed 3 Jan 2017

Mistry J, Nelwamondo FV, Marwala T (2008) Investigating a predictive certainty measure for ensemble based HIV classification. In IEEE International Conference on Systems, Computational Cybernetics. ICCC, pp 231–236

Pires MM (2005) American option pricing using computational intelligence methods. Master's Thesis, University of the Witwatersrand

Pires MM, Marwala T (2004) American option pricing using multi-layer perceptron and support vector machine. In: Proceedings of the IEEE international conference on systems, man, and cybernetics, pp 1279–1285

Pires MM, Marwala T (2005) American option pricing using bayesian multi-layer perceptrons and bayesian support vector machines. In: Proceedings of the IEEE 3rd international conference on computing cybernetics, pp 219–224

Russell SJ, Norvig P (2003) Artificial intelligence: a modern approach. Upper Saddle River, New Jersey

Teweldemedhin E, Marwala T, Mueller C (2004) Agent-based modelling: a case study in HIV epidemic. In: Proceeding of the fourth international conference on hybrid intelligent systems, pp 154–159

Tim TN, Marwala T (2006) Computational intelligence methods for risk assessment of HIV. In Imaging the Future Medicine, Proceedings of the IFMBE, vol 14, pp 3581–3585

Chapter 14
Causality

Abstract Causality is a powerful concept which is at the heart of markets. Often, one wants to establish whether a particular attribute causes another. As human beings, we have perceived causality through correlation. Because of this fact, causality has often been confused for correlation. This chapter studies the evolution of causality including the influential work of David Hume and its relevance to economics and finance. It studies various concepts and models of causality such as transmission, Granger and Pearl models of causality. The transmission model of causality states that for causality to exist, there should be a flow of information from the cause to the effect. Simple example of the study on the link between circumcision and risk of HIV are used in this chapter.

14.1 Introduction

The problem of causality is at the core of economic modelling. Policy makers require to know whether a stimulus package during economic downturn revitalizes the economy. President Barack Obama when the automotive industry was facing difficulties bailed it out and this was based on the assumption that bailing it will result in the industry performing better. When President Obama was conceiving that strategy, he had to have some idea about the causal relationship between bail out and economic performance. The problem of understanding causality has pre-occupied philosophers, economists and scientists for a long time. From the times of Plato and Aristotle and even before that period, mankind has been asking why and how they exist in this planet and various answers to these questions involved causality e.g. "We are here because God created us". The significance of understanding causality to satisfy human curiosity and enhance the functioning of the social, economic, political and technological aspects of society is enormous. The medical field is based on the premise that some medicines cause healing of diseases (Marwala 2014, 2015). To link specific medicines to the curing of diseases requires a good understanding of causality and as long as this understanding is not complete, the results of clinical trial studies will always be sub-optimal. One example to

© Springer International Publishing AG 2017   159
T. Marwala and E. Hurwitz, *Artificial Intelligence and Economic Theory: Skynet in the Market*, Advanced Information and Knowledge Processing,
DOI 10.1007/978-3-319-66104-9_14

illustrate this is the avocado that was thought of as being very dangerous because the causal relation between avocado consumption and cholesterol was poorly understood. Today avocado consumption is considered very healthy for one's cholesterol.

This example illustrates a very simple explanation of what a cause is and what a correlation is. On trying to understand causality, it is vital to understand the principle of correlation because within any causal model lies correlation principles.

14.2   Correlation

There is an example used by Marwala (2014) which stated that whoever is born will die implying that birth causes death. In this example, we can study the relationship between people being born and where they are after 90 years. In this example, the two variables, x indicating a vector of individuals born and each being assigned a value of 1 because they are born, and y indicating a vector of individuals whether alive or dead after 90 years with 1 indicating dead and 0 indicating alive. In this case, variable x is positively correlated to variable y. According to www.dictionary. com, correlation is defined as: "the degree to which two or more attributes or measurements on the same group of elements show a tendency to vary together". The degree to which variables vary together can be quantified. Two variables are correlated if their underlying substructures are connected. For example, if one was to measure the heart rate and blood pressure of patient John, then these parameters may be correlated primarily because they are measurements from a common super-structure and in this case a patient called John. Marwala (2014) studied a concept called the correlation machine which is a conventional predictive system that is primarily based on mapping of variables to themselves and this is called autoassociative network (Kramer 1992). This means that, whenever an input vector is presented to the network, the output is the predicted input vector. It is a process through which a system is able to recreate a complete set of information from a small piece of information. For example, one could easily complete the following statement if one is familiar with the former USA President J.F. Kennedy: "Ask not what your country can do for you but....". In order to achieve this task, the autoassociative memory is used. The autoassociative networks are sometimes called auto-encoders or memory networks. These networks have been used in a number of applications including novelty detection, image compression (Rios and Kabuka 1995) and missing data estimation (Marwala 2009). An illustration of the autoassociative network is shown in Fig. 14.1.

The principles governing the autoassociative network are as follows (Marwala 2009):

1. A correct model that describes inter-relationships that exist amongst the data variables and defines the rules that govern the data is identified. This is achieved using an autoassociative memory network.

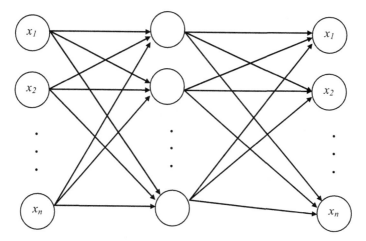

Fig. 14.1 An autoassociative network

2. In order to estimate an unknown variable(s), the correct estimated variable(s) are those that when identified, they obey all the inter-relationships that exist amongst the data as defined in Step 1 and the rules that govern the data. In order to ensure that the estimated values obey the inter-relationships in the data, an optimization method that treats the unknown variable(s) as design variable(s) and the interrelationships amongst the data and rules that govern the data as the objective to be reached, is formulated. Therefore, the unknown variable(s) estimation problem is fundamentally an optimization problem where the objective is to estimate unknown variable(s) by ensuring that the rules and interrelationships governing the data are maintained.
3. It is vital to have a good idea of the bounds that govern the unknown variable(s) in order to aid the optimization process.

14.3 Causality

According to the Oxford English dictionary, causality is defined as "the relationship between something that happens and the effect it produces" and defines a cause as "making something" while an effect is defined as "a change which is a result of an action". The cause does not necessarily have to be one dimensional. For example, in a causal relationship between sunlight, minerals, air and water causing the tree to grow, the cause has 4 dimensions as explained here and one could add more variables. Causality has also been defined in terms of counterfactuals. In this regard, if A causes B, it means one needs to establish the truthfulness of the counterfactual,

A not causing B to not be true. According to Suppes (1970), there are many different types of causes and these are *prima facie* causes, spurious causes, direct causes, supplementary causes, sufficient causes and negative causes.

According to Suppes (1970), the event B is the *prima facie* cause of event A if event A happened after event B has happened, the probability of event B happening, $p(B)$, is greater than zero and the probability of event A happening given the fact that event B has happened, $p(A|B)$, is greater than the probability of event A happening, $p(A)$. Spurious cause is the cause of an event in which an earlier cause is the real cause of the event. According to Suppes (1970), "an event $B_{t'}$ is a spurious cause of A_t if and only if $t' > t''$ exists and that there is a partition $\pi_{t''}$ such that for all elements $C_{t''}$ of $\pi_{t''}$, $t' < t$, $p(B_{t'}) > 0$, $p(A_t|B_{t'}) > p(A_t)$, $p(B_{t'}C_{t''}) > 0$ and $p(A_t|B_{t'}C_{t''}) = p(A_t|C_{t''})$". Again according to Suppes (1970), "an event $B_{t'}$ is a direct cause of A_t if and only if $B_{t'}$ is a *prima facie* cause of A_t and there is no t'' and no partition $\pi_{t''}$ such that for every $C_{t''}$ in $\pi_{t''}$, $t' < t'' < t$, $P(B_{t'}C_{t''}) > 0$ and $p(A_t|B_{t'}C_{t''}) = p(A_t|C_{t''})$". Supplementary causes are more than one cause supplementing one another to cause an event. Suppes (1970) defines $B_{t'}$ and $C_{t''}$ as supplementary causes of A_t "if and only if $B_{t'}$ is a *prima facie* cause of A_t, $C_{t''}$ is a *prima facie* cause of A_t, $p(B_{t'}C_{t''}) > 0$, $p(A|B_{t'}C_{t''}) > \max(p(A_t|B_{t'}), p(A_t|C_{t''})$". Sufficient causes are those causes that cause the event to definitely happen. Accordingly, Suppes (1970) defines that "$B_{t'}$ is a sufficient cause of A_t if and only if $B_{t'}$ is a *prima facie* cause of A_t and $p(A_t|B_{t'}) = 1$". Negative cause is an event that causes another event not to occur. According to Suppes (1970), "the event $B_{t'}$ is a *prima facie* negative cause of event A_t if and only if $t' < t$, $p(B_{t'}) > 0$ and $p(A_t|B_{t'}) < p(A_t)$".

Hume (1896) advanced the following eight principles of causality:

1. The cause and effect are connected in space and time.
2. The cause must happen before the effect.
3. There should be a continuous connectivity between the cause and effect.
4. The specific cause must at all times result in the identical effect, and the same effect should not be obtained from any other event but from the same cause.
5. Where a number of different objects give the same effect, it ought to be because of some quality which is the same amongst them.
6. The difference in the effects of two similar events must come from that which they are different.
7. When an object changes its dimensions with the change of its cause, it is a compounded effect from the combination of a number of different effects, which originate from a number of different parts of the cause.
8. An object which occurs for any time in its full exactness without any effect, is not the only cause of that effect, but needs to be aided by some other norm which may advance its effect and action.

The eight statements by Hume can be reduced to three principles with regards to causality and these are that the cause and effect are associated or correlated, that the cause happens before the effect and that the cause and effect are connected. These three factors are in essence the necessary conditions for causality.

There are a number of different theories of causality and the first one described here is the transmission theory of causality. In the transmission theory of causality, causal information is transmitted from the cause to the effect (Ehring 1986; Kistler 1998; Salmon 1984; Dowe 1992). What this transmitted information is depends on the specific case being analyzed. Because of the transmission of such information from the cause to the effect, there should be a correlation between the cause at the time of the transmission of this information and the effect at the time of the arrival of the information. In simple terms, the effect at the time of the arrival of the information is correlated to the cause at the time of the departure of the information. It is because of this reason that whenever correlation is observed, causality is wrongly inferred and human intuition has evolved such that it has learned to identify causality through correlation. This is because of the inability to detect a time lag between a cause and effect which necessarily implies causality.

The second one is the probability theory of causality, which is based on the premise that some classes of causality are probabilistic. This of course is in violation of the principle advocated by Hume, which states that the specific cause must at all times give the identical effect, and the same effect should not be obtained from any other event but from the same cause. For example, there is a controversial topic on whether *HIV causes AIDS*. There is clearly a correlation between HIV and AIDS, but not all people with HIV necessarily develop AIDS. In the deterministic world, HIV does not cause AIDS because all people who have HIV will not necessarily develop AIDS. However, in the probabilistic world, indeed HIV causes AIDS. To be precise, the statement should be framed as follows, the probability of AIDS being there given that HIV is there is very high but not necessarily 100%. Therefore, a generalized causal model is necessarily probabilistic with the deterministic version being a special case when the probability is 100%.

The third one is the causal calculus and structural learning. Suppose we would like to estimate the hypothesis that HIV causes AIDS. Causal calculus allows us to estimate the interventional probability that a person who is forced to have HIV develops AIDS which is written as $P(AIDS|forced(HIV))$ from the conditional probability $P(AIDS|HIV)$ using Bayesian networks. When this process is defined on a directed acyclic graph, it is possible to infer causal relationships amongst variables. More details on this can be found in Pearl (2000) who treated a counterfactual as a structural equation model. Causal calculus assumes that the structure that connects variables is in existence. There are cases where the structure does not exist and has to be identified from the observed data. This can be achieved by using the Bayesian networks.

The fourth one is the Granger causality which is a technique for revealing directed functional connectivity based on time series analysis of causes and effects. Suppose we have variable observations $y_k, y_{k-1}, \ldots, y_1$ and $x_{k-1}, x_{k-2}, \ldots, x_1$, then there is a causal relationship between the variables if when predicting future values of y from its past values, you get worse predictions than when you predict future values of y from its past values as well as the past values of x (Granger 1969).

The fifth one is the manipulation theories of causality. Consider causal relationships between causal variable x and effect variable y, and evaluate changes in *x* called Δ*x* and assess whether it leads to change in *y* (Δ*y*) in the model *y* = *f*(*x*). If it does, then there is a causal relationship between *x* and *y*. If this is not the case, then there is another variable which both *x* and *y* depend on.

The sixth one is the process theories of causality. Consider the causal relationship between variables *x* and *y*, and identify the actual process of causality, not its mirror. Anderson and Scott (2012) studied process causality and social context. They presented a process perspective of causality that permitted qualitative researchers to infer causal relationships from the practice settings.

Causality machine is a system that takes an input vector (*x*), which is the cause and propagates it into the effect (*y*). One example of a model that inherently exhibits causal characteristics is the multilayer perceptron. It is a feed-forward neural network model where the input variables are fed-forward until they become the effect. It, therefore, estimates a relationship between sets of input data (cause) and a set of appropriate output (effect). It is based on the standard linear perceptron and makes use of three or more layers of neurons (nodes) with non-linear activation functions, and is more powerful than the perceptron.

The multi-layer perceptron neural network has multiple layers of neural units, which are interconnected in a feed-forward configuration (Bishop 2006) and is shown in Fig. 14.2. Each neuron in one layer is directly connected to the neurons of the subsequent layer.

One of the most important questions on causation are how do we detect causation and possibly how to measure it. If we are to adopt the transmission model of causation, we could possibly observe whatever information is transmitted from the cause to the effect. Another way to sense causation is to frame a question differently by inquiring how relevant the cause is on the effect, rather than asking how the cause is transmitted into the effect. By asking the question on how relevant the cause is on the determination of the effect and ruling out correlation, this can allow one to use relevance determination models such as factor analysis to possibly sense causality.

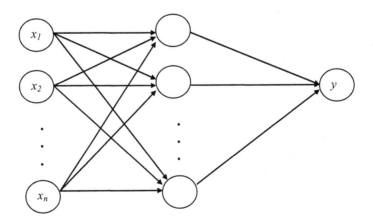

Fig. 14.2 A multi-layer perceptron neural network

14.4   Granger Causality

In Granger causality model, if there are two sets of time series variables, x and y, then relations exist between these two variables if by estimating the future values of one variable (y_{t+1}) from its previous values (y_t, ..., y_{t-p}) when compared to predicting the future values of the same variable (y_{t+1}) from the combined previous values of both variables (y_t, ..., y_{t-p} and x_t, ..., x_{t-p}), it is observed that the latter case gives more accurate results than the former case.

The first model for implementing Granger causality is to use $\{y_1, y_2, y_3, y_4\}$ to predict y_5 and then the second network is trained with input values being the combined values of $\{y_1, y_2, y_3, y_4\}$ and $\{x_1, x_2\}$ to predict y_5 as shown in Figs. 14.3 and 14.4. The accuracies of the models in Figs. 14.3 and 14.4 are then compared and if the model in Fig. 14.4 is higher than model in Fig. 14.3, then there is a Granger causality relation.

The model proposed is sensitive to the dependency between two sets of variables because the autoassociative model captures the character of the causal dynamics of the two sets of variables through the cross correlation analysis.

Given the availability of historical values of x and y, the next step is to apply system identification techniques to identify the weights that will map the input-output relationship (Bishop 2006).

14.5   Pearl Causality

This section introduces Pearl causal model, which is a model concerned with primarily inferring interventional probabilities $p(y|do(x))$ from conditional probabilities $p(y|x)$ using directed acyclic graphs (Pearl 1995). The Pearl causality model uses what is called directed acyclic graphs (DAGs), which is directed in the sense that it is pointing at a direction and if we assume the transmission theory of causality, it indicates the direction which information that emanated from the cause is taking. Furthermore, it is thought to be acyclic because it goes from one variable

Fig. 14.3 Estimation of future value of y from 4 previous values of y

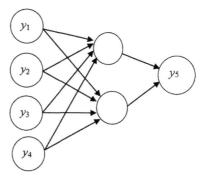

Fig. 14.4 Estimation of
future value of *y* from 4
previous values of *y* and 2
past values of *x*

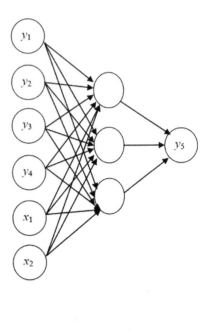

Fig. 14.5 Direct and indirect
causation

to another rather that from one variable to itself. There are three causal substructures
that define causal relationships between variables and these are direct and indirect
causation (Fig. 14.5), common cause confounding (Fig. 14.6) and a collider
(Fig. 14.7).

X and Y are conditionally dependent. Furthermore, X and Y are conditionally
independent given Z. The effect of this on causal model is that it intercepts the
causal pathway.

X and Y are conditionally dependent. Furthermore, X and Y are conditionally
independent given Z. To explain Fig. 14.7, suppose X represents the fact that it has
rained and Y represents that the sprinkler was on and Z represents the fact that the
grass is wet.

Fig. 14.6 Common cause
confounding

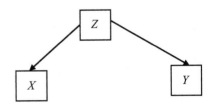

Fig. 14.7 The collider

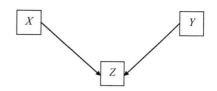

The fact that it has rained is independent from the fact that the sprinkler is on. However, if we know that the grass is wet, Z, and that it has rained, then this reduces the probability that the sprinkler was on. Therefore, the knowledge of X and Z gives us some information on Z. Therefore, for a collider, X and Y are conditionally independent. Furthermore, X and Y are conditionally dependent given Z. The effect of this on a causal model is termed endogenous selection bias. The aim of this was to identify properties of conditioning on a common effect to detect conditional independencies within layers of the conditioning variable, not obvious on DAGs without the expression of sufficient causes.

In Figs. 14.5 and 14.6, X and Y are dependent and are independent given Z and, therefore, are statistically indistinguishable from cross-sectional data. Figure 14.7 is uniquely identifiable because X and Y are independent but are dependent given Z and, therefore, can be identified from cross-sectional data.

The concept of d-separation defines conditions in which a directed acyclic graph path transmits causal information and DAGs are viable inference techniques for identifying causal relationships from conditional independence relationships (Spirtes 1996; Geiger and Pearl 2013). A path, p, is considered d-separated by a set of nodes Z if and only if:

1. p comprises a chain $x \to n \to y$ or a fork $x \leftarrow n \to y$ in such a way that the middle node n is in Z, or
2. p comprises a collider $x \leftarrow n \to y x \to n \leftarrow y$ in such a way that the middle node n is not in Z and such that no descendant of n is in Z.
3. A set Z is considered to d-separate X from Y if and only if Z blocks all paths from X to Y.

Using these rules, y and x are d-separated by z or x and y are d-separated by a collider while y, p and q are d-connected. A back-door adjustment is a procedure for estimating the probability of observing one variable y given the fact that another variable x has occurred by using conditional probabilities that relate variables x, y and z where z influences directly x and y. A variable set z meets the back-door criterion with respect to variables x_i and x_j in a DAG if none of the variables in z descend from x_i and z d-separates or blocks all paths between x_i and x_j which include arrows leading to x_i. According to Pearl (2000), a variable set z fulfils the front-door criterion with respect to variables x_i and x_j in a DAG if and only if every directed path from x_i to x_j contains variable z and there is no back-door route from x_i to z, and x_i blocks all back-door paths to x_j. There are three sets of rules that are essential in transforming conditional probabilities into interventional calculus. Of the three do-calculus rules that were identified by Pearl (2000), the first one is insertion or deletion of observation and it is based on the concept of *d*-separation. Insertion or deletion of observation (*d*-separation) does not have any consequences if the variables are conditionally independent. The second of do-calculus states that, actions and observations can be interchanged if all the back-doors are blocked. The third do-calculus rule states that inserting or deleting of actions after the action does not change anything.

14.6   Use of Do-Calculus

In South Africa in the 1800's there was a powerful King called Shaka who ruled over a nation called Zulu. He was a military general who was pre-occupied with conquest of other nations. There are many innovations that this great King introduced and was successful in his endeavors. The Zulus that this great King ruled are the same people as the Xhosas and their language as well as cultures and customs are practically identical. One of these customs that were shared by these groups was circumcision. In these groups, circumcision was usually done at the age of 18 and normally required these young men to spend a month in the forest healing from the circumcision operation. King Shaka realized that this was a waste of time for young men who according to him should be in the army conquering other nations and decided that the Zulus will no longer undergo circumcision. This basically left the Zulus still very similar to Xhosas except that the Zulus did not circumcise while the Xhosas circumcised. Another difference between Xhosas and Zulus that emerged later was that the Zulus seemed to have a higher incidence of HIV infection than the Xhosas even though the two groups remain virtually identical in all other respects. The only other explanatory variable for this difference in HIV infection rate was circumcision. Previous studies by many researchers have demonstrated that circumcision can be used to minimize HIV transmission. Given the evidence that circumcision reduces the incidence of HIV, the King of the Zulus, Goodwill Zwelithini, reintroduced circumcision in 2010. In order to study these causal relationships, Fig. 14.8 can be used.

From Fig. 14.8, we can calculate or estimate the interventional probability of a person being *HIV* positive given the fact the person is circumcized and observe that this depends on the probability that the person is sexually active, *S*, and the conditional proability that a person is HIV positive given the fact that the person is sexually active and is circumcized integrated over the number of sexual encounters.

Fig. 14.8 The DAG illustrating the relationship amongst unprotected sex, circumcision and HIV

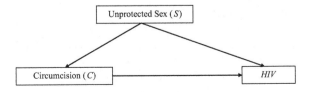

14.7 Conclusions

This chapter studied the evolution of causality including the work of David Hume on causality. It studied various concepts such as correlation and causality (transmission, Granger and Pearl models). Simple example on the link between circumcision and risk of HIV was used to illustrate these concepts.

References

Anderson GL, Scott J (2012) Toward an intersectional understanding of process causality and

Bishop C (2006) Pattern recognition and machine learning. Springer, Berlin. ISBN 0-387-31073-8

Dowe TP (1992) Wesley Salmon's process theory of causality and conserved quantity theory. Philos Sci 59:195–216

Ehring D (1986) The transference theory of causation. Synthese 67:249–258

Geiger D, Pearl J (2013) On the logic of causal models. Proceedings of the Fourth Conference on Uncertainty in Artificial Intelligence (UAI1988). ArXiv:1304.2355. Last accessed 1 May 2017

Granger CWJ (1969) Investigating causal relations by econometric models and cross-spectral methods. Econometrica 37:424–438

Hume D (1896) In: Selby-Bigge (ed) A treatise of human nature. Clarendon Press

Kistler M (1998) Reducing causality to transmission. Erkenntnis 48:1–24

Kramer MA (1992) Autoassociative neural networks. Comput Chem Eng 16(4):313–328

Marwala T (2009) Computational intelligence for missing data imputation, estimation and management: Knowledge optimization techniques Information Science Reference Imprint. IGI Global Publications, New York, USA

Marwala T (2015) Causality, correlation, and artificial intelligence for rational decision making. World Scientific, Singapore. ISBN 978-9-814-63086-3

Marwala T (2014) Artificial intelligence techniques for rational decision making. Springer, Heidelberg. ISBN 978-3-319-11423-1

Pearl J (2000) Causality: models, reasoning, and inference. Cambridge University Press

Rios A, Kabuka M (1995) Image compression with a dynamic autoassociative neural network. Math Comput Model 21(1–2):159–171

Salmon W (1984) Scientific explanation and the causal structure of the world. Princeton University Press, Princeton

Spirtes P (1996). Using d-separation to calculate zero partial correlations in linear models with correlated errors. Carnegie Mellon University Technical Report

Suppes P (1970) A probabilistic theory of causality. North-Holland Publishing Company, Amsterdam

Chapter 15
Future Work

Abstract This chapter concludes this book and summarizes the general direction of artificial intelligence and economics. It summarizes all the key concepts addressed in this book such as rational expectations and choice, bounded rationality, behavioral economics, information asymmetry, game theory, pricing, efficient market hypothesis, mechanism design, portfolio theory, rational counterfactuals, financial engineering and causality. Additionally, it evaluates how all these ideas are influenced by the advent of artificial intelligence. This chapter also studies the concept of decision making which is based on the principles of causality and correlation. Then it proposes a way of combining neoclassical, Keynesian and behavioral economics together with artificial intelligence to form a new economic theory. Furthermore, it postulates on how the interplay between advances in automation technologies and human attributes that can be automated determine a limit of the extent of automation in an economy or a firm.

15.1 Conclusions

This book presented some of the major thoughts that have pertained economics and finance in the last 300 years. These thoughts comprise of Marxist thinking, the theory of invisible hand, the theory of equilibrium and the theory of comparative advantage (Austin and Vidal-Naquet 1980; Screpanti and Zamagni 2005; Ekelund and Hébert 2007). Methods of artificial intelligence (AI) such as learning, optimization and swarm intelligence were used to better understand economic theories.

This book also examined the law of demand and supply which is the basic law of economic trade (Mankiw and Taylor 2011; Fleetwood 2014). The demand characteristics of the customer describes the relationship between price and quantity of goods, and if the price of a good is low, the customer will buy more goods and services than if the price is high. The relationship between price and the willingness of the customers to buy goods and services is called the demand curve. The other aspect of the demand and supply law is the supply curve which stipulates the relationship between the price and the quantity of goods suppliers are willing to

© Springer International Publishing AG 2017

T. Marwala and E. Hurwitz, *Artificial Intelligence and Economic Theory: Skynet in the Market*, Advanced Information and Knowledge Processing,
DOI 10.1007/978-3-319-66104-9_15

produce. For example, the higher the price the more the goods and services the suppliers are willing to produce. Conversely, the lower the price the lesser the goods and services the suppliers are willing to produce. The point at which the suppliers are willing to supply a specified quantity of goods and services, which are the same as those that the customers are willing to buy is called equilibrium. This book examined how the law of demand and supply has been changed by the advent of AI. It is observed that the advent of AI allows the opportunity for individualized demand and supply curves to be produced and reduces the degree of arbitrage in the market. Furthermore, it brings a certain degree of fairness into the market which is good for the efficiency of the economy.

The theory of rational choice was also studied in this book and it assumes that when people make decisions, they choose the option that maximizes their utility (Arrow 1989; Anand 1993; Allingham 2002; Amadae 2003). To accomplish this objective, they must use all the information obtainable and study all the choices accessible to select an optimal choice. This book explored the impact of a scenario when decisions are made by AI machines rather than human beings. The expectations of the future were found to be more reliable if they were executed by an AI machine than if they were conducted by human beings. This is because the bias and the variance of the error of the predictions were reduced by the AI machine. Additionally, the decisions that were conducted by AI machines were more rational and consequently making the marketplace to be more rational.

Rational decision making encompasses using information which is practically always imperfect and incomplete with an intelligent machine which if it is a human being, it is inconsistent to make a decision that maximizes utility (Simon 1990, 1991). For the reason that the world is imperfect, the theory of bounded rationality has been advanced. In the theory of bounded rationality, decisions are executed irrespective of the fact that the information to be used is incomplete and imperfect and that the human brain is inconsistent. Recent advances in artificial intelligence and the continual improvement of computer processing power due to Moore's law have implications for the theory of bounded rationality. These advances expand the bounds within which a rational decision making process is exercised and, thereby, increases the probability of making rational decisions.

Behavioural economics is a branch of economics which takes into account human behaviour in understanding economic phenomena (Tversky and Kahneman 1973; Kahneman and Tversky 1979; Kahneman 2011). In his book "Thinking fast and slow" Kahneman described human thought as being divided into two systems i.e. System 1 which is fast, intuitive and emotional and System 2 which is slow, rational and calculating. He further described these systems as being the basis for human reasoning or the lack thereof and the impact of these on the markets is phenomenal. With the advent of decision making using AI machines, all these effects and biases are eliminated. System 1, which is intuitive is eliminated altogether while System 2 becomes the norm. System 2 then becomes fast because contemporary computational machines work faster and faster due to Moore's Law.

Frequently, when human beings make decisions, a human agent may have more information than the other and this notion is called information asymmetry (Akerlof

1970; Spence 1973; Stiglitz and Greenwald 1986). In general, when one human agent is set to manipulate a decision to its advantage, the human agent can signal misleading information. On the other hand, one human agent can screen for information to diminish the influence of the asymmetry of information on decisions. With the advances of AI, signaling and screening are simpler to accomplish. This book investigated the impact of artificial intelligence on the theory of asymmetric information and the simulated results validated that AI agents reduce the degree of information asymmetry. This result is found to make markets more efficient. Furthermore, the more AI agents deployed in the market, the less is the volume of trades in the market because for trade to happen, asymmetry of information should exist thereby creating an arbitrage opportunity.

Game theory was also studied in this book and in game theory, agents with rules interact to obtain pay-off at an equilibrium point called Nash equilibrium (Nash 1950). Nash equilibrium is a position where interacting players in a game cannot gain any further utility by playing some more times. The advent of AI enriches the ability to simulate complex games especially by using autonomous, intelligent and adaptive agents. In this book, intelligent multi-agent system based on AI was successfully applied to study the game of Lerpa.

Pricing theory is a well-established mechanism that illustrates the constant push-and-pull of buyers versus consumers and the final semi-stable price that is found for a given good (Dewey 1939). Embedded in the theory of pricing is the theory of value. Various pricing models were considered in this book and how they are changed by advances in artificial intelligence was evaluated. The pricing models studied in this book are game theory, rational pricing, capital asset pricing model, Black-Scholes pricing model and the law of demand and supply. In game theory based pricing, AI based agents interact with each other until they reach a Nash equilibrium. Multi-agent system was found to enhance this model and, thereby, facilitating pricing. In rational pricing, pricing is conducted such that the amount of arbitrage is minimized and AI was found to improve this model. Advances in AI technique of evolutionary programming was found to improve the capital asset pricing model. AI technique of fuzzy logic was found to improve the Black-Scholes pricing model by better modelling volatility. For the law of demand and supply, the advent of artificial intelligence within the context of online shopping infrastructure resulted in individualized pricing models.

The efficient market hypothesis (in its varying forms) has allowed for the creation of financial models based on share price movements ever since its inception (Fama 1970). This book explored the impact of AI on the efficient market hypothesis and investigated theories that influence market efficiency. It was concluded that advances in AI and its applications in financial markets make markets more efficient.

In game theory, players have rules and pay-off and they interact until Nash equilibrium is attained. In this manner, we are able to observe how a game with sets of rules and a pay-off reaches Nash equilibrium. Mechanism design is the inverse of game theory and it is closely related to control systems. In mechanism design, the Nash equilibrium end-state is known and the task is to design a game (identify the rules and pay-off function) which will ensure that the desired end-state is achieved. This is done by assuming that the agents in this setting act rationally. This book discussed how AI, big data and mechanism design offer exciting avenues for economics.

The basis of portfolio theory is rooted in statistical models based on Brownian motion (Markowitz 1952; Hurwitz 2014). These models are surprisingly naïve in their assumptions and resultant application within the trading community. The application of AI to portfolio theory has broad and far-reaching consequences. AI allows us to model price movements with much greater accuracy than the random-walk nature of the original Markowitz model, while optimizing a portfolio can be performed with greater optimality and efficiency using evolutionary computation. In this book, a portfolio rebalancing method was described and AI was applied for portfolio rebalancing problem to achieve the results demanded by investors within the framework of portfolio theory.

The concept of rational counterfactuals is an idea of identifying a counterfactual from the factual (whether perceived or real), and knowledge of the laws that govern the relationships between the antecedent and the consequent, that maximizes the attainment of the desired consequent (Marwala 2015). In counterfactual thinking, factual statements like: 'Greece was not financially prudent and consequently its finances are in tatters', and with its counterfactual being: 'Greece was financially prudent and consequently its finances are in good shape'. This chapter used AI to build rational counterfactuals.

Financial engineering has grown with the advents of computing and this growth has accelerated in the last decade with the growth of artificial intelligence (Marwala 2013). This book explored how AI is changing the effectiveness of quantitative finance. This book explored the problem of estimating risk, simulating the stock market using multi-agent systems, applying control systems to inflation targeting and factor analysis. The results demonstrated that AI improves the estimation of risk, makes stock markets more homogeneous and efficient, is a good basis for building models that target inflation and enhances the identification of factors that drive inflation.

Causality is a powerful concept which is at the heart of markets (Marwala 2015). Often, one wants to establish whether a particular attribute causes another. Often as human beings, we have perceived causality through correlation. Because of this fact, causality has often been confused for correlation. This book investigated the evolution of causality including the influential work of David Hume and its relevance to economics and finance. It investigated a number of concepts and models of causality such as transmission as well as Granger and Pearl models of causality. The transmission model of causality states that for causality to exist, there should be a flow of information from the cause to the effect. Simple example of the study of the link between circumcision and risk of HIV were used. HIV risk was used because it has serious consequences for the economies of nations.

15.2 Decision Theory

Decision theory is a theory of choice and this book has explored various mechanisms for making decisions. The first group of mechanisms is based on the theory of rationality. The limitation of rationality in decision making is then encountered due to the developments in the theory of bounded rationality and behavioral economics. Game theory and mechanism design were presented as aids for decision making. The causal decision making based on the theory of counterfactuals was also presented. A generalized decision making framework based on AI which encompasses causality, correlation, counterfactuals and rationality can be developed.

When decision making is made, there are few factors that are important and these are information, various decision options, prediction of the future and selection of the optimal decision. Making decisions require information and information requires processing. Advances in information processing makes the processing of information easier to handle. Some of the information processing methods are in the time domain, frequency domain such as the Fourier transform and time-frequency domain such as wavelet transform. The second aspect of decision making is the generation of options. For example, if the objective is to fly from London to Brussels at a cost effective manner, the options would be to fly there directly or to fly from London to Holland to Brussels or to fly from London to Berlin to Holland. All these are options because they are viable trips. AI is able to efficiently generate these options. The other factor that should be taken into account is the prediction of the implication of each option in terms of its respective utilities. Because these options have not yet been executed and that they will only be executed sometime in the future, there is an element of the prediction of the future implications of these options. Rational expectations is a theory that has been used extensively to predict the future in an unbiased way. Again, AI is a tool that has been successfully used to achieve this because it is able to fuse information from different sources such as text, voice, images etc. The selection of an optimal solution requires one to be able to compute respective utilities and in an easier scenario, one only chooses the option that gives the most utility. However, in complex examples, there are numerous options and, therefore, it is necessary to use some complicated AI optimization method to select the optimal solution.

There are other decision making procedures that are important to take into account. For example, one can use Bayesian statistics to build the theory of rational expectations. In Bayesian statistics, one evaluates the probability of action X happening given the fact that action Y has happened, which is equivalent to the probability of Y happening given that X has happened multiplied by the probability of X happening divided by the probability of Y happening. In this way, future expectations are interpreted probabilistically and, therefore, allowing for probabilistically building future expectations (Bernardo 1979). There are other non-probabilistic methods that are able to achieve the same goal such as possibilistic models e.g. fuzzy logic.

15.3   Developmental Economics

In developmental economics there is a theory, which was developed by Nobel Laureate Arthur Lewis, which prescribes how countries can move from a developing to a developed state (Lewis 1954, 2003). In this theory, suppose in a country there are many people who are located in the subsistence economy (e.g. 80%), and this is called the second world economy, and 20% in the formal advanced economy, which is called the first world economy. The first world economy can then absorb 10% from the second world economy, without the need to increase the wages of the first world economy. The profits in the first world economy that are obtained from the introduction of 10% of labor from the second world economy can be used to improve the productive forces of the first world economy and thus advance capital formation. This can be repeated until such that it is no longer economically beneficial to migrate labor from the second world economy to the first world economy and the only way the first world economy can expand capital is by increasing the cost of labor in the first world economy and this point is called the Lewis turning point. This model was used by China, to expand its productive forces by bringing cheap labor from the hinterland to the first world economy without much increase in the aggregate cost of labor. Now the aggregate cost of labor in China is increasing because China has reached its Lewis turning point.

Arthur Lewis theory can be used to understand the development of the economy into the fourth industrial revolution where absolutely everything in the economy will be automated by artificial intelligent agents and other related technologies. In this scenario, a point of equilibrium is when it does not make economic sense for labor to move from humans to machines. There are various reasons why not all labor can possibly be automated and these include the fact that some human capabilities are simply too expensive or difficult to automate. These include attributes such as judgment and empathy. On the other hand, there is a limit in technological progress and as such there comes a point where technological progress can no longer return sufficient marginal profits. Some of the limits of technological progress include physical laws such as the fact that the most efficient heat engine, which is the Carnot engine, is only 33% efficient and this is practically unreachable. The interplay between technological progress on the one hand and difficulties in automating certain human capabilities on the other hand, determines the maximum levels of automation that are attainable. And once this equilibrium is reached, automation stops expanding. Thus, to paraphrase Arthur Lewis, in the area of automation, the turning point is a point where the surplus human labor reaches a financial zero. This theory is applicable to both microeconomics (in the case of a firm) and macroeconomics (in the case of a country).

15.4 New Economic Theory

Classical economics is based on the idea of a self-organizing economic system that is guided by the principle of the invisible hand (Smith 1776). The concept of self-organization is a complex notion that has been observed in nature. For example, swarm of bees self-organize themselves such that they work tirelessly for the queen bee (Michener 2000). These worker bees are assigned tasks and they even have a caste system. They have a goal and that is to take care of the queen bee. The unintended consequence of their actions is that in doing their work, they are crucial for pollination, a concept that forms a key aspect of our ecosystem. Adam Smith thought the economy of the country can self-organize itself with the resulting emergent behaviour being the greater good of its population. He further postulated that the greater good can be achieved even though the individuals are acting to maximize their own utility. The value of goods and services in classical economics is the cost of labour and the cost of materials. Embedded in the classical economics is free competition and free trade. What can go wrong in self-organization? People can capture states for their own selfish reasons and the resulting effect is not the greater good for the population but the impoverishment of a nation. On pursuing their individual wants, human rights can be violated and child labor can be used resulting in the reduction of the collective happiness of the population. Inequality can result from unchecked classical economy. Adam Smith's invisible hand in the economy is not as guided as that of the swarm of bees and perhaps it is because the social organization of the social bees has evolved over hundred thousand years whereas that of the economic system only at best few thousand years.

Neoclassical economics is based on the principle of rationality where each individual acts to maximize utility and the principle of value depends on the individual and this has an impact on the principles of demand and supply (Kauder 1953). Neoclassical economics uses mathematics to study economic phenomena and is the dominant economic approach. Neoclassical economics claims that these processes of customers acting in order to maximize their wants leads to efficient allocation of capital. This approach to economics has a number of problems such as the fact that human agents are not rational and, therefore, the concepts of rational choice and efficient markets are limited and to use the words of Herbert Simon, bounded rationally. The other criticism directed at neoclassical economics is from Keynesian economics where state intervention is advocated.

Keynesian economics was developed by John Maynard Keynes primarily to explain what happened in the Great depression (Keynes 1936). Keynes advocated increased government spending and lower taxes to stimulate aggregate demand and increase economic expansion. This is in contrast with classical economics which advocated that cyclical changes in the economics are self-correcting. In this regard, when the aggregate demand is low, then the wages will be low and this will stimulate production which will in turn expand economic activities and thus ulti-mately adjust the aggregate demand.

Behavioural economics is based on the principles of psychology (Kahneman 2011). Neoclassical economics has faced a number of criticisms especially from behavioural economics, which basically states that human beings are governed by the field of psychology and, therefore, they have fears, prejudices, biases and are often irrational and, therefore, all these factors must be taken into account when studying economics.

Artificial intelligence has ushered new forms of decision makers such that the concept of homo economica is more and more merged with machines along the lines of cyber-physical-biological systems. A new economic system that accounts for the emergence of man-machine systems needs to be developed.

References

Akerlof GA (1970) The market for 'lemons': quality uncertainty and the market mechanism. Quart J Econ 84(3):488–500

Allingham M (2002) Choice theory: a very short introduction, Oxford

Amadae SM (2003) Rationalizing capitalist democracy: the cold war origins of rational choice liberalism. University of Chicago Press, Chicago

Anand P (1993) Foundations of rational choice under risk. Oxford University Press, Oxford

Arrow KJ (1989) Economic theory and the hypothesis of rationality. in The New Palgrave

Austin MM, Vidal-Naquet P (1980) Economic and social history of Ancient Greece. University of California Press

Bernardo JM (1979) Reference posterior distributions for Bayesian inference. J Royal Stat Soc 41:113–147

Dewey J (1939) Theory of valuation. University of Chicago, USA

Ekelund RB Jr, Hébert RF (2007) A history of economic theory and method. Waveland Press

Fama E (1970) Efficient capital markets: a review of theory and empirical work. J Financ 25 (2):383–417

Fleetwood S (2014) Do labour supply and demand curves exist? Camb J Econ 38(5):1087–1113

Hurwitz E (2014) Efficient portfolio optimization by hybridized machine learning. Doctoral Thesis, University of Johannesburg

Kahneman K (2011) Thinking. Macmillan, Fast and Slow

Kahneman D, Tversky A (1979) Prospect theory: an analysis of decision under risk. Econometrica 47(2):263

Kauder E (1953) Genesis of the marginal utility theory from aristotle to the end of the eighteenth century. Econ J 63:638–650

Keynes JM (1936) The general theory of employment, interest and money. Macmillan, London

Lewis WA (2003) The theory of economic growth. Taylor and Francis, London

Lewis WA (1954) Economic development with unlimited supplies of labour. Manch Sch 22: 139–191

Mankiw NG, Taylor MP (2011) Economics (2nd edn, revised edn). Cengage Learning, Andover

Markowitz HM (1952) Portfolio selection. J Financ 7(1):77–91

Marwala T (2015) Causality, correlation, and artificial intelligence for rational decision making. World Scientific, Singapore

Marwala T (2013) Economic modeling using artificial intelligence methods. Springer, Heidelberg

Michener CD (2000) The bees of the world. Johns Hopkins University Press

Nash JF (1950) Non-cooperative games. PhD thesis, Princeton University

Screpanti E, Zamagni S (2005) An outline of the history of economic thought (2nd edn). Oxford University Press

Simon H (1990) A mechanism for social selection and successful altruism. Science 250 (4988):1665–1668

Simon H (1991) Bounded rationality and organizational learning. Organ Sci 2(1):125–134

Smith A (1776) An inquiry into the nature and causes of the wealth of nations. 1(1edn). W. Strahan, London

Spence M (1973) Job market signaling. Q J Econ 87(3):355–374 The MIT Press

Stiglitz JE, Greenwald BC (1986) Externalities in economies with imperfect information and incomplete markets. Quart J Econ 101(2):229–264

Tversky A, Kahneman D (1973) Availability: a heuristic for judging frequency and probability. Cogn Psychol 5(2):207–232

Appendix A
Multi-layer Perceptron Neural Network

A *neural network* is an information processing technique that is inspired by the way biological nervous systems, like the human brain, process information (Haykin 1999; Marwala 2012). It is a computer based procedure, designed to model the way in which the brain performs a particular function of interest. A multi-layer perceptron neural network is viewed as generalized regression model that can model both linear and non-linear data (Marwala 2009, 2012). The construction of a neural network involves four main steps (Haykin 1999; Marwala 2012):

- the processing units u_j, where each u_j has a certain activation level $a_j(t)$ at any point in time;
- weighted inter-connections between a number of processing units;
- an activation rule, which acts on the set of input signals at a processing unit to produce a new output signal; and
- a learning rule that stipulates how to update the weights for a given input or output.

A trained neural network can be viewed as an expert in the class of information that it has been given to analyze. This expert can then be applied to offer predictions when presented with new circumstances. Because of its ability to adapt to non-linear data, neural network has been applied to model a number of non-linear applications. The architecture of neural processing units and their inter-connections can have a significant influence on the processing capabilities of a neural network. Accordingly, there are many different connections that define how data flows between the input, hidden and output layers.

Neural network has been successfully applied to both classification and regression problems. It is a broad structure for describing non-linear mappings between multi-dimensional spaces where the form of the mapping is overseen by a set of free parameters (Bishop 1995) which are estimated from the data.

In the architecture of the MLP, each connection between inputs and neurons is weighted by adjustable weight parameters. In addition, each neuron has an adjustable bias weight parameter which is denoted by a connection from a constant input $x_0 = 1$ and $z_0 = 1$ for the hidden neurons and the output neuron, respectively.

© Springer International Publishing AG 2017
T. Marwala and E. Hurwitz, *Artificial Intelligence and Economic Theory: Skynet in the Market*, Advanced Information and Knowledge Processing,
DOI 10.1007/978-3-319-66104-9

The advantage of a multi-layer perceptron network is the interconnected cross-coupling that occurs between the input variables and the hidden nodes, with the hidden nodes and the output variables. If we assume that x is the input to the multi-layer perceptron and y is the output of the MLP, a mapping function between the input and the output may be written as follows (Bishop 1995):

$$y = f_{\text{output}} \left(\sum_{j=1}^{M} w_j f_{\text{hidden}} \left(\sum_{i=0}^{N} w_{ij} x_i \right) + w_0 \right) \qquad (A.1)$$

here:

- N is the number of inputs units;
- M is the number of hidden neurons;
- x_i is the ith input unit;
- w_{ij} is the weight parameter between input i and hidden neuron j; and
- w_j is the weight parameter between hidden neuron j and the output neuron.

The activation function $f_{\text{output}}(\cdot)$ is sigmoid and can be written as follows (Bishop, 1995):

$$f_{output}(a) = \frac{1}{1 + e^{-a}} \qquad (A.2)$$

The activation function $f_{\text{hidden}}(\cdot)$ can be any complex function. The weights, of the neural network in Eq. A.1, are estimated by minimizing the error between the prediction of Eq. A.1 and the observed data.

The process of identifying a minimum error is conducted through methods that are classified as optimization techniques. Traditionally optimization has been performed by identifying the gradient of the function to be optimized and then equating this to zero and solving for the design variables (here network weights). In many practical problems, this is not possible and, consequently, techniques such as gradient descent and conjugate gradient methods have been developed to tackle this problem (Bishop 1995). These techniques rely on the accurate estimation of the gradient of the error and methods to achieve this are described in detail by Bishop (1995). Alternatively, instead of estimating the network weights that minimize the error, probability distributions of the network weights are identified. Methods that are based on Bayesian statistics such as the Markov Chain Monte Carlo simulation have been developed to estimate the network weights probability distributions. Again more details on these can also be found in a book by Bishop (1995). Evolutionary computation is a new class of algorithms that is inspired by natural and biological phenomena and these include particle swarm optimization as well as genetic algorithm and they too can be used for optimization. An overview of these techniques was conducted in a book by Marwala (2009).

References

Bishop CM (1995) Neural networks for pattern recognition. Oxford University Press, Oxford
Haykin S (1999) Neural networks. Prentice-Hall, NJ
Marwala T (2009) Computational intelligence for missing data imputation, estimation and management: knowledge optimization techniques. IGI Global Publications, NY
Marwala T (2012) Condition monitoring using computational intelligence methods. Springer, Heidelberg

Appendix B
Particle Swarm Optimization

Particle swarm optimization (PSO) is a stochastic, population-based evolutionary algorithm that is used for optimization. It is based on socio-psychological principles that are inspired by swarm intelligence, which offers understanding into social behavior. Society enables an individual to maintain cognitive robustness through influence and learning. Individuals learn to tackle problems by communicating and interacting with other individuals and, thereby, develop a generally similar way of tackling problems (Engelbrecht 2005; Marwala 2010). Swarm intelligence is driven by two factors: group knowledge and individual knowledge. Each member of a swarm acts by balancing between its individual knowledge and the group knowledge.

To solve optimization problems using particle swarm optimization, a fitness function is constructed to describe a measure of the desired outcome. To reach an optimum solution, a social network representing a population of possible solutions is defined and randomly generated. The individuals within this social network are assigned neighbors to interact with. These individuals are called particles, hence the name particle swarm optimization. Thereafter, a process to update these particles is initiated. This is conducted by evaluating the fitness of each particle. Each particle can remember the location where it had its best success as measured by the fitness function. The best solution of the particle is named the *local best* and each particle makes this information on the local best accessible to their neighbors and in turn observe their neighbors' success. The process of moving in the search space is guided by these successes and the population ultimately converges by the end of the simulation on an optimum solution.

The PSO technique was developed by Kennedy and Eberhart (1995). This procedure was inspired by algorithms that model the "flocking behavior" seen in birds. Researchers in artificial life (Reynolds 1987; Heppner and Grenander 1990) developed simulations of bird flocking. In the context of optimization, the concept of birds finding a roost is analogous to a process of finding an optimal solution. Particle swarm optimization has been very successful in optimizing complex problems.

PSO is applied by finding a balance between searching for a good solution and exploiting other particles' success. If the search for a solution is too limited, the simulation will converge to the first solution encountered, which may be a local

© Springer International Publishing AG 2017
T. Marwala and E. Hurwitz, *Artificial Intelligence and Economic Theory: Skynet in the Market*, Advanced Information and Knowledge Processing,
DOI 10.1007/978-3-319-66104-9

optimum position. If the successes of others are not exploited then the simulation will never converge.

When using PSO, the simulation is initialized with a population of random candidates, each conceptualized as particles. Each particle is assigned a random velocity and is iteratively moved through the particle space. At each step, the particle is attracted towards a region of the best fitness function by the location of the best fitness achieved so far in the population. On implementing the PSO, each particle is represented by two vectors: $p_i(k)$, which is the position of particle i at step k; and $v_i(k)$, which is the velocity of particle i at step k.

Initial positions and velocities of particles are randomly generated and the subsequent positions and velocities are calculated using the position of the best solution that a particular particle has encountered during the simulation called $pbest_i$ and the best particle in the swarm, which is called $gbest(k)$. The subsequent velocity of a particle i can be identified as:

$$v_i(k+1) = \gamma v_i(k) + c_1 r_1 (pbest_i - p_i(k)) + c_2 r_2 (gbest(k) - p_i(k)) \qquad (B.1)$$

where γ is the inertia of the particle, c_1 and c_2 are the 'trust' parameters, and r_1 and r_2 are random numbers between 0 and 1.

In Eq. B.1, the first term is the current motion, the second term is the particle memory influence and the third term is the swarm influence. The subsequent position of a particle i can be calculated using:

$$p_i(k+1) = p_i(k) + v_i(k+1) \qquad (B.2)$$

The inertia of the particle controls the impact of the previous velocity of the particle on the current velocity. These parameters control the exploratory properties of the simulation with a high value of inertia encouraging global exploration while a low value of the inertia encourages local exploration.

The parameters c_1 and c_2 are trust parameters. The trust parameter c_1 indicates how much confidence the current particle has on itself while the trust parameter c_2 indicates how much confidence the current particle has on the successes of the population. The parameters r_1 and r_2 are random numbers between 0 and 1 and they determine the degree to which the simulation should explore the space.

The position of the particle is updated, based on the social behavior of the particles' population and it adapts to the environment by continually coming back to the most promising region identified.

References

Engelbrecht AP (2005) Fundamentals of computational swarm intelligence. Wiley, London
Heppner F, Grenander U (1990) A stochastic non-linear model for coordinated bird flocks. In: Krasner S (ed) The ubiquity of Chaos, 1st edn. AAAS Publications, Washington DC

Kennedy JE, Eberhart RC (1995) Particle swarm optimization. In: Proceedings of the IEEE international conference on neural network, pp 942–1948

Marwala T (2010) Finite element model updating using computational intelligence techniques. Springer, London

Reynolds CW (1987) Flocks, herds and schools: a distributed behavioral model. Comput Graphics 2:25–34

Appendix C
Simulated Annealing

C.1 Simulated Annealing

Simulated Annealing (SA) is a Monte Carlo method that is used to identify an optimal solution (Marwala 2010). Simulated annealing was first applied to optimization problems by Kirkpatrick et al. (1983). It is inspired by the process of annealing where objects, such as metals, recrystallize or liquids freeze. In the annealing process, a metal object is heated until it is molten and then its temperature is slowly decreased such that the metal, at any given time, is approximately in thermodynamic equilibrium. As the temperature of the object is lowered, the system becomes more ordered and approaches a *frozen* state at $T = 0$. If the cooling process is conducted inadequately or the initial temperature of the object is not sufficiently high, the system may become quenched, forming defects or freezing out in meta-stable states. This indicates that the system is trapped in a local minimum energy state.

The process that is followed to simulate the annealing process was proposed by Metropolis et al. (1953) and it involves choosing an initial state and temperature, and holding temperature constant, perturbing the initial configuration and computing the error at the new state. If the new error is lower than the old error then the new state is accepted, otherwise if the opposite is the case, then this state is accepted with a low probability. This is essentially a Monte Carlo method.

The SA technique replaces a current solution with a "nearby" random solution with a probability that depends on the difference between the corresponding fitness function values and the temperature. The temperature decreases throughout the process, so as temperature starts approaching zero, there is less random changes in the solution. The SA technique keeps moving towards the best solution and has the advantage of reversal in fitness. The SA technique identifies the global optimum if specified, but it can take an infinite amount of time to achieve this. The probability of accepting the reversal is given by Boltzmann's equation (Bryan et al. 2006):

$$P(\Delta E) = \frac{1}{Z} \exp\left(-\frac{\Delta E}{T}\right) \tag{C.1}$$

© Springer International Publishing AG 2017
T. Marwala and E. Hurwitz, *Artificial Intelligence and Economic Theory: Skynet in the Market*, Advanced Information and Knowledge Processing,
DOI 10.1007/978-3-319-66104-9

here ΔE is the difference in error between the old and new states. T is the temperature of the system; Z is a normalization factor that ensures that when the probability function is integrated to infinity it becomes 1. The rate at which the temperature decreases depends on the cooling schedule chosen.

C.2   Simulated Annealing Parameters

On implementing simulated annealing, several parameters and choices need to be specified. These are the state space, which are the variables to be estimated; the objective or cost function; the candidate generator mechanism which is a random number; the acceptance probability function; and the annealing temperature schedule. The choice of these parameters has far-reaching consequences on the effectiveness of the SA technique as far as identifying an optimal solution is concerned.

C.3   Transition Probabilities

When simulated annealing is implemented, a random walk process is embarked upon for a given temperature. This random walk process entails moving from one temperature to another. The transition probability is the probability of moving from one state to another. This probability is dependant on the present temperature, the order of generating the candidate moves, and the acceptance probability function. A Markov Chain Monte Carlo (MCMC) method is used to make a transition from one state to another by creating a chain of states and accepting or rejecting them using the Metropolis algorithm.

C.4   Monte Carlo Method

The Monte Carlo (MC) method is a computational method that uses repeated random sampling to calculate a result (Mathe and Novak 2007). MC methods have been used for simulating physical and mathematical systems. The Monte Carlo method is usually used when it is not possible or not feasible to compute an exact solution using a deterministic algorithm.

C.5 Markov Chain Monte Carlo

The Markov Chain Monte Carlo (MCMC) method is a process of simulating a chain of states through a random walk process. It consists of a Markov process and a Monte Carlo simulation (Liesenfeld and Richard 2008). Here a system is now considered whose evolution is described by a stochastic process consisting of random variables $\{x_1, x_2, x_3, \ldots, x_i\}$. A random variable x_i occupies a state x at discrete time i. The list of all possible states that all random variables can possibly occupy is called a state space. If the probability that the system is in state x_{i+1} at time $i + 1$ depends completely on the fact that it was in state x_i at time i, then the random variables $\{x_1, x_2, x_3, \ldots, x_i\}$ form a Markov chain. In the Markov Chain Monte Carlo, the transition between states is achieved by adding a random noise (ε) to the current state as follows:

$$x_{i+1} = x_i + \varepsilon \tag{C.2}$$

C.6 Acceptance Probability Function Metropolis Algorithm

When the current state has been achieved, it is either accepted or rejected using methods such as the Metropolis algorithm (Bedard 2008). This algorithm which was invented by Metropolis et al. (1953) has been used extensively to solve problems of statistical mechanics. In the Metropolis algorithm, on sampling a stochastic process $\{x_1, x_2, x_3, \ldots, x_i\}$ consisting of random variables, random changes to x are considered and are either accepted or rejected according to the following criterion:

$$
\begin{aligned}
&\textit{if } E_{new} < E_{old} \textit{ accept state } (s_{new}) \\
&\textit{else} \\
&\textit{accept } (s_{new}) \textit{ with probability} \\
&\exp\{-(E_{new} - E_{old})\}
\end{aligned}
\tag{C.3}
$$

C.7 Cooling Schedule

A *Cooling scheduling* is the process through which the temperature T should be reduced during simulated annealing (De Vicente et al. 2003). Lessons from the physical simulated annealing dictate that the cooling rate should be sufficiently low for the probability distribution of the present state to be close to the thermodynamic equilibrium at all times during the simulation. The time it takes during the simulation for the equilibrium to be achieved after a change in temperature depends on the shape of the objective function, the present temperature and the candidate generator.

References

Bedard M (2008) Optimal acceptance rates for metropolis algorithms: moving beyond 0.234. Stoch Process Appl 118:2198–2222

Bryan K, Cunningham P, Bolshkova N (2006) Application of simulated annealing to the biclustering of gene expression data. IEEE Trans Inf Technol Biomed 10519–10525

De Vicente J, Lanchares J, Hermida R (2003) Placement by thermodynamic simulated annealing. Phys Lett A 317:415–423

Kirkpatrick S, Gelatt CD, Vecchi MP (1983) Optimization by simulated annealing. Sci New Ser 220:671–680

Liesenfeld R, Richard J (2008) Improving MCMC, using efficient importance sampling. Comput Stat Data Anal 53:272–288

Marwala T (2010) Finite element model updating using computational intelligence techniques. Springer, London

Mathe P, Novak E (2007) Simple monte carlo and the metropolis algorithm. J Complex 23:673–696

Metropolis N, Rosenbluth A, Rosenbluth M, Teller A, Teller E (1953) Equation of state calculations by fast computing machines. J Chem Phys 21:1087–1092

Appendix D
Genetic Algorithms

D.1 Genetic Algorithms

Genetic algorithm (GA) is a population-based, probabilistic method that operates to find a solution to a problem from a population of possible solutions (Goldberg 1989; Holland 1975; Marwala 2010). It is applied to identify approximate solutions to difficult problems through the analogy of the principles of evolutionary biology to computer science (Michalewicz 1996; Mitchell 1996). It was inspired by Darwin's theory of evolution where members of the population compete to survive and reproduce whereas the weaker members are eliminated from the population. Every individual is allocated a fitness value according to how well it satisfies the objective of solving the problem. New and more evolutionary-fit individual solutions are produced during a cycle of generations, where selection and recombination operations take place, similar to how gene transfer happens to the current individuals. This continues until a termination condition is satisfied, after which the best individual thus far is considered to be the estimation for missing data. GA views learning as a competition between populations of evolving candidate problem solutions. The fitness function evaluates each solution to decide whether it will contribute to the next generation of solutions. Through operations analogous to gene transfer in sexual reproduction, the algorithm creates a new population of candidate solutions (Goldberg 1989).

D.2 Initialization

In the beginning, a large number of possible individual solutions are randomly generated to form an initial population. This initial population is sampled so that it covers a good representation of the updating solution space. The size of the population depends on the nature of the problem.

© Springer International Publishing AG 2017

T. Marwala and E. Hurwitz, *Artificial Intelligence and Economic Theory: Skynet in the Market*, Advanced Information and Knowledge Processing, DOI 10.1007/978-3-319-66104-9

D.3 Crossover

The crossover operator fuses genetic information in the population by cutting pairs of chromosomes at random points along their length and swapping the cut sections over. This has a potential for assembling successful operators (Gwiazda 2006). Crossover occurs with a certain probability. For simple crossover, one crossover point is chosen, a binary string from the beginning of a chromosome to the crossover point is copied from one parent, and the rest is copied from the second parent. For instance, if two chromosomes in binary space $a = 11001011$ and $b = 11011111$ undertake a one-point crossover at the midpoint, then the resulting offspring is $c = 11001111$. For arithmetic crossover, a mathematical operator is performed to make an offspring. For example, an AND operator can be executed on $a = 11001011$ and $b = 11011111$ to create an offspring 11001011.

D.4 Mutation

The *mutation* operator chooses a binary digit in the chromosomes at random and inverts it. This has a potential of adding new information to the population, and in so doing avoids the GA simulation from being trapped in a local optimum solution. Mutation takes place with a certain probability. In many natural systems, the probability of mutation is low (i.e., less than 1%) (Goldberg 1989). When binary mutation is applied, a number written in binary form was selected and one bit value was inverted. For instance: the chromosome 11001011 may become the chromosome 11000011. Non-uniform mutation operates by increasing the probability of mutation such that it will approximate 0 as the generation number increases adequately. It avoids the population from stagnating in the early stages of the evolution process, and then allows the procedure to improve the solution in the end stages of the evolution.

D.5 Selection

For each generation, a selection of the proportion of the existing population is selected to breed a new population. This selection is accomplished by using the fitness-based procedure, where solutions that are fitter are given a higher probability of being chosen. Some selection approaches rank the fitness of each solution and select the best solutions, whereas other techniques rank a randomly selected sample of the population for computational efficiency. Numerous selection functions have a tendency to be stochastic in nature and are, therefore, designed such that a selection procedure is performed on a small proportion of less fit solutions. This ensures that diversity of the population of possible solutions is preserved at a high level and, consequently, avoids convergence on poor and incorrect solutions.

D.6 Termination

The procedure explained is recurred until a termination criterion has been realized, either because a desired solution that meets the objective function was identified or because a stated number of generations has been achieved or the solution's fitness has converged (or any combination of these).

References

Holland J (1975) Adaptation in natural and artificial systems. University of Michigan Press, Ann Arbor

Goldberg DE (1989) Genetic algorithms in search, optimization and machine learning. Addison-Wesley, Reading

Gwiazda TD (2006) A Genetic algorithms reference Vol. 1 cross-over for single-objective numerical optimization problems. Adobe eBook, Lomianki

Holland J (1975) Adaptation in natural and artificial systems. University of Michigan Press, Ann Arbor

Marwala T (2010) Finite element model updating using computational intelligence techniques. Springer, London

Michalewicz Z (1996) Genetic algorithms + data structures = evolution programs. Springer, NY

Mitchell M (1996) An introduction to genetic algorithms. MIT Press, Cambridge

Appendix E
Fuzzy Logic

Fuzzy logic is a procedure that relates an antecedent to a consequent using linguistic rules entailing the *if-then* statements (von Altrock 1995; Cox 1994). It consists of four objects: fuzzy sets, membership functions, fuzzy logic operators and fuzzy rules. In classical set theory a set is either an element or is not an element of a set (Johnson 1972). Accordingly, it is possible to explain if an object is an element of a set because of clear boundaries. Classically a characteristic function of a set has a value of 1 if the object is an element of that set and a value of zero if the object doesn't belong to the set (Cantor 1874). In this regard, there is no middle road in terms of membership or non-membership of a set.

Fuzzy logic offers a flexible representation of sets of objects by introducing a concept of a fuzzy set which does not have as clear cut boundaries as a classical set and the objects have a degree of membership to a particular set (Wright and Marwala 2006). A membership function defines the degree that an object is a member of a set. The membership function is a curve that maps the antecedent space variable to a number between 0 and 1, representing the degree to which an object is a member of a set. A membership function can be a curve of any shape. For example, if we are studying the problem of height, there would be two subsets one for tall and one for short that overlap. Accordingly, a person can have a partial membership in each of these sets, therefore, determining the degree to which the person is both tall and short.

Logical operators are applied to create new fuzzy sets from the existing fuzzy sets. Classical set theory offers three basic operators for logical expressions to be defined: intersection, union and the complement (Kosko and Isaka 1993). These operators are also applied in fuzzy logic and have been adapted to deal with partial memberships. The intersection (AND operator) of two fuzzy sets is given by a minimum operation and the union (OR operator) of two fuzzy sets is given by a maximum operation. These logical operators are applied to determine the final consequent fuzzy set.

Using fuzzy rules conditional statements which are applied to model the antecedent-consequent relationships of the system expressed in natural language are created. These linguistic rules which are expressed in the *if-then statements* use

© Springer International Publishing AG 2017
T. Marwala and E. Hurwitz, *Artificial Intelligence and Economic Theory: Skynet in the Market*, Advanced Information and Knowledge Processing,
DOI 10.1007/978-3-319-66104-9

logical operators and membership functions to infer consequents. A characteristic of fuzzy logic are linguistic variables which use words or sentences as their values instead of numbers (Zadeh 1965; Zemankova-Leech 1983; Lagazio and Marwala 2011). As described by Marwala and Lagazio (2011), linguistic variable *weight* can be assigned the following set values {*very fat, fat, medium, thin, very thin*} and then a fuzzy rule is of the form:

$$\textbf{if } x \textbf{ is } A \textbf{ then } y \textbf{ is } B \qquad\qquad (E.1)$$

where A and B are fuzzy sets defined for the antecedent and consequent space, respectively. Both x and y are linguistic variables, while A and B are linguistic values expressed by applying membership functions. Each rule consists of two parts: the antecedent and the consequent. The antecedent is the component of the rule falling between the *if-then* and maps the antecedent x to the fuzzy set A, applying a membership function. The consequent is the component of the rule after the then, and maps the consequent y to a membership function. The antecedent membership values act like weighting factors to determine their influence on the fuzzy consequent sets. A fuzzy system consists of a list of these *if-then* rules which are evaluated in parallel. The antecedent can have more than one linguistic variable, these antecedents are combined by applying the AND operator.

Each of the rules is evaluated for an antecedent set, and corresponding consequent for the rule obtained. If an antecedent corresponds to two linguistic variables then the rules associated with both these variables will be evaluated. Also, the rest of the rules will be evaluated, however, they will not have an effect on the final result as the linguistic variable will have a value of zero. Therefore, if the antecedent is true to some degree, the consequent will have to be true to some degree (Zadeh 1965). The degree of each linguistic consequent value is then computed by performing a combined logical sum for each membership function (Zadeh 1965) after which all the combined sums for a specific linguistic variable can be combined. These last steps involve the use of an inference method which maps the result onto a consequent membership function (Zadeh 1965; Mamdani 1974).

Finally, de-fuzzification process is performed where a single numeric consequent is produced. One method of estimating the degree of each linguistic consequent value is to take the maximum of all rules describing this linguistic consequent value, and the consequent is taken as the center of gravity of the area under the effected part of the consequent membership function. There are other inference methods such as averaging and sum of mean of squares. The application of a series of fuzzy rules, and inference methods to produce a de-fuzzified consequent is called a Fuzzy Inference System (FIS).

There are several other types of fuzzy inference systems which vary according to the fuzzy reasoning and the form of the *if-then* statements applied. One of these methods is the Takagi-Sugeno-Kang neuro-fuzzy method (Takagi and Sugeno 1985). This technique is similar to the Mamdani approach described above except that the consequent part is of a different form and, as a result, the de-fuzzification procedure is different. The *if-then* statement of a Sugeno fuzzy system expresses the consequent of each rule as a function of the antecedent variables and has the form (Sugeno and Kang 1988; Sugeno 1985):

$$\text{if } x \text{ is } A \text{ AND } y \text{ is } B \text{ then } z = f(x, y) \tag{E.2}$$

References

Cantor G (1874) Über eine Eigenschaft des Inbegriffes aller reellen algebraischen Zahlen. Crelles J f. Math 77:258–262

Johnson P (1972) A history of set theory. Weber & Schmidt, Prindle

Kosko B, Isaka S (1993) Fuzzy Logic Sci Amer 269:76–81

Mamdani EH (1974) Application of fuzzy algorithms for the control of a dynamic plant. In: Proceedings of IEE 121:1585–1588

Marwala T, Lagazio M (2011) Militarized conflict modeling using computational intelligence. Springer, London

Sugeno M (1985) Industrial applications of fuzzy control. Elsevier Science Publication Company, Amsterdam

Sugeno M, Kang G (1988) Structure identification of fuzzy model. Fuzzy Sets Syst 28:15–33

Takagi T, Sugeno M (1985) Fuzzy identification of systems and its applications to modeling and control. IEEE Trans Syst Man Cybern 15:116–132.

von Altrock C (1995) Fuzzy Logic and NeuroFuzzy applications explained. Prentice Hall, NJ

Wright S, Marwala T (2006) Artificial intelligence techniques for steam generator modelling. arXiv:0811.1711

Zadeh LA (1965) Fuzzy sets. Info Control 8:338–353

Zemankova-Leech M (1983) Fuzzy relational data bases. PhD Dissertation, Florida State University

Appendix F
Granger Causality

Granger causality is a technique which is used to detect the so-called Granger causality. It is premised on the assumption that given a time series y then an autoregressive linear model can be constructed using the following mathematical equation (Granger 1969):

$$y(t) = \sum_{j=1}^{p} B_j y(t-j) + E_1(t) \tag{F.1}$$

here p is the maximum number of past data points while E is the error of this model and B_j is the jth coefficient. If we introduce variable x which also has a time history available, is stationary and can also be modeled using linear assumptions to predict future values of y, then Eq. F.1 may then be re-written as:

$$y(t) = \sum_{j=1}^{q} A_j x(t-j) + \sum_{j=1}^{p} B_j y(t-j) + E_2(t) \tag{F.2}$$

A_j is the jth coefficient while q is the past time points to be included. Granger observed that given Eqs. F.1 and F.2, then variable x Granger causes variable y if the introduction of variable x to Eq. F.1 to form Eq. F.2 results in Eq. F.2 being better at predicting variable y than Eq. F.2.

Reference

Granger CWJ (1969) Investigating causal relations by econometric models and cross-spectral methods. Econometrica 37(3):424–438

© Springer International Publishing AG 2017   201
T. Marwala and E. Hurwitz, *Artificial Intelligence and Economic Theory: Skynet in the Market*, Advanced Information and Knowledge Processing,
DOI 10.1007/978-3-319-66104-9

Index

© Springer International Publishing AG 2017
T. Marwala and E. Hurwitz, *Artificial Intelligence and Economic Theory: Skynet in the Market*, Advanced Information and Knowledge Processing,
DOI 10.1007/978-3-319-66104-9

Printed in the United States
By Bookmasters